# ANNE GILCHRIST

## HER LIFE AND WRITINGS

**AMS PRESS**

NEW YORK

Painted by Herbert Harlakenden Gilchrist.

ANNE GILCHRIST

# ANNE GILCHRIST

## HER LIFE AND WRITINGS

EDITED BY

HERBERT HARLAKENDEN GILCHRIST

With a Prefatory Notice by

William Michael

Rossetti.

SECOND EDITION.

LONDON:

T. FISHER UNWIN

1887

**Library of Congress Cataloging in Publication Data**

Gilchrist, Anne (Burrows) 1828-1885.
 Anne Gilchrist, her life and writings.

 1. Gilchrist, Anne (Burrows) 1828-1885.
I. Gilchrist, Herbert Harlakenden, 1857-     ed.
PR4715.G5Z6  1973          820'.9'008  [B]      74-148783
ISBN 0-404-02767-9

Reprinted from the edition of 1887, London
First AMS edition published in 1973
Manufactured in the United States of America

AMS PRESS INC.
NEW YORK, N. Y.      10003

# PREFACE.

THAT a correspondence covering a period of forty years should have been preserved, is due to the fact of my mother's life-long friendships ; and to the methodical care of those to whom her letters were addressed—I sincerely thank those friends. Some of " her most beautiful, characteristic and copious letters" were written to her friend Walt Whitman. I suggested to Mr. Whitman, the giving of these letters or rather extracts from them, for publication in the present volume. But the poet was not entirely favourable or willing. " I do not know," he says in a late letter to me, " that I can furnish any good reason, but I feel to keep these utterances exclusively to myself. But I cannot let your book go to press without at least saying—and wishing it put on record—that among the perfect women I have known (and it has been my unspeakably good fortune to have had the very best, for mother, sisters and friends)

I have known none more perfect in every relation, than my dear, dear friend, Anne Gilchrist."

My mother never imagined that her Memoir would be written ; but a fortnight before her death, she placed in my hands a slip of paper containing a list of her published essays faintly written in pencil—a sacred warrant, which has had effect in strengthening my purpose to the execution of this labour of love.

By no means the least pleasant part of my duty is that of acknowledging my indebtedness to a valued friend— Mr. Rossetti.   I thank Mr. and Mrs. Carwardine for furthering the reproduction, which has been made from the beautiful picture by Romney, of " Mrs. Carwardine and Child," at Colne Priory.

HERBERT HARLAKENDEN GILCHRIST.

KEATS CORNER, WELL ROAD, HAMPSTEAD,
                                    *November 22, 1886.*

# Prefatory Notice.

WHEN Mr. Herbert Gilchrist undertook to write and edit the life and some of the writings of his mother, he honoured me with an invitation to say something by way of preface. I assented with the utmost readiness; feeling it a satisfaction to associate myself in any such way in a project for honouring the memory of so dear and valued a friend. Nevertheless, now that I sit down to write my preface, I feel a certain embarrassment. The manuscript of the work has been in my hands meanwhile, and I find that the name of Rossetti figures in it more largely than I had fully anticipated. I note that Dante Gabriel Rossetti and his doings bear their part in the book—which was indeed indispensable, and that Christina Rossetti is not wholly below the horizon; and (what is the main point at present) that letters addressed to myself, and extracts from my own letters in reply, occupy no inconsiderable space. It is difficult to avoid feeling that some readers will consider that I am thus amply, and more than amply, represented already in this record, and that a preface from my hand in addition is something delicately poised between a superfluity and an impertinence. However, my duty to the memory of Mrs. Gilchrist, and to her son and biographer, remains. As I really had something to do with two of the important occurrences of Mrs. Gilchrist's life—her occupation upon the *Life of Blake*, and her enthusiastic rally to the cause of Walt Whitman—I have abstained from interfering (except in some minor particulars) with the biographer's discretion in the treatment of these copious items of correspondence; and, as to the further general question, I commit myself to the indulgent construction of the reader.

My acquaintance with Mrs. Gilchrist must have begun in the autumn or winter of 1860. Her husband was then engaged in the composition of his *Life of William Blake*, and my brother had entrusted to him a precious MS. volume, his own and my joint property, containing a rich store of Blake's writings in prose and in verse, and of his designs. This is the volume, famous among the students of Blake, which my brother bought towards 1847 from Palmer, an attendant in the British Museum, at the modest price (produced from my pocket) of ten and sixpence, and which remained ever afterwards in our possession until, in the sale of my brother's effects which took place soon after his death in 1882, it fetched the sum of £110 5s., and even that, in the eyes of experts, was rather below than above its intrinsic worth. Along with this volume my brother had lent Mr. Gilchrist Varley's pamphlet of *Zodiacal Physiognomy*, containing some engraved heads by Blake; a precious and almost undiscoverable *brochure* which through the misdeed of a cheap bookbinder (acting under my orders, but certainly contrary to my intention), had been wofully cut down at its edges amid other items bound into the same volume, so that even the engravings showed clippings and manglings. I doubt whether Mr. Gilchrist ever quite forgave my involuntary share in this outrage, which remained for my brother a standing joke against me for years—always on hand when convenient. I can still remember something of that evening which I spent with Mr. and Mrs. Gilchrist in 1860. They were then living in Cheyne Row, Chelsea, next door to Carlyle. This proximity, of itself, made the meeting an interesting one to me. To know the author of the *Life of Etty* (a book which I had myself reviewed in the *Spectator*), now engaged on the still more important and attractive subject of Blake's career, and to inspect the numerous Blake drawings and engravings which he had got together, was of course a matter to me of even higher and more direct interest than any quasi-Carlylean environment. I passed a very cordial and pleasant evening with the Gilchrists, finding in both of them a large fund of intelligence and sympathy, and in neither the least pretence or affectation. A more evidently well-assorted couple there could hardly be : the husband animated, clear-headed, and bent upon producing good work—he was then regarded, in my own circle, as the best-equipped and ablest of the various art-critics on the periodical press ; the wife entering with zest into all his ideas, and capable not only of serving but of furthering their development.

Notwithstanding this favourable beginning of my acquaintance with Mr. Gilchrist, and the intimacy which my brother, my friend Mr. Madox Brown, and probably some others of my friends, maintained with him during the brief remainder of his life, I cannot remember that I saw him more than once or twice again. We were both busy men, and one casualty or another kept us apart. It was not until some little while after his death (December 1861), that my brother offered to Mrs. Gilchrist, for himself and for me, that we would do anything which we could to aid her in bringing the *Life of Blake* to completion. The biography was already indeed substantially finished by Mr. Gilchrist; and his widow undertook, and very efficiently accomplished, those connecting and amplifying details which were really wanted. But my brother acted as selector, editor, and elucidator of the poems and prose-writings of Blake, and supplied some important comments upon some of his works of art; while I set-to at compiling a *catalogue raisonné* of his paintings and designs. This was a task of no small compass, requiring me to go about to various localities to look up the works, besides the time and attention needed for the actual criticism, compilation, and arrangement. Not long after I had undertaken the cataloguing I paid a visit of a day or two to Mrs. Gilchrist in her cottage-home, Brookbank, Shottermill, near Haslemere. Here our previous acquaintance ripened into what I am proud to remember as a frank and unreserved friendship. The young widow surrounded by her three small children (the elder boy was, I think, absent), presented a touching picture of sorrow borne wisely and bravely, with a constant sense that the duties of life, though they may change with its changing and sometimes heart-rending conditions, never intermit, but have to be met with the whole strength of will and affection, and the whole force of character. Brookbank, on the very confines of three counties, Surrey, Hampshire, and Sussex, with an uncommon plenty of noticeable old fashioned farm-houses about, was a most pleasurable residence for persons who, while indifferent to luxury, had a true feeling for home-like comfort, and a genuine enjoyment of fine scenery. Mrs. Gilchrist was of these. It always appeared to me that she was excellently well suited at Brookbank; indeed, after seeing her there on three or four successive short visits spread over about as many years, the ideas of her personality and of her locality seemed to be so identified that her ultimate removal to London told as the break-up of a natural and pleasant affinity.

In London, and afterwards when (upon returning to England from a sojourn in America lasting three years) she had settled in Hampstead, we met oftener, yet still not extremely often; although, if there was one house more than another in which I felt myself always at home, and the object of cordial welcome, it was that of Mrs. Gilchrist. The last time I saw her was in August 1885, soon after I had come back from my annual holiday at the sea-side. I remember walking up to Hampstead on a Sunday of steady sultry heat, and passing in her house as friendly and agreeable an afternoon as I ever enjoyed. Her reminiscences of Carlyle and his wife, an interesting project which she entertained of vindicating his character from misconstructions by a narrative of her personal experiences, and many other matters (in which Turner and British painting in landscape and other forms bore a part), furnished forth a discursive and unflagging talk of three or four hours. She had then for a long while suffered from an illness, of which the chief obvious symptom was an oppression of breath. It affected her voice to some extent, and prevented her from moving about with much freedom, even in her sitting-room; but her manner, her readiness of conversation, and the vivacity of her mind, remained wholly unimpaired. I left the house without the faintest idea that this was to be our last meeting. Soon afterwards, however, I learned that her malady had taken a very serious turn, confining her to bed; and after an anxious interval the news of her death reached me from her son Herbert. Thus passed out of my life one of its sincere and firm friendships : a friendship never clouded, so far as my own share in it goes, by a breath of coldness or dissatisfaction. That it was reciprocated with fully equal warmth I am amply convinced : if perchance the warmth was coupled with more indulgence, the reason is obvious —that there was more to indulge.

As already observed, I was closely associated with Mrs. Gilchrist in two of the leading literary interests of her life : those which concern William Blake and Walt Whitman. As regards Blake, I co-operated with her— so far as my limited share in the matter goes—both when the biography was preparing for the press in 1862, and again when the second and revised edition was forthcoming in 1880. As regards Whitman, it will be seen in the Memoir that the selection which I made and published in 1868 from the works of the great-souled American introduced Mrs. Gilchrist to a knowledge of his work, and laid the foundation for that heart-stirring enthusiasm of hers in his cause which astonished me at first, and which I have ever since continued to regard as the most moving and important outcome—fertile perhaps of much in the future—from my comparatively humble doings in selection and exposition. I say that her enthusiasm astonished me: for indeed it revealed to me a greater susceptibility on her part to new and strong impressions—a greater and deeper passion of sentiment as governing and transfusing the conclusions of a strong reasoning and inquiring faculty—than I had hitherto supposed to be within the scope of her character. It was a new and unexpected link of sympathy between her and myself—a new and signal proof that the friendship which united us was a matter of essence, and not merely of circumstances. It need hardly be said that after her return from America, where she had known Whitman on a footing of intimate friendship, his personal character and demeanour were frequently the topic of conversation between us. I learned with pleasure— assuredly with no surprise—that the man individually was just as loveable and large-natured as the poet in his books. One small but thoroughly symptomatic point which particularly pleased me was to hear that, in the family circle or amid a small company of friends, he not only arrogated to himself nothing which he would not willingly allow or promote in others, but even showed a special disposition to bring out the younger members of the party—encouraging them to express themselves freely, and to bear their full share in the talk. This is exactly, on a small scale, the mood of mind which informs Whitman's poems with a rich and vigorous life, reaching out to a universal relation.

I shall say here little about Mrs. Gilchrist's writings: my high opinion of what she wrote concerning Walt Whitman being very amply expressed in the course of the ensuing pages. Her letters speak for themselves; and it would not befit me, to whom so many of them are addressed, to enlarge upon the qualities of thought and composition which mark them. I will therefore only observe that her longest production, the *Memoir of Mary Lamb* (in the series entitled *Eminent Women*), appears to me to be a very substantial, able, and even masterly piece of work; full without wordiness, and remarkable for that true and nice discrimination of character which neither sympathy without comprehension, nor comprehension unprompted by sympathy, could supply.

There are three portraits of Mrs. Gilchrist, done by her son and biographer, each of which gives a very true impression of her appearance: a life-sized half-figure in oil colour, pen in hand; a life-sized crayon-drawing, full-faced; and a smaller oil full-length, executed within a year of her death. She had an eminently *speaking* face: not merely in the ordinary sense that the countenance was genuinely expressive of the mind and character, but it seemed besides to be full-charged with some message to which the mouth would give word: it was at once a mirror and a prelude. The eyes were the marked feature—full, dark, liquid, and extremely vivacious. There was a humorous glance in them, free from causticity. Falsehood or pretence stood little chance with that pair of eyes : they would look through and through all ambiguity and all flimsiness, but the scrutiny was not barbed with the malicious pleasure of exposure.

As to the mind and character of which the face was the index, I should say that their foundation lay in strong sense ; common sense and mental acumen combined.   Mrs. Gilchrist was in manner remarkably cordial, without 'gushingness'; genial, courageous, steady in all her likings and habits.   I never knew a woman who, while maintaining a decorous social position from which she never deviated or derogated by a hair's-breadth, showed less propensity towards any of those social distinctions which are essentially factitious and arbitrary.   Solid worth suited her taste : whether with or without varnish was to her a matter of indifference. She never appeared to me out of temper, querulous, or languid—not even fidgety ; but she could be honestly indignant (as what generous-minded person cannot ?) upon sufficient cause. Constantly the same, clear-headed and alert, she never seemed to be taken at unawares. She was a good and rather copious talker—serious, and amusing as well ; and could maintain an argument with spirit, firmly grounded in the essentials of the matter, and seeing them with so much plain sense as to be difficult to dislodge from her position.   If she talked well, she listened well also; and, while she never shirked her own views, neither did she try to impose them.   To sum up, hers was a life of earnest, warm, and unfrittered simplicity, holding an even and sensitive balance between the claims of family-affection and those of intellectual activity. To make the home a centre of mental as well as family vital energy may perhaps have been her ideal; it was, at any rate—so far as I may be permitted to form an opinion—her lifelong practice.

WM. M. ROSSETTI.

*London, September* 1886.

# TABLE OF CONTENTS.

## BIOGRAPHY.

### CHAPTER I.

Ancestry — Colne Priory — Mary Wale — Sir Thomas Cawarden — Hayley's letters to Carwardine — George Romney — Mrs. Butler and Sir Joshua Reynolds — Ann Carwardine.

### CHAPTER II.

#### 1828—1838. Age 1—10.

Childhood — John Parker Burrows — "Lost in the Wood" — Falls into the Well, sensation of drowning — Returns to Gower Street.

### CHAPTER III.

#### 1839—1851. Age 11—23.

School-days — A calamity — Miss Cahusac — Mrs. Pugh, the Hermit of Eartham and 'the lovely young damsels of Baddow' — Tenniel's designs — Fondness for music — Rousseau's Confessions — Her first letter — Loses her only brother — Thinks deeply upon religious questions — Meets Alexander Gilchrist — Leaves London for Colne — Marriage.

### CHAPTER IV.

#### 1851—1852. Age 23—24.

The Wedding-journey — Windermere — Etty's native county — Delightful evenings — Letter by Alexander Gilchrist.

*b*

### Chapter V.
#### 1852—1856.  Age 24—28.

Lyme Regis — Description of their first home — Walter White — First letter from Carlyle about Etty — Letter of Alexander Gilchrist to William Haines in which Thomas Carlyle is described — Eight letters from Carlyle — Frederick's old Palace — "Take care of Dowb" — Countess D'Aulnoy — Removal to London.

### Chapter VI.
#### 1856—1859.  Age 28—31.

Life at Chelsea — Samuel Palmer — Carlyle's opinion of Blake — Miss Muloch — Lady Stanley of Alderley, Miss Brown and Marshal Brown — 'A poor Knight of Windsor' — Carlyle's conversation, his opinion of magazines and books — Anne Gilchrist's first Essay — Madame Vestris — A strange character — Jane W. Carlyle writes to Alexander Gilchrist.

### Chapter VII.
#### 1859.  Age 31.

Letter from Jane W. Carlyle — The Essay, "Whales and Whalemen" — Conversations with Carlyle — G. H. Lewes — Lady Jersey — Barnum and Everett — Carlyle's opinion of Burns.

### Chapter VIII.
#### 1860—1861.  Age 32—33.

Letter from J. W. Carlyle — Charles Dickens and Thomas Carlyle — Thackeray and Lady Airlie — Carlyle's liking for Ruskin — Captain Matthew Baillee, a noted border robber — — Mrs. Carlyle and her husband's proofs — Her opinion of his writing.

### Chapter IX.
#### 1861.  Age 33.

Dante Gabriel Rossetti — Mrs. E. Burne Jones — *The Italian Poets* — Boswell — Woodward the architect, and the Union Debating Club at Oxford — Water-colour picture of Dr. Johnson — Mrs. Wells.

CHAPTER X.

1861.  Age 33.

Last year of life at Great Cheyne Row — [Memoir of Alexander Gilchrist quoted from] — Letters from Jane W. Carlyle and from Dante G. Rossetti — Death of Alexander Gilchrist.

CHAPTER XI.

1861—1862.  Age 33—34.

Jane W. Carlyle writes to her neighbour — Letters from D. G. Rossetti, Samuel Palmer, Madox Brown — The new scene.

CHAPTER XII.

1862.  Age 34.

Brookbank — Associations — Turner and Dickens — Walter White quoted.

CHAPTER XIII.

1862—1863.  Age 34—35.

Death of Mrs. G. Rossetti — Letter from the widower — Anne Gilchrist writes to William Rossetti for the first time — Autobiographical letter to Mrs. Burnie — Mrs. Blake and Linnell — Disraeli — D. G. Rossetti and Blake's poetry.

CHAPTER XIV.

1863.  Age 35.

Completion of the Blake — Anne Gilchrist offers to lend Brookbank to Carlyle — Letters from Jane and Thomas Carlyle and from Samuel Palmer — Christina Rossetti at Brookbank.

CHAPTER XV.

1864—1867.  Age 36—39.

Letter from Christina Rossetti — Jean Ingelow — John Carwardine's account of the Secession War — [Lord Alfred] Tennyson — "The Indestructibility of Force" — Sidney Gilchrist Thomas — Hayley's composition — Madox Brown's Exhibition — Anne Gilchrist meets with a carriage accident — Tennyson and old Tom Campbell — Tennyson and Blake — The walk to High Hollow — Greenhill.

CHAPTER XVI.

1868—1870.   Age 40—42.

Letter from Christina Rossetti — Jonathan Hutchinson — Rossetti tells a good story about Carlyle and Browning — Anne Gilchrist reads "Leaves of Grass" for the first time — The first letter from Walt Whitman — Stillman's meeting with Walt Whitman — A Mediæval Troubadour.

CHAPTER XVII.

1870—1871.   Age 42—43.

Anne Gilchrist writes to Dante Gabriel Rossetti about "Jenny" — Her first Essay upon Whitman — Dixon of Sunderland — Shelley and *The Devil's Walk* — Serious illness.

CHAPTER XVIII.

1871—1876.   Age 43—48.

George Eliot at Brookbank — Letters from George Henry Lewes and his wife — Buchanan's letter in *The Daily News* — Letter from Walt Whitman, in which he speaks of [Lord] Alfred Tennyson — Visits America.

CHAPTER XIX.

1876—1879.   Age 48—51.

The new country — Description of Philadelphia — Edward Carpenter — Walt Whitman at the play — Joaquin Miller comes to tea — Walt Whitman recites *Ulysses* — Sir Edward Thornton — Miss Bremer —Count Gurowski — Thoreau — The visit to New England — Letter published in *The Daily Advertiser* — Emerson and Longfellow.

CHAPTER XX.

1879—1882.   Age 51—54.

The return — Durham — Haslemere — Letter from Walt Whitman — Settles at Hampstead — Begins the second edition of The Life of Blake — The new Blake letters — Letter from D. G. Rossetti — Conversation with Mr. Richmond — Letter from Walt Whitman, in which John Burroughs is mentioned — Frederic J. Shields — Death of D. G. Rossetti.

CHAPTER XXI.

1882—1885.   Age 54—57.

Mary Lamb — John Burroughs — Interesting letter upon London
— Cary's reminiscence of Charles and Mary Lamb — Mrs.
Cowden-Clarke — George Sand — Wordsworth — Coleridge
— Last words — THE END.

ESSAYS.

AN ENGLISHWOMAN'S ESTIMATE OF WALT WHITMAN.

THREE GLIMPSES OF A NEW ENGLAND VILLAGE.

A CONFESSION OF FAITH.

# LIST OF ILLUSTRATIONS.

Autograph . . . . . . . *Half-title.*

Anne Gilchrist. Painted by Herbert Harlakenden Gilchrist,
    1882-1884. Photogravure . . . . *Frontispiece.*

PAGE

Mrs. Butler [Anne Gilchrist's great-aunt]. Drawn by Herbert
    Harlakenden Gilchrist, from the picture by George
    Romney, at Colne Priory . . . . . . 6

Mrs. Carwardine and Child. From the picture at Colne
    Priory, painted by George Romney. Photogravure . 10

Silhouette of Anne Burrows (Gilchrist), 1835. Engraved on
    wood by W. H. Hooper . . . . . . 20

Alexander Gilchrist. Drawn by Herbert H. Gilchrist from
    a daguerreotype made in 1851 . . . . . 32

Monument of Thomas de Vere, the eighth Earl of Oxford.
    Died September 18, 1370 . . . . . . 40

Brookbank. Drawn by Herbert H. Gilchrist, 1884 . . 116

William Blake. Sketched from memory by Frederick Tatham
    for Alexander Gilchrist, one evening at 6 Great Cheyne-
    row, in 1860 . . . . . . . . 131

William Hayley. Drawn by Herbert H. Gilchrist, from a
    sketch in oil-colour by George Romney, at Colne Priory 154

Map upon which Walt Whitman had traced his journey to
    the Rocky Mountains . . . . . . . 253

Anne Gilchrist. Painted by Herbert H. Gilchrist, June, 1885.
    Photogravure . . . . . . . . 280

Angel of *Hope*. Designed, in water-colour, by William Blake 284
    (Reproduced by Walker and Boutall.)

# ANNE GILCHRIST.

## CHAPTER I.

### ANCESTRY.

THE life of Anne Gilchrist is the life of a woman of letters, who in a measure renounced literature until she had reared her children, giving to each a profession; whose strength of character stemmed adverse fortune, made life a success under difficult circumstances, and enabled her to emerge through sorrow with a spirit only more finely tempered. A life too, which, when seen through family association, touched the slower pulse of the eighteenth century; that century forming a background to the scientific and political events of her own.

As life itself is a fragment, a fragment albeit of greatness, how fragmentary must a biography appear! When we catch reflected in a pool a tall elm or hurrying cloud, seen at intervals through long rifts driven by the wind, our mind unconsciously completes the forms so obscured. Even such a partial reflection, the biographer perforce must set before his reader.

Anne Gilchrist, whose maiden name was Burrows, was born at number seven, Gower Street, on the twenty-fifth of February, 1828—year of Schubert's

death, and of Dante Rossetti's birth. She was the surviving child of three, one of whom died in infancy; she
lost the other, a brother, John Burrows, twenty-one
years later. The fact of death as revealed to her when
a child of three, in the form of an only baby-sister
shrouded in black velvet, left a lasting impression.

Henrietta Burrows, *née* Carwardine, was a gentle-
woman of the old school. Descended from a long line
of small squires, she was drilled in the now despised
accomplishments, being a mistress of those graceful
amenities of life that a daughter learns in a family where
bringing up is insisted upon, with its high traditions of
conduct and unflinching obedience to self-imposed
duties: traditions duly instilled into little Annie. A
witty and delightful grand-dame she seemed to us,
whose stately manners were reminiscent of the " grand
old style." It seemed wonderful to look into Henrietta
Burrows' aged face, whilst conversing about the past;
for were we not face to face with one out of those very
audiences held spell-bound by Mrs. Siddons, when the
actress, as Lady Macbeth, in the fifth act began—" Yet
here's a spot."

Could we give some delineation of the Carwardines,
and their environment at Earls Colne, would it not
help us to appreciate the influences that most combined
to mould Anne Gilchrist's character? for Colne was the
background to leisure hours in early and middle life.

Earls Colne, the garden of Essex, as it is called, possessed once a beautiful church and priory. From whatever point we approach the village, we see rising mid
elms the church tower, encircled beneath the battlements

with stars picked out in flint, which sparkle in the sun.
The sluggish Colne, winding through pastures, skirts
Colne Priory, a monastery founded by Aubrey de Vere,
A.D. 1100; its chapel enriched with four richly carved
tombs, three of which are to the Earls of Oxford.

These are the same monuments about which there
was a controversy in the public journals, June, 1884.
More than a hundred years ago the Priory chapel fell into
disuse, when it rapidly became a ruin : the four tombs
were removed, and were lent by Henry Carwardine
to Colne Church, pending a rebuilding of the Priory ;
he subsequently removed them back to a sort of
cloister on the Priory.   The monuments to the De Veres
received many embellishments from the bucolic clasp-
knife during their incarceration in Colne Church ; in fact,
had they been allowed to remain there, would have been
well nigh destroyed : beyond doubt, Henry Carwardine
was well within his legal rights in the matter.

The earliest and most beautiful tomb is that sur-
mounted by the effigy of Robert de Vere, the fifth Earl
of Oxford, who died A.D. 1296.   It is carved in stone.
The Earl lies with his legs crossed ; he is clothed in a
hauberk or shirt of mail, reaching nearly to the knees,
with a hood, or coif de maille, secured round the fore-
head by a fillet, or, perhaps, covered with a basenet,
or iron skull cap.   'Both the opening for the face
and the lower edge of the hood terminate in a point.
The legs and feet are encased in mail, the knees being
further protected by poleyns or genouillières.   The
spurs are attached to the heels by straps which pass
round the instep.   The shield is gone, but the guige by

which it was slung from the right shoulder remains, and passes under the coif de maille.

'A sleeveless surcoat, worn over the mail, reaches below the knees, is fastened round the waist with a narrow belt, and is open below, showing the lower part of the hauberk and the legs. A large sword is suspended at the left side by a broad belt, the buckle of which is in front. At the feet is a boar, couchant, with his head turned towards the figure. The free-stone tomb supporting it is of Decorated work of high artistic merit, apparently of the middle of the fourteenth century.'

Round the Priory we find art and nature playing into each other's hands. One marvels at some dainty sculptured angel shining through an ivied setting ; at figures impregnated with the religious sentiment which is among the sweet possessions of Gothic art. And what of the humanity ? the succession of soldiers and ecclesiastics whose feet have trodden this ancient ground ; of the loves, the quarrels, the intrigues, and of those silent workers recording their deeds in stone? Round this monastery stands a Norman wall : what experiences its battered face could tell ! Of all this, it is not in our power to chronicle ; though one brief word we will give, tracing the Holgates and Carwardines *ab ovo*.

Alberic de Vere, son of Alphonsus de Vere, and Earl of Ghisnes in Normandy, came over with William the Conqueror, who gave to the Earl in marriage his half-sister Beatrix and the manor of Colne. The occasion of the foundation of Colne Priory is said to have been owing to the skill in physic of the Abbot of

Abingdon, who by it recovered Geoffrey, eldest son of the above-named Aubrey, from illness. William Harlakenden came over at the Conquest as 'Esquier' to Alberic de Vere; and the former seems also to have received a present of land (at Woodchurch, Kent) from the Conqueror. Some of Harlakenden's descendants lived at Colne, and for many years were land-stewards to the Earls of Oxford, till at length these Harlakendens in their turn became land proprietors; they bought the monastery with its lands from the De Vere family.

In Colne Church there is a relief of one Roger Harlakenden (d. 1602), with his four wives kneeling behind him; his daughter, Dorothy, was married to Samuel Symonds, who emigrated to America in 1637, and the latter was Deputy Governor of New England: John Addington Symonds is collaterally descended from Dorothy (Harlakenden) Symonds.

Old Quarles (Emblems) is the only literary figure discoverable among Anne Gilchrist's ancestors.

In 1770 Ann Holgate represents the Harlakendens; she is a ward, guarded by a dragon, in the form of a maiden aunt—Mary Wale, who assumed the name of Holgate. "Molly" does not however seem to have stood in the way of Ann Holgate's marriage with Thomas Carwardine. In the published diary of Thomas Wale, the young people's courtship is mentioned:—"June 9th, 1770. The next day, after breakfast with Miss Bridge, we set out and got to Colne before two o'clock, in good time for dinner with Miss Holgate, and found her and her niece Nancy and sweetheart (Mr. Carwardine) all

well.  We spent ye 10th, 11th, and 12th with fishing,
walking [and] driving."

Tradition has it that Nancy's sweetheart, Thomas
Carwardine, of Thinghill Court, is collaterally descended
from Sir Thomas Cawarden, of Bletchingley Castle :
certainly, this squire's courtly manners and *savoir
faire* stamp him as a worthy representative of the *Knight*
who served four sovereigns without losing either his
head, or the bulk of his estate ; though Queen Mary
confiscated part of Sir Thomas's fine armoury, but
probably Queen Elizabeth paid him compensation.

'Sir Thomas Cawarden (or Cawerden, familiarly
Carden) was a gentleman of the Privy Chamber to
Henry the Eighth, Master of the Revels, and Keeper of
the King's Tents, Hales, and Toyles.  It belonged
to his office as Master of the Revels to take charge
and custody of all the garments and properties necessary for the pageants, masks, and other diversions of
the Court ; to provide for the erection and decoration of
all such temporary buildings as might be required for
those entertainments.  To this office, therefore, was
very naturally joined that of keeper of the king's tents
and temporary lodgings, used in military expeditions or
other occasions in the field.

'Sir Thomas Cawarden seems to have stood high in
the favour of King Henry VIII.  He had a grant from
that monarch of the manor of Hextalls, in Surrey,
which had belonged to Sir Nicholas Carew, of Bedding-
ton, near Croydon. . . . "Cawarden is said to have
entertained Henry VIII., and his Queen Ann Boleyn, at
his castle at Bletchingley. . . . He was at the siege

*Drawn by Herbert H. Gilchrist, from the picture by George Romney at Colne Priory.*

MRS. BUTLER—MISS CARWARDINE.

of Boulogne (doubtless in his capacity of Master of the King's Tents), where he was knighted by his sovereign."

Alfred John Kemp, F.S.A., in his notes on the Loseley Manuscripts, has more to say about this worthy knight; as William More was one of Sir Thomas's executors, so that most of Cawarden's papers have been preserved in the muniment-room at Loseley. His arms were—A bow between two pheons; Aubrey calls him bow-bender to Henry VIII.

But to return to Anne Gilchrist's grandfather, Thomas Carwardine. He was married to Ann Holgate at Earls Colne, Essex, July 9, 1771. During the first fifteen years of their married life, Ann Carwardine's aunt (Miss Wale) refused to leave Colne Priory. Thomas Carwardine possessed a legal friend in Lord Thurlow,—" lose half your estate, rather than go to law," was the lawyer's advice to the young people. Miss Wale died August 30, 1786; not, however, before burning a budget of Cromwell's letters, and a lock of the Protector's hair. Lord Thurlow's opinion had been previously sought for, as to a profession. Carwardine leaning towards art, the Chancellor reminded him that a friend can only have his portrait painted once. The Church was suggested, and a living spoken of, this suggestion was adopted.

The Rev. Thomas Carwardine was " a pleasant and good friend " of Romney's, says Allan Cunningham, and of Hayley's too: indeed, the three travelled together in Italy (1773); the divine being the only one of the trio unaccompanied by a fair but unwedded companion—noticeable rectitude in those days.

Hayley liked Carwardine: here is a passage taken
from one of a pile of old letters, written by the
"Hermit of Eartham" in 1815, and addressed care of
Mrs. Butler, 1, James Street, Buckingham Gate:—
"Come when you can! my very dear sympathetic
Comrade, and we will hobble and laugh together, as
gaily as a group of merry Beggars in a Barn, who have
not met for years, and have a thousand curious adventures to relate for their reciprocal Diversion."

"The amiable Divine" knew through his sister, Mrs.
Butler (a miniature painter second only to Ozias
Humphrey) what Lord Thurlow called the other
"faction in art"—Sir Joshua Reynolds—at whose
studio Carwardine visited: the amateur was struck with
the great artist's rapidity of execution, as contrasted
with "old Phillips' slow fumbling!" Anne Gilchrist's
grandfather (the Rev. Thomas Carwardine) was
genuinely fond of art, and we trace the artist in sayings
such as, "the most beautiful eye is of a colour impossible to name," and "green is nature's colour."

'Mistress' Carwardine's frugal care in saving a small
fortune out of the entailed Priory estate, proved of
service; and could her gentle soul have foreseen the
premature widowhood of both daughter and grand-
daughter, Ann Carwardine would have felt some compensation for all the pains taken in the diligent admin-
istration of her affairs.

The good housewife was somewhat formal, never
addressing her husband otherwise than as "Mr. Carwardine," though she would unbend in the nursery;
her rendering of "Auld Robin Gray," in a clear sweet

soprano, was listened to with breathless attention by the little ones.

Ann Carwardine died March 2, 1817, in the 66th year of her age, of the same cruel malady that sixty-eight years later carried off her grand-daughter. When Ann Carwardine's bier was placed in Colne Church, a robin redbreast flew in and perched upon her coffin, singing sweetly the while. As we look at Romney's portrait, the mother's arms encircling her eldest boy, one of twelve, cannot we believe all good things of this grandmamma, and say with Locker,—

> " If Romney's art be true,
> What a lucky dog were you,
> Grandpapa ! "

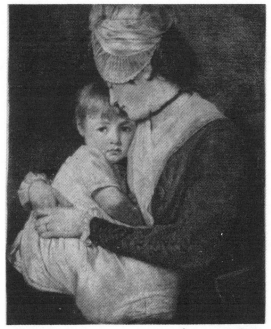

G. Romney      Mistress Carwardine & Child

# CHAPTER II.

## CHILDHOOD.

### 1828—1838. AGE, 1—10.

WE may find a suggestion of John Parker
Burrows' personal appearance in the fact that
the lawyer, when walking, would not unfrequently be
mistaken for Sir Thomas Lawrence by friends of the
latter. A solicitor, fond of his profession, John P.
Burrows brought large executive powers to bear upon
his work; indeed, to those who watched the rapid
growth of the lawyer's practice, it seemed a pity that
such ability should not have been called to the bar. In
common with his daughter, John P. Burrows was never
too busy to help a friend; (in the solicitor's case),
working for those not well able to afford law.

Mrs. Burrows spoke of the physician's admiration for
her little one. The old doctor would come daily,
during bath time, to study "the most beautifully formed
baby" that he had ever seen. The child must have
had a memory to remember her first lesson—that of
toddling from mother to nurse! Annie (Gilchrist)
possessed "a kind and good father," who recognised
ability in his daughter, and did all he could to develop

the child's mind and character. John P. Burrows was
fond of music, and often would little Annie be taken to
hear a fine chorister; or sometimes, on Sunday afternoon, the two would walk from Gower-street to the
Zoological Gardens. No wonder if the little feet ached
upon those occasions! At other times this companion-
able father would empty his pockets of coppers (before
dressing) for Annie's benefit, Ann Carwardine's grand-
child taking care of their bright faces until there had
accumulated enough to buy a rose-wood desk. It must
have been a pretty sight to see the father listening to his
daughter's first piece, " La Petite Surprise," the chubby
fingers of five summers rendering the small intricacies of
this French composition upon the piano with painstaking
fidelity.

In common with many fathers, John P. Burrows was
somewhat hasty, enforcing his will with quick punishment. With his daughter an occasion for punishment
occurred but once, and, whatever the occasion, the little
woman's pride was ruffled by it. In after years Anne
Gilchrist expressed disapproval of punishment, holding
that a parent should avoid conflicts with a child's mind
in small matters, and always resort to gentle means when
possible.

Anne has a playmate in John T. Burrows, the
typical brother, who burns the dollies of a yielding and
half-hearted devotee of dolly.

From a tale, " Lost in the Wood," one of the *Magnet
Stories*, published in the autumn of 1861, we get a
glimpse of the brother's and sister's childhood. " When
I was about nine or ten years old," writes Anne

Gilchrist, " I was taken to pay a long visit to an uncle, who lived in a wild country place—Tolleshunt-Knights, Essex—of which he was the clergyman. . . . We went in a coach, which, though it had four horses to draw it, and fresh ones every ten miles, took nearly the whole day to go the sixty miles to Tiptree, near which place my uncle lived. But oh! were we not wild with delight, I and my brother! When we felt the coach no longer rattling over stones, but bowling along a road with hedges on each side, that seemed scampering away from us instead of we from them; when we passed golden cornfields, sprinkled here and there with beautiful scarlet poppies; and green meadows with dear, white, woolly sheep nibbling away in them—it was hard work to sit still and not to jump for joy, and shout and sing, and otherwise torment the grave grown-up people in the coach. Well, the journey came to an end at last. And, to say the truth, we were rather tired of it before it was over, and were glad enough to change from the inside of a coach to open air in the four-wheeled chaise, which stood ready waiting for us at the inn where the coach stopped. Off we go again, across a broad common, past the tall windmill, which I remember, was swinging round its great arms merrily, as if resolved to do a good day's work, for the wind blew fresh.

" Then down a winding, shady lane, and just as the sun was sinking, we turned in at the white gate of Elmwood Rectory. In the porch, to welcome us, stood my aunt and her little son Frank, a merry-looking fellow, with bright hazel eyes—just the playfellow for the coming six weeks. I hardly know which is pleasantest,

the first arrival—when, hungry and tired, you sit down
at table, with kind faces round, looking a welcome, and
delicious country fare—new milk and eggs, and home-
made bread, and swan-shaped pats of butter spread out
before you—or when you stretch out your limbs in the
snow-white bed, the sheets, the room, everything
smelling sweet, and looking strange and bright, and the
last sound you hear before dropping off to sleep is the
rustling of the leaves and the scratching of the boughs
of the great tree outside against your window ; or when
the sun, shining in brightly, wakes you in the morning,
for a moment wondering where you are, till the sound
of the gardener whetting his scythe to mow the lawn tells
you that you are really in the country ; that what you
have been dreaming and longing for, for weeks, has come
to pass, and you jump up briskly, that you may get into
the garden while yet the flowers are covered with
dewdrops.

"Cousin Frank and brother [Johnny] were already out,
and together we explored the garden. Such a garden !
I am afraid none will ever seem so beautiful to me
again. There was a broad lawn, and on each side of it
a flower-border, in which tall white lilies glistened
against a background of dark evergreens ; and roses
and mignonette, and all sweet-smelling flowers, bloomed
there in abundance ; evening primroses, too, which it
is so pretty to watch towards sunset, shutting themselves
up by fits and starts for the night. The lawn sloped
down towards a haw-haw, which is neither more nor less
than a ditch. But a ditch, not with ragged sides and
muddy bottom, such as you see under a hedge, but made

trim and fit for the garden ; with sides of smooth short
grass which slope till they meet, so that there is no flat
bottom to hold mud or water. What a capital place for
trap-ball that lawn was ! Every evening, when the
shadows lengthened and the air grew cool, we used to
have a game, while the old folks sat by on the bench
··nder the great pear-tree, with honeysuckle climbing
.ound it, which stood in the middle.

"No small treat, too, was it to fetch up the cow from
the field, and sometimes she would let the smallest of us
ride on her back ; and then we stood in a corner of the
cow-house to watch the milking. Also, there was piggy
—ugly, but funny—and very grateful if you took him
a few wind-fall apples, or scratched his head with a stick.

"One morning, my mother and aunt went to spend the
day with friends, a few miles off, and we children were
left to do almost what we pleased. For Uncle [Billy]
was much engaged in his study, and did not concern
himself with our doings.

"There was a wood about a couple of miles off ; nuts
were ripe, what could be pleasanter than to go nutting ?
To this we all agreed ; and my brother, Cousin Frank,
and myself, set off as gay as the lark. What a delicious
place a wood is on a hot sunny day ! You feel as if
you would like to live there always. The boys cut some
famous long hooked sticks to draw down the branches
with, and we gathered nuts till our teeth grew tired
of cracking, and our pockets and handkerchiefs were
stuffed quite full.

"'I think we've had enough of this,' said Frank.
'What shall we do now?'

" 'I vote for birdsnesting,' answered Johnny. For some time I stood watching the boys as they climbed about ; but I don't think they found many nests, except, perhaps, a few old ones from which the young birds had long since flown. If we had been country children, or if Frank had been older, we should have known it was not much use to search for eggs in autumn, when nuts were ripe. When I grew tired of watching them, I wandered away hunting for wild flowers, and trying to sing, as I was very fond of doing, some of my mother's favourite old songs. There was one broad path through the wood, full of ruts, which the waggons used when they came to cart brushwood or timber, and there were narrow green paths winding in all directions, so narrow that I had to hold the boughs aside with my hands, and even then tore my clothes sadly in pushing through. But somehow the narrower and wilder the path, the more inviting it looked. The sound of my companions' voices shouting and laughing grew fainter and fainter, and at last I could not hear them at all ; but I felt very happy, and not a bit lonely. There was velvety moss to sit down on, and the air was full of pleasant sounds ; soft cooing of wood pigeons, the little tapping noise of the woodpecker's beak against the bark of a tree, and a buzzing and humming, and chirping of all sorts of merry little creatures, which seemed enjoying the summer's day and the shady wood as much as I did. And then, as nobody was by to listen, I sang my favourite tunes louder than ever, till the wood rang with them. . . . "

" One morning, Frank and Johnny were high busy in the fir grove, with carpentering tools and a block of wood, which they were trying to scoop out and shape into a ship. [Johnny] was head-carpenter, and worked upon the hull, while Frank got ready straight and smooth pieces for the mast and spars. And when this was finished, there was to run to the shop for a ball of string to rig it with, and to beg of aunt some nice pieces of calico for the sails. Then they went hunting about for some one who could cut them out nicely; and at last Frank came upon me. I was busy in the yard, with a large handful of grain, feeding the pigeons ; and I intended to give the rabbits a treat of some nice, fresh green food.

"'Oh, cousin! I'm so glad I've found you. Do come this very minute and help us to cut out our sails,' said Frank.

"'I can't come directly,' answered I. 'You must just wait till I have finished feeding my dear pigeons.'

"'Oh, do come, Annie.'

"'Well, I will, if you will only wait patiently a few minutes.'

"'But we can't wait—we won't wait. You shall come now.'

"And my cousin took tight hold of me, and tried to drag me along, while I struggled violently to get free, and in doing so, stepped back—forgetful of what was behind me—into the well; the top of which was level with the ground, not bricked round or protected in any way. I remember the splash, the plunge down under water—the feeling of suffocation—and then I remember no more till I opened my eyes and found myself on a bed, with many anxious faces round.

c

" But I was afterwards told that my little brother had saved my life: for hearing Frank give a scream of terror, he came running into the yard, and had the sense to lie down by the well, and when I came up the second time, lay hold of my hair, and then by means of that, of my head, and managed to keep hold, too, till their continued shouts and screams brought the gardener running to see what was the matter, and to pull me out, as he had pulled out poor Grim, only a week before."

The " little brother " Johnny was ten years old. In after years, this experience of so nearly drowning was referred to, as not unpleasant ; ' with the consciousness of the memories of my life flashing past, as in an instant, and then the sensation of dreamily floating past green fields to unconsciousness.' As near to the sensation of death as it was possible to approach.

" Our visit to [Tolleshunt-Knights] was soon to end. Six happy weeks had glided away, and the morning came at last for saying ' Good-bye.' Once more we drove along the pleasant lanes to meet the coach. The days had shortened since the journey down ; and it was night before we rumbled into the inn yard in Holborn, where the stage put up, and where they packed us, bag and baggage, into a great old lumbering hackney-coach.

" Was there not something pleasant in coming back once more to the grand old smoky familiar place ? Something happy, too, when we stopped at the door of our own dear home, to be warmly welcomed by the faithful servants, whose pride and pleasure it had been to make everything clean, neat, and comfortable for our return ? "

# CHAPTER III.

## SCHOOL-DAYS.

### 1839—1851.  AGE, 11—23.

A CALAMITY was in store for the Gower-street
household.  One day John Parker Burrows met
with an accident—a fall from his horse—soon to be
followed by an illness, to which the strong but over-
worked man of fifty-one succumbed in three days
(April 18, 1839).  Upon the heels of this dire calamity
succeeded a hurried winding up of the large practice;
the widow with her son and daughter moving into a
smaller house at Highgate.

Annie Burrows, though only eleven, is already a
school-girl of five years' standing at the Misses Cahusacs';
an evangelical school at Highgate, which gave some
advantages in education; not that the scholars thereof
would now, any of them, take honours at Girton.
Nevertheless, the Cahusacs' curriculum was an advance
upon that in vogue some eighty years ago; for instance,
where Mrs. Burrows was at school, at Baddow, the head-
mistress's share of instruction consisted in teaching
deportment, of stepping in and out of a carriage, or of
walking magnificently through the school-room once a

day, as a lady should walk. Mrs. Pugh's example is significant surely to us, living in a time when round shoulders and a shuffling gait are but too common.

Amongst Hayley's letters to the Rev. Thomas Carwardine, beginning " My dear Prior," we notice a postscript in which the school just referred to, is mentioned by the Hermit of Eartham :—" Pray give my *love to Mrs. Pugh !* and tell her I often recollect with pleasure, how satisfactorily I said my prayers *with her* and her *evening congregations of lovely young damsels* of Baddow." Mrs. Pugh was Carwardine's sister, and at whose school, no doubt, he first saw Nancy Holgate.

School life for Annie at eleven, fortunately was not to receive any check from the break-up of the home in Gower-street, Miss Cahusac being desirous to keep so promising a pupil.

Miss Julia Newton tells us that her school friend " Annie was a favourite with the masters, because of her ability and painstaking application. The 'English Master' would turn to my companion when none of the other pupils could follow him in the problems of Euclid. Together with an understanding of the elements of mathematics, Annie showed a retentive memory. Upon one occasion a page of Boileau's Satires had to be learnt within the space of ten minutes. When my friend's turn came to repeat the lesson, she was able to take up her part in the book at the right time : and twenty years afterwards Anne Gilchrist remembered the lesson, though she had never looked at the book in the interim !"

At the Cahusacs' " deportment " was in safe hands,

Ami~ 1835

viz., under the guidance of the celebrated dancing master Tenniel, an indefatigable teacher, with his "round your elbows," a perpetual word of command to pupils whose angular arms could not be made to take the graceful contour. "How well I remember Tenniel bringing a portfolio of his son's designs for the Pilgrim's Progress, and showing them with great pride to Miss Cahusac. The illustrations were by the student who has since become the political cartoonist for *Punch*. Tenniel said that his son's drawings had won a prize at the Society of Arts."

A fondness for music was soon to show itself; an announcement that her mistress would play a sonata of Beethoven's, Annie always greeted with a beaming face.

' As early as fifteen my school-fellow began to think about spiritual questions. With a love of freedom for herself in theology, was combined an anxiety not to unnecessarily shock those who thought orthodoxy essential. No wonder, then, that such a zealous student disliked the needle. It was a rule at Miss Cahusac's that we should do some needlework for "the poor," two hours a week; a task which was enlivened with reading aloud. The governess's inquiry as to who would like to read, was always answered by Anne. Sometimes Elizabeth Cahusac would say with a smile : "I think you had better do a little needlework this evening, Anne." The latter's poor work was always list run upon calico. I once asked my companion why she always did the same thing? "Because I need not think about it."' Though years afterwards, as a mother, Anne Gilchrist's needle went swiftly enough.

Ten years of school-life came to an end in 1844.
Anne is now sixteen. A few months after her release
from school, we find the diligent student deep in
" Rousseau's Confessions." When, upon one occasion,
Annie was studying Jean Jacques, walking upon the
Terrace at Highgate Cemetery, the Vicar put in a
rather unexpected appearance. After the usual saluta-
tion, Clericus asked, " What is your book Miss
Burrows? " Realizing the situation, Annie replied, almost
inaudibly, " Rousseau's Confessions," of which the last
word only caught the parson's ear. " ' St. Augustine's
Confessions.' Ah! good reading ; very good book,
my dear."

A letter written to Julia Newton by Annie Burrows
when seventeen, is the first utterance of hers that comes
to us :—

"*July* 21*st*, 1845.

" How long it is, dearest Julia, since I have heard
from you, and still longer since you have from me.
Indeed I should have written sooner, but not knowing
your direction in France, thinking my letters were not
worth the postage, and daily expecting your return, I
consoled myself with the prospect of your paying us a
long visit, and delayed writing till I feel quite ashamed
to do so, lest you should have thought me very unkind.
And now, dearest, we shall not meet probably till about
November, as I am staying in Essex, and have three long
visits to pay in different parts of the country ; but we
will keep up a regular correspondence ; indeed I will
try to be a good girl, and write often, and in return I
shall expect such an interesting journal from you of all

you have seen, heard, and thought while on the Continent. Have I asked too much in saying, what you *think* as well as see? Nay, that is the most interesting part to your friend.

"Did you enjoy the trip quite as much as you expected? It is the height of my ambition to travel through Italy, Switzerland and Germany. And yet I don't know either—I sometimes think I derive more pleasure in reading descriptions of lovely scenery by authors I very much admire. You see it, as it were, through the medium of their brilliant imaginations; and a tide of interesting, of beautiful associations, invest it with a thousand charms, which, if I gazed on it myself, my dull intellect would fail to supply.

"Very likely what I have just written is nonsense. Whenever I try to write what I feel, I am quite at a loss how to express myself; but tell me if you understand what I mean; have you ever thought the same?

"I am staying at a very pretty, retired place, within sight of the sea; and we have delightful water parties and picnics. In an excursion of this kind, I fell into the water the other day, and a tall gentleman on the top of me. However, they soon hauled me out again.

"Rhoda and I have already commenced correspondence, and she tells me she is going to be confirmed. Poor girl, she is very pleased. I never will be confirmed with my own consent. If I am forced, I must submit; but I trust I shall escape."

'No sooner had Annie left school than the sister made herself a perfect companion to the brother; giving up her time wholly to him when he was at home; and if

" Johnny " is late in returning from the law-office or
opera, Annie will sit up to chat with the amusing, good-
natured brother.   " Play me something, Annie," was a
frequent request, readily granted then, as in after years
such a request would be by Anne Gilchrist to her children and friends.   My school-friend told me that there
were many little things that she, as a sister, could advise
her brother in.'

    ' Wholly unprepared was Annie for the terrible blow
that followed eight years after her father's death.   In the
sister's nineteenth year, that only brother, so full of
promise, from whom she had never been separated for
long together, was snatched away by a malignant fever
(16th July, 1847) ; and the sister was not allowed even
the sad satisfaction of seeing her brother from the time
that he was taken ill to the day of his death.   The loss
of her " angel brother " put the sun out of her sky for
many a day.   The suddenness of the shock, too, stunned
her : and the thought of death so environed Annie that
she owned to a surprise, " at finding any young man of
her acquaintance alive."'

    Six months after the death of John T. Burrows,
Annie wrote to her friend ' Julia ' from 10, Heathcote
Street—a house which Mrs. Burrows rented of Mrs.
James Gilchrist.   The former had moved from Highgate
in the Michaelmas of 1846, in order that her son might
the better be enabled to study law.

    " ' Do write soon, dear Annie,' is the closing petition
of your letter ; and what shall Annie say to make you
forgive her having allowed three weeks to slip away
before answering you ?   In truth, dear Julia, I feel

reluctant to enter into the discussion you wish : not because my interest in the subject has diminished ; on the contrary, it increases greatly ; but because it is one on which I am conscious that my mind is in a state of darkness and perplexity. And I have suffered lately, too, from such almost unconquerable depression. However, I will try and begin the New Year better ; indeed, I do not give way to it, and can always disguise it from those who surround ; but I could not do so in writing to my friend.

" I feel deeply grateful for the warm, true affection that prompts your anxiety about my views of religion. May I speak freely, dearest ? It seems to me that such anxiety betrays a want of confidence in the power of truth and in the goodness of God. Can you believe that one who earnestly and humbly seeks the truth, will be permitted to embrace vital error ?

"I cannot help thinking you attach too much importance to creeds and doctrines. They are mere definitions, after all ; and definitions are better calculated to circumscribe truth, and bring it down to the narrow level of our half-awakened understandings, than to raise our minds to deep, elevated, life-giving comprehension of it ; and this, I feel persuaded, is not bestowed upon us at once by the Creator, but is to be earned slowly, by years of labour, by struggling resolutely to crush the evil and develop the good that is in us. ' To me, I confess, it seems a very considerable thing just to believe in God ; difficult indeed to avoid honestly, but not easy to accomplish worthily, and impossible to compass to perfection. A thing not lightly to be professed, but rather humbly sought; not to be found at the end of any syllogism, but in the inmost fountains of purity and affection; not the sudden gift of intellect, but to be earned by a loving and brave life. It is, indeed, the greatest thing allowed to mankind, the germ of every lesser greatness.' The greatest thing allowed to mankind. Oh, this is so true! The soul pants to worship God. Could it but catch a glimpse of its Creator, it would at once be filled with love and adoration, with joy unspeakable, mingled with awe and deep humility, with love to man, with divine energy, and with the thirst for perfection.

"You ask me if I believe in the doctrine of man's total depravity? I do not. I believe that there is much evil in the human heart, and also much that is good; that the Creator has endowed it with noble capabilities; and the Scriptures are full of blessed promises of light and strength from above to those who seek it earnestly.

"The Gospels, the Psalms and Job, I read, but not the Epistles yet: they are so hard of interpretation.

"It pains me to hear from your lips such a doctrine as this : ' That the least guilty of men deserve a doom so dreadful, that eternity will not exhaust their punishment;' whilst at the same time you confess that we are born with an irresistible tendency to sin. I can find no warrant in the Gospels for such a belief.

"I think, dear Julia, we start with a different aim; those who take your view of religion (the Calvinists) think that our sole object is to get to Heaven and escape damnation; and this necessarily results from their view of human nature and of God. But to me it seems, that our great aim should be to fulfil the ends for which we were created; that is to say, develop to the utmost the nature which God has given us; and I cannot think of Heaven as a place, but as a state of Being. How I long to see you again, my dear friend. I count the days till your return."

Henry Carwardine—Anne Gilchrist's uncle—in one of his numerous letters to James Gillman (Coleridge's friend), tells us something about his niece :—

" *November*, 1847.

" My sister (Mrs. Burrows) has been at her old quarters—No. 10, Heathcote Street, for four or five weeks—but since the death of her son, having *no object* for living in London, and her daughter not liking it, they are both coming to live at a snug cottage of mine, close to the entrance gate of the Priory. I am going to add a bedroom on the ground-floor; for she cannot mount a stair." [Mrs. Burrows suffered from rheumatism for twenty-five years.]  "She will be near her own family and many of her early friends, and I shall be able in many ways to render her assistance, and minister to her little comforts and requirements; and I think we can get her into a bath-chair in fine weather, and wheel her about the old Priory grounds—a mode of enjoying air and exercise which she cannot obtain in London. All this cannot take place till after Midsummer next. . . . The pleasure with which she [Mrs. Burrows] looks forward to her residence at Colne, is not unmixed with dread of the painful effort of the journey ; however, she will make the attempt about August [1848]

by which time I hope to have everything ready to afford
her as much comfort as her sad state admits of."

Annie Burrows writes to Julia Newton from Colne
Priory, September 24, 1848 :—.

"Your charming little note, after a journey round
Essex, found me at the Priory; and here we shall
remain till Friday next, when we enter our new abode.

"So you may fancy what a busy, bustling lady I
am just now, making curtains and superintending
carpenters.

"Poor Mamma got through the journey [from 10,
Heathcote Street] pretty well, but I grieve to say her
rheumatism is worse rather than better : however, I
try to persuade myself this is owing to our being near a
great deal of water, for there is a large pond a hundred
yards from the Priory, and the river close by ; and that
when we are settled in our little cottage, she will not be
so great a sufferer.

"And so at last, you do confess that chimney pots,
brick walls, and a sky of smoke, are not so pleasant to
look upon as fields and woods, and the azure heavens.
I had really begun to think you were as hopeless a case
as Dr. Johnson, who said : ' Sir, when you have seen one
green field, you have seen all green fields.  Sir, I like
to look upon men ; let us walk up Cheapside.'  And
yet, now I have left dear old London, I feel great affection
for it, but I own I like it best at a distance, and have no
wish to return, if my friends will come to me.  How I
long for your promised visit !  Shall we not walk and
talk of things human and divine ?  Apropos of things
human, I agree in what you say of Miss Bremer.  Her

truthful simplicity and earnestness of feeling make her a beautiful painter of domestic life. Do read the 'Home;' you will be quite enchanted with it.

"And your remarks on Miss Edgeworth, too, which three or four years ago I should fiercely have disputed, I now cordially assent to. She gives us fine deeds and fine talk, but never a human being. She sees only the outside of life, appearances instead of realities, and is evidently one who observed acutely but neither thought nor felt deeply.

"You ask me what I have been reading lately. To confess the truth, I am in a state of mental starvation. I am afraid all my cares have been devoted to the body, that is to say, to preparing our new home. When we are in it I mean to do great things, but you know I am one who always 'means to do.' If I ought to judge of the future by the past, it won't end in much.

"Meanwhile, what little reading time I have, has been spent on the writings of the Transcendentalists, such as Emerson, as a sort of balance to my usual studies in Comte.

"Comte and Emerson are the two opposite poles of the present intellectual world. Comte is, I think, essentially a materialist. Emerson's writings are treated with a good deal of contempt and ridicule now, but I think the next generation will call him a great man. If people would have patience to study him, in spite of his apparent affectation and mysticism, they would, per-haps, find him a profound thinker.

"However, after all, eclecticism is a fine thing. Truth is to be found complete in no man's system, but a portion of it in all systems. It is for the reader to collect it, and reconcile apparent contradictions.

"Just eleven o'clock! and I must rise with the lark to-morrow, and be as industrious as the bee. So good-night and good-bye, dear friend."

The announcement of Anne Burrows's engagement to Alexander Gilchrist, is made so prettily by the former, in a letter written in 1848 to Julia Newton, that we are tempted to give the epistle—though in doing so we shall have 'sold cheap what is most dear':—

"I am driven up to the last corner of my note-paper, simply because I could not make up my mind to begin.

"Do you remember Mr. Gilchrist, and a long conversation we once had about him? Perhaps this question will make you guess the rest—guess that your friend is very happy, for she loves and is beloved by one who can fulfil her aspirations, realize her ideal of a true marriage, one who is her friend and helper, as well as her lover. But when I speak of marriage, do not think, dear, that that will come to pass next week, or next month, or within the next four or five years. In the first place, he is at present only a student for the Bar, and cannot afford to have a wife. And in the next place, I should not like to run away from mamma so soon—indeed I do not think I could ever make up my mind to do so—should not bear it unless she promised to live either with me, or next door to me. But this is looking a long way into the future.

"I know not how to describe him to you, dear Julia, except by telling you that he is altogether, both in intellect and heart, great, noble and beautiful.

" I am still engaged upon my old studies, which, together with general reading, very fully occupy the time that is at my own disposal.

" By the bye, have you read yet ' Modern Painters ' by a Graduate of Oxford ? If not, pray do so forthwith, and I feel sure you will thank me for the suggestion."

Three years later, Annie writes from Earls Colne, 5th Jan., 1851:—

" Dear Julia little dreamed what sorrow had befallen her friend when her affectionate Christmas greeting reached Colne. The same post brought tidings that Alex. was taken suddenly and dangerously ill, and another hour saw me on the road to London. I found him past the worst. My Christmas was spent in nursing him.

" Dear Julia will understand me, I think, when I tell her it was the sweetest Christmas I have yet passed. I left him on the Saturday after, all fear of relapse being then over, and he rapidly regaining his strength, which the severity of the attack had entirely prostrated. And so I left him, with a heart full of gratitude to God, and renewed happiness. And though, of course, his visit to Colne was entirely relinquished, he would not exchange those few days for *months* of our usual happy, serene Colne meetings."

One month after this, Anne Burrows and Alexander Gilchrist were married quietly at Colne Church—on Tuesday morning, February 4th, 1851.

ALEXANDER GILCHRIST.

# CHAPTER IV.

## The Wedding Journey.

### 1851—1852. Age 23—24.

WITH marriage began a new horizon and a larger intellectual life; from varied pursuits, ranging over science and literature, the bride and bridegroom were not likely to experience ennui. In a letter of Anne Gilchrist's to Julia Newton, we are given a glimpse of the honeymoon :—

"*July* 30, 1851. *Keswick, Cumberland.*

MY DEAREST JULIA : Surely you have been expecting a letter from me this long time? Travelling accumulates such a heap of material that it makes one, strange to say, quite shrink from the effort of writing. For the material is so crude and undigested that it takes months to get into an articulate shape with me. By which I mean to say, that I shall not attempt to describe anything except perhaps those things least worth describing.

"After I last saw you, we spent nearly a week at Aldermaston. Then a few very busy days winding-up our affairs, packing, and so forth, at Barnet. Then, last

Monday three weeks, set out on our travels northward, going, however, by a circuitous route, in order to visit Lincoln Cathedral; and were well repaid for the *détour*, I need not say. In fact, we shall not have such another architectural treat at York itself. Next day we went on to Leeds, slept there, and early the following morning started for Windermere, *via* Lancaster. Arrived there at mid-day, walked on to Bowness, a small town seated at the edge of the Lake. Next day went up the Lake by steamer to Ambleside, where we lodged for above a week. Thence on to Grasmere, spending a week there also, and thence to Keswick, which we leave on Saturday next for Patterdale.

"Think how strange we must have felt when the railway set us down on the border of Windermere, among mountains. (N.B.—Highgate Hill was the greatest elevation, I think, I had previously seen.) However, a mountain is but a big hill after all.

"What I delight in most are the mountain streams and waterfalls, and woods and lakes, with just a peep of the mountains through the trees. These latter are best seen at a distance: when actually walking amongst them, their grandeur and solitariness and barrenness are depressing and chilling. After all, the sunny, fertile, woody plain for me, with gentle hills around, with a deep, calm river smiling in the sunshine, not darkly frowning in the shade, as here, flowing through it. I could not make a *home* here, glorious and lovely and sublime—it is all these in turns—as the scenery is here. But the climate is dismal to a degree—so wet and cloudy and sunless. I am told, that in many of the

valleys here the ground is unvisited by the sunbeams
for three months at a time in winter.

"We shall go to York the week after next, and then
return by the West; visiting the Wye, and, if possible,
finding a six months' resting-place there for the winter.
Next spring, I think, we shall settle for something like
a permanence.  My dear husband most thoroughly
enjoys the life we are now leading, and he says I am a
very brave little traveller, though I have not yet been
up a mountain—at least, only up a moderate one."

The object of a visit to York has been mentioned in
the 'Memoir of Alexander Gilchrist.'   "We went into
Yorkshire, Etty's native county, to collect materials for
the 'Life,' which took us into some curious old-world
nooks and corners, and among people with a fresh
flavour of their native soil about them.  The following
winter was spent within sight and sound of the sea at
Lyme Regis."

*Marine Parade, Lyme Regis, Sunday,*
*December* 21—24, 1851.

"  . . . Seven weeks have glided by as swiftly and
noiselessly as a river through sunshine, not through
shade.  Happy, sunny days which unexpectedly soon
have to be reckoned by the week and month.  But
how is it all this time, dear Julia, no tidings of you?
How and where is life spending itself with you?  I
trust this will reach you on Christmas morn—a blithe
Christmastide and a fruitful New Year to you! as glad
a Christmas as ours will be still and quiet.  What a
funny Christmas Day it will be; us two all alone, and
enough to one another.  Every day is such a happy

one, we have no margin left, and being more than a
hundred miles away from all dear friends, we have no
means of changing the *kind* of happiness.

" You will be glad to hear what a fortunate environment we have contrived and been blessed with for this
new era of my life. Every arrangement was made
weeks ago, and our quarters are most homelike and
comfortable. . . . Dear husband has kept me up to being
very active and industrious these two months; daily
writing, daily practice, and daily walks. Most of all,
delightful are our evenings—the reward and crown of
the day, when he reads aloud earnest books to me, I
working (with the needle) the while; and I ' read ' music
to him. He has selected for me all the music he thinks
worth anything, and as I play and sing it all, we have
variety and freshness.

" Carlyle's ' Sterling ' is one of the books we have
thus read together. Mrs. Browning's ' Casa Guidi
Windows,' a poem which elevates my notions of
women's capabilities in verse; Herbert Spencer's
' Social Statics ; ' Guyot's ' Earth and Man,' a suggestive
though faulty book on physical geography ; Mariotti's
' Italy in 1848,' a still less satisfactory book as a whole,
but giving some insight into Italian affairs. As for
Carlyle's ' Life of Sterling,' it is a book to vivify one's
very heart, revealing to us as it does the tender, gentle,
beautiful, loving and lovable nature of *him* (Carlyle),
the great, stern, earnest thinker, before whose burning
intensity, like that of an old Hebrew prophet, as it has
been said, we almost tremble. Surely never before was
there in any man the union of such Titan strength and

keenest insight, with soft, tenderest, pitying gentleness. Never surely a man who had so the power of winning deep, reverent heart's love from his readers. Do you remember his interpretation, so to speak, of Giotto's portrait of Dante in ' Hero Worship ? ' It might stand word for word as a description of himself.

" Herbert Spencer's ' Social Statics ' has taken great hold of us, but I have not left myself a corner to gossip more."

The following " Sunday, December 28, 1851," Alexander Gilchrist writes an important announcement to his wife's friend :—

" Dear Miss Newton : You will hear with pleasure, yesterday, about two p.m. the long-expected little guest arrived in these parts, in good condition, and nowise belated. . . . *Monday January 5.*

" Our first-born is strong and healthy, and decidedly pretty for his years—I mean *days!* Little Percy Carlyle (so we have already named him), protests vehemently against the operations of the toilette, and proclaims his hungry sensations on first waking, which latter little noise is soon quieted. He has been otherwise disturbed only twice, during his short span of life. . . . "

# CHAPTER V.

## THE FIRST HOME.

### 1852—1856.   AGE, 24—28.

THE year succeeding the departure of Anne and
Alexander Gilchrist from Lyme Regis (April 30,
1852) was spent in travel; before they finally decided to
settle in the " cheerful, picturesque town of Guildford."
In the Memoir of her husband, Anne Gilchrist speaks of
' Stoke' near Guildford :—" Our roomy old, gabled,
weather-tiled house, standing a little back from the high
road, was a home after our own heart.   It seemed to have
a particularly comfortable, sleepy way of basking in the
sun, as a thing it had been used to do on summer afternoons for two or three centuries ; but in rough weather
it was like a ship at sea, so did the winds, from whatever
quarter, buffet it, and surge along the hollows of its
many gabled roof.   In the hall, which was the largest
room, stood a long oak table, lustrous with age and the
polishings of many hands, which must have been made
in the house to remain there till both should crumble, for
at no door nor window could it have been got in or out ;
and with it were the high oaken stools on which less
luxurious generations had sat at meat.   There was a great

open fireplace with niched seats in the chimney corner
where to rest with a friend over the glowing, fragrant
logs when stiff and chill, but in happiest mood, after a
twenty-mile walk, was an enjoyment that made a man
' o'er all the ills of life victorious.' Often the friend
was Walter White, than whom no man knows better how
to enjoy, and to make his readers enjoy, such a tramp
and such a rest."

Now and again, Anne Gilchrist accompanied her
husband in the shorter " country rambles which had for
their goal some old church, every stone of which was
scanned till it yielded up its quota of the history, as well
as of the meaning and beauty of the whole." But
oftener at this time, the young housewife would be
hospitably occupied in their Manor-like house ; immersed
also in maternal responsibilities.

On the eighteenth of September, 1854, Anne Gilchrist gave birth to a second child. In a letter to Isabella Ireland (November 7) the mother says :—" We
have named our little girl Beatrice Carwardine. Beatrice
we chose for its own sake ; and Carwardine because
it was my mother's maiden name."

Alexander Gilchrist's first book was nearing completion ; and in the beginning of 1855 the " Life of Etty "
made its appearance.

The book brought an appreciative letter from Carlyle,
who wrote from " Chelsea, 30th January, 1855 :—

" DEAR SIR : I have received your *Life of Etty;*
and am surely much obliged by your kind Gift and by
the kind sentiments you express towards me. I read,
last night, in the Book, with unusual satisfaction : a

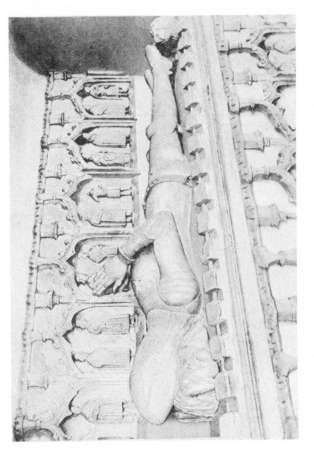

MONUMENT OF THOMAS DE VERE, EIGHTH EARL OF OXFORD, AT
COLNE PRIORY: DIED SEPTEMBER 18, 1370.

(See page 3.)

Book done in a vigorous sympathetic vivacious spirit, and promising me the delineation, actual and intelligible, of a man extremely well worth knowing. Beyond doubt I shall finish steadily what I have begun,—and small thanks to me in this instance. Etty's name was, naturally, familiar to me; but his physiognomy of body and mind, and his great merits as painter and man were a mere rumour to me hitherto.

I believe I may congratulate you on accomplishing a good work, of its kind, among your fellow creatures; and it is a real favour to me that I have the opportunity of enjoying myself over it, and instructing myself by it.

" I wish you all good speed in your enterprises; and solicit a continuance of your goodwill towards me.

" I am, with many thanks and regards,

Yours sincerely,

T. CARLYLE."

The letter led to acquaintance with Thomas Carlyle: 30th May, 1855, a note came from 5, Cheyne Row :—

" DEAR SIR: If you call here any afternoon about half-past three, you will commonly find me disengaged, and ready for a little speech with a friend."

Six months later, Alexander Gilchrist called, and describes his second visit, in a letter to William Haines :—              [*November 29th*, 1855.]

" At half-past seven on Friday evening last, an omnibus set me down in Great Cheyne Row. Shown up into the large, comfortable drawing-room, I found Mrs. Carlyle alone (Carlyle downstairs fetching a short allowance of sleep over night), and was more favourably impressed by her than I had expected. After exchanging a few words, as she was making the tea, Carlyle appeared in his long brown indoors coat, and shook me cordially by the hand; was from that moment to the last *very* kind. 'I have brought you here on false pretences.' Ruskin was coming the *following* night; Mrs. Carlyle was engaged out to a party. 'You must not suppose,' she had before said, 'the wife of a philosopher sits at home over the fire in white satin shoes.'

"Carlyle was very pleased with all I had brought him; was 'like a wild man,' said Mrs. Carlyle, the night before, over the pamphlets. These were nearly all new to him, and nearly all more or less worth seeing." [Alexander Gilchrist was helping Thomas Carlyle to find prints of costumes and portraits: "Frederick's Military Instructions" was among the *pamphlets*.]

"After tea, Mrs. Carlyle left. And for the rest of the evening (till twelve) I sat with him alone, he pouring himself out as is his wont; sitting the latter part of the time on a footstool by the fire, smoking, and looking in his old long brown kind of great-coat, as he was bewailing the pass men and things had come to, and as he thought of it hardly caring to live,—looking like a veritable Prophet, mourning in sackcloth and ashes the sins of the world.

"Carlyle gave me a new and heroic view of Marlborough and his Duchess, among other things. Which led to Macaulay and his [C.] blackening of M.'s face, and to a long imaginary address to Macaulay for flying at great men—as the *canaille* of themselves are ever prone to do. 'Come out of that, I tell you, you big blockhead—big as you look, you low miserable creature, you.'

[At another time Carlyle, after reading in Macaulay's "History of England," laid down the book and said, "Flow on, thou shining river." !]

"Carlyle took me up into his study, showed his daguerreotype from Cooper's 'Cromwell,' for which he has a great fondness; his screen covered with small prints relative to Frederick; a (framed) Albert Durer, that had once belonged to the Elector of Saxony; who saved Luther. *Gave* me also a plaster mask of Dante's face, which he has had many years.

"Carlyle spoke affectionately of Hollar—despondingly of literature. 'If he were on his death-bed' (Carlyle spoke this with intense sincerity), the only thing he had done would give him any pleasure was the 'Cromwell;' some little pleasure to have done that—to have dispersed the lies, and shown him as some day all men would see him to have been!' 'One might as well go on the stage and be a mountebank as take to literature'—with other 'splenetic words,' as on my interposing he confessed them to be. Carlyle showed himself truly lovable, as well as grand, throughout."

From the time of this visit, Gilchrist was in constant correspondence with Carlyle over the "Frederick:" letters wherein the historian is seen at work upon his last great book. For full enjoyment, the communications presuppose close knowledge of the "History of Frederick the Great." As eight of Carlyle's letters to Gilchrist follow one another closely in date, we give them in sequence :—

"*Chelsea*, 28 *Nov.*, 1855.

" My Dear Sir,

Last night your messenger brought down the Pictures
framed,—four new ones among the lot, besides the 3
Fredericks :—thanks for your singular and useful goodness to me.   One of these new Pictures, *Lascy* (I write
Lacy) is extremely good ; indeed they seem all good,—
except *Loudon*, whom I know otherwise with a better
physiognomy extremely *Scotch*.  This Garret will become
quite a Gallery, were all these Portraits hung in their
places here ;  my wife, skilful in such things, has undertaken that part of the business ;—and indeed is now
actually engaged in the preliminary parts of it.

"But there is one thing you must do straightway : solve
me this couple of Enigmas, the two Prints, Lady and
old Gentleman who have no name !  No name the
remarkable old gentleman (whom I could *wish* to prove
Anhalt-Dessau, whose other portraits he does slightly
resemble,— but no, no, Anhalt has always *whiskers*),—
and the Lady almost worse than no name, for her
signature seems to be written in Persic or Arabic: who
on earth is she ?  Not the Czarìna Elizabeth surely ?
And she does not resemble Maria Theresa, to my understanding, hardly at all.

"Of the Frederick Books I have read  three ; all of
them worth looking at ; one of them a conspicuously
excellent Piece, which I had never seen before, his
*Instructions Militaires*, extremely *physiognomic* of the
man, and in all ways demanding to be read.  I think
the Prussians must still keep it secret,—or I know not
what they do with it ?  No trace of it hitherto in any of

the collections of his books; nor did I know it had ever been translated into English. Were I Commander in Chief I would study that book to the last fibre of meaning in it; and make all my officers, down to the lowest corporal who had sense in his head, read it and again read it.—Alas, I fear if *our* "Commander-in-Chief," so-called, did read it till he really *understood* it,—the first effect would be, said Commander-in-Chief would go distracted, and do himself a mischief, with rope or otherwise! It is certain our highest War-Secretary, Duke of Newcastle or whoever he might be, if he applied to Frederick to be made a Drummer, would not even be allowed to drum: " Go first and learn it, then apply to me!"— — But enough of all that. Please solve me the enigma at once, for I shall be unhappy till then, more or less!

" Ruskin took my copy of *Etty* with him; hopes to make your acquaintance before long. . . ."

" *Chelsea*, 10 *Dec.*, 1855.

" I yesterday found your new Gift of Prussian Pamphlets waiting for me when I came down. Really I am almost ashamed of your kindness, tho' very heartily obliged. . . .

The *Letter on Patriotism* I never saw, never distinctly heard of, before: I almost guess they are really not by Frederick (tho' nobody can at once say, such unutterable *Editors* are these Prussian ones), but I will read, I will examine; a Book even with such a title, in that year 1760, must be curious, and throw light on a thing or two. I suspect the Frederick in sky blue coat (dark blue is the real colour) may really be a copy by Hogarth from the Chodowiecky Portrait,—not a quite unsuccessful Copy.   The other reproduction from Chodowiecky teaches us at least (so bad is it) how happy we are to possess the excellent original.

"Smith is quite right : " It is an *error* " (very considerable indeed !) " that the science of war needs not to be taught," rule of thumb is by no means adequate to said science !—The " Instructions to the Cavalry " is a genuine Piece ; I already have it in German (somewhere), with Notes by the Prince de Ligne.   Frederick, I find, wrote several sets of " Instructions," general or special, which at length got into print ; that of De Ligne's is the only one I had ; and that *first* one you gave me was reckoned by far the most important : every General had a copy in writing ; sworn to keep it secret, and not to carry it to the war with him ;—I see it was written before the 7-Years' War (probably about 1750) ; by what chance it got to the Public is not said ; but, about the time of that English one, it was getting printed in various places—the Prussian Editors do not give it ; a very notable set of Editors !—

" We go on Monday, as I said ; but shall be back, if all go right, punctually on the 17th of next month ; shortly after which date let me have the pleasure of seeing you again, and thanking you for all this kindness.

" Yours, with many regards,

" T. CARLYLE."

" *Chelsea, 3rd February,* 1856.

" Beyond doubt you are one of the successfullest hunters up of Old Books now living ; and one of the politest of obliging men !   Once more I have to declare myself very much your debtor, and grateful to be helped,—in such a spirit, and also with such effect.

"The *Bielefeld* is quite a conquest; vainly tried, in all manner of ways, for four years past: it would have saved me, and will still save me, many missions (*missions*, since visits are really impossible for me) to that dismal labyrinth of a British Museum; nay I may get out of it what no missions or visits would ever have given. . . .

"I find in that old book of military Pictures, something of *costume* to learn from; and at least three portraits I was interested in,—Prince de Ligne (Prince of Puppies, as I call him) for one. N.B. all his pamphlets about Frederick (indifferent all, but unique some of them) are under my hand already."

"*Chelsea, 5th March,* 1856.

"Thanks again for your new Gift,—which I must endeavour again to accept without confusion of face! There is a certain interest in witnessing the actual Installation of Frederick's grandfather by Dutch William and "Mr. Johnston" (a countryman, whom I do not know), —though the main profit is to make good the allusions (Louis XIV.'s *second* attack upon mankind, treaty of Ryswick still in the womb of Time, &c.), and to spell out the Prussian personages, one or more of whom are beyond my might in this dreadfully mangled condition, "Fulks" for Fuchs, "Denherff" for *Donhoff* etc. etc.

" "*Serena*" is rather a curious book for Toland's sake, and may become a little more so if the Goddess herself should ever be better known to English mankind. It was worth picking up.

"I kept, or at least keep, the Dutch Book, after all. I find there are controversial discussions in it, Mynheer even getting satirical :—I learned one thing of interest to me, out of one of the old Plates : the situation of the Vielle Cour at Loo ; *Frederick's* old Palace there, "a place all hung with cobwebs," out of which Voltaire often dates letters to Frederick and others. It is hard to say, out of what one may *not* learn, by keeping one's eyes well open !

"Your book, *Müller on the* 2 *Silesian Wars,* will be particularly welcome to me,—and *Quàm Vivendum,* for I am just in that affair, hoping to wind myself out of it in, a fortnight or so ; Heaven knows what bother I have had with mere masses of dark rubbish (dark though authentic), and no Books upon it that were not irrational. Please let me have that ; it will be welcome any day.

"Francke is Father of the Prussian *Pietists,* founder of a grand orphan Asylum at Halle, etc. ; "*ce chien de Francke,*" as Frederick's sister calls him for making them all take to psalm-singing and family prayers during the very dinner time, when her Father fell into the blues ! I do not care about Francke ; though as being a famed man of those days any book of his has a certain claim on one.

"As to the hypothetical or prospective list, do not purchase at all. *Bielefeld* (tho' I did not know he *was* in English, before), thanks to your virtuous search, is here in French original. *Vie du Prince Henri* I also have, —a mere "hoohoo !" of empty laudation and court-wind ; as is another *Vie* of him which I have :—

nothing else is well possible in that country, the man being truly an oblique-eyed (*squinting*), jealous, lean, vain creature, tho' very sharp in war; whom it is handier to say *nothing* plain about.

" *Mèm. de Bareith* is a famed Book, and of first-rate moment (tho' very obscure to the English reader): I have at last got an English copy of my own. . . .

" A clever creature this Wilhelmina, " the Margravine," Frederick's eldest sister, loved by him beyond all other beings, and loving him with the like intensity: her Book is extremely curious (I often say, the one *human* Book there yet is on that matter); and with all her shrill vehemency and reckless exaggeration, Wilhelmina has grown quite a love of mine too. . . . "

" *Chelsea,* 12*th April,* 1856.

" . . . Again and again I give you thanks; and am astonished at your assiduity, zeal and marvellous success in these fields of generous adventure. On that head I will say no more.

" Frederick's *signatures* are excessively abundant: about 3,000 or so of autograph letters by him are in existence (not a few in the *Mitchell Papers,* British Museum); and of *Orders,* Cabinet Officialities and the like, he *signed* perhaps 20 or 30 every day of his long reign, from 1740 to 1786.—I have a *facsimile* (or perhaps it is an original?) of a reply he makes, to certain Town Magistrates on some proposal or other, in German,—dreadfully ill-spelt (as all his writings in all his languages are) but with plenty of sharp sense in it, as likewise is always the case."

" We have been rather out of sorts in the late

intemperate weather,—my wife confined with cold, and
myself, what is more unusual, making signals of distress
now and then in that way. The wet westerly winds
are repairing such damages.—I think I must keep
Guildford ahead of me as a *bonne bouche* for getting
through some other Section of this deplorable muddy
business of mine! I am given to claim a *holiday* at the
end of every stage in my journey, sometimes at the end
of very short stages. At all events we must let the
weather dry, and the flowers get out."

" *Chelsea, 6th May,* 1856.

" . . . These are again capital Books several of
them; you surpass all people, of my experience, in the
chase of Books!—Riesbuk (or Risbuk) the Traveller
is a cleverish fellow by nature, and actually *lived* in
many of the places he describes. An Advocate first or
some kind of lawyer, about the Mentz region; he then
took to literature (Passau, Lintz, Vienna), then to Play
acting; died (still under 40) as Newspaper Editor
at Zürich, where he had translated *Coxe* &c. His
Book is very *like* all that made great noise in its
day; and is still worth reading, especially by me.—The
*Letters* by *Main du Maitre,* I soon found after you
went, are also a decidedly authentic and curious Piece:
Published by Frederick's *Youngest Brother,* striving to
vindicate himself against the fierce condemnation Frederick had passed on his unlucky retreat (from Prag, after
the Battle of Kolin) in 1757.—"If justice were done,"
said he to the Generals and him, " your heads would all
lie there!" (fiercely pointing to the ground), and so
turned his mare's hips on them, and went off at a canter.

The Brothers, I think, never met more; the younger (great-grandfather of the present King of Prussia) demanded his demission, fell into worse and worse health, and died within 2 years.—I wonder what Frederick would have said, to certain Gentlemen returning from the Crimea, with Panmure and " Doub" at the head of them! Such sight as that he was not condemned to . . ."

*Take care of Dowb.* The Secretary at War (an officer superseded when the present office, Secretary of State for War, was created) was for many years Mr. Fox Maule, who became Lord Panmure. In the early and alarming days of the Crimean war, the Commander-in-Chief Lord Raglan received a telegraphic despatch from Lord Panmure giving various directions about the campaign, and ending with the words " Take care of Dowb." Lord Raglan could not understand " Dowb," but supposed it must be some local strategic point of importance, from which perhaps a formidable Russian attack might be impending. He had to telegraph back for an explanation, and then received the full name " Dowbiggin." There was a young subaltern officer, Dowbiggin, in the army (perhaps on the staff of Lord Raglan), son of Doubiggin, a large upholsterer (in or near Oxford Street) who was somehow connected with Lord Panmure; and Lord Panmure's meaning was that Lord Raglan should keep a friendly eye on " Dowb," and take any convenient opportunity of promoting him. It was General Sir De Lacy Evans, M.P., who brought this matter before the House of Commons (say some few months afterwards); and it was matter—as many of our readers well remember—of much laughter and some scandal.

As early as 1856 Alexander Gilchrist formed a project of writing a Life of Countess D'Aulnoy. Thomas Carlyle writes from " *Chelsea*, *12th May*, 1856. " . . . I unluckily know next to nothing about D'Aulnoy, and fear there is not much that can be known. She has come athwart me early in excerpts from her *Spanish*, and other Court Delineations, done, I think, in the form of *Tours*, *Mèmoires*; in which, tho' very lively and pleasant, she is said to be extremely indifferent to known and Not-known, and even to True and False. Of her *Fairy* Productions, again, I hear a highly favourable account from several quarters.—Perhaps in the very *latest* of the Editions of Morèri's Dictionary (1740 or so) there may be something of her? In that of 1709 there is nothing whatever. Bayle only quotes her once, and with a slight shake of the head: *Biographie Universelle* is utterly meagre.

Perhaps you are right to give up Rogers's affair; as to the man himself you are certainly right: his poetic sense of beauty was trifling from the first, and had all got contracted into the *dilettante* and *upholsterish* form. . . ."

" *July*, 1856.

" I have again to thank you for many fine things. " These strange coloured Prints of Costumes (all as *true*, we may fancy, as the " English lord " is) are very curious to look upon, and awaken many thoughts. I cannot rightly make out the *time*, guessing from internal evidence; the place seems to be Vienna, Artist one I never heard of before.　"*Kaiser Leopoldus*" died 1705 (but the Portrait here resembles his son, Carl VI, rather);　the *Imperatrix* given is *Leopold's*, however: on the other hand, the female *Archidux* "Maria Anna" is his *grand*-daughter come to maturity; and takes on to about 1740 or later.　"Prince Eugenius" too (strangely walking a minuet, or walking the tight-rope as they mostly do!), takes us to about the same date,—not quite.　Probably they were published at Wien, now and then, for a long series of years.

"That Prussian Picture is a very old acquaintance and a first-rate favourite of mine!　I have seen an older Engraving, more elaborate, but not so like as this: the oil Picture is still in Charlottenburg as fresh as when *new;* and Lord Ashburton here has an unsurpassable copy of it,—done, I believe, for my sake, tho' I get but little good of it.　We are both of us, my wife and I, in love with the Picture;—must have this Engraving *framed,* if you will give it leave to hang here till— you become our neighbour, and one can step in to look at it and other things!

"I read *Carr* thro', with great interest: a really curious old talk he keeps up, and is an authentic man . . . Not another moment is left: 'Breakfast ready, sir!' (for I have been up too early), and so good-bye till we return.　I send many regards to Mrs. Gilchrist, and hope I may be in good case to enjoy a little of her music, against my getting back into these parts.

"With many good wishes and thanks,

Yours always truly,

T. CARLYLE.

Surely the letters which we have been reading, throw a
pleasant light upon the great biographer, at work in his
"garret"?  They also remind us of the special skill that
the collector must possess; a skill amounting to talent;
the fruits of which, historians and artists feed upon.
That this, though a recognized opinion, is one which is
not acted upon in some quarters, was shown some eighteen
years ago, when Sir Samuel Meyrick's unique collection of armour was first offered the nation for as little as
£40,000, which offer was refused.    " By  far the finest
collection in Europe," said Sir Coutts Lindsay, who tried
to make Robert Lowe, then Chancellor of the Exchequer,
understand this; but the statesman declined to "give
£40,000 for a lot of old iron."   What happened?  The
" old iron " was sold really to Sir R. Wallace, to dealers
in France and Germany, and a certain amount to Sir
Coutts Lindsay; realizing between £60,000 and £70,000.
Doubtless, it was very generally believed, that the
superb collection could easily be brought together again!
Perhaps we do not realize, that fine judgment, unerring
instinct and patience are necessary qualifications for the
sport of collecting.

A secluded life of four years at Guildford was soon to
end for Anne and Alexander Gilchrist:—"Allan Cunningham's sketch in ' Lives of the Painters ' and  the well-
known illustrations to ' Blair's Grave ' were, up to this
time, all the acquaintance my husband had with Blake.
But, in a visit to London, he now came upon some
designs, and upon the 'Illustrations of the Book of
Job,' which filled him with enthusiasm, and his mind
was quickly made up to the task of gathering together

as complete a record of Blake's life and works as was yet possible. This and other literary plans made removal to London desirable, and in the course of a visit to Mr. Carlyle the idea was mooted of our taking a house next door to him. Soon afterwards Mr. Carlyle wrote, ' I dare not advise anybody into a house (almost as dangerous as advising him to a wife, except that divorce is easier) ; but if Heaven should please to ' rain you, accidentally, into that house, I should esteem it a kindness.' And Heaven did rain us down there, much to our satisfaction, in the autumn of 1856."

# CHAPTER VI.

## LIFE AT CHELSEA.

### 1856—1859   AGE 29—32.

" WE had been settled at Chelsea only a few months
when a domestic sorrow,—the accidental
drowning of a much-loved elder brother,—came upon him
[Alexander Gilchrist].  The two succeeding years had
to be wholly devoted to the harassing task of winding up
large and complicated business affairs, left in disorder by
this sudden death.  That done, Alexander turned with
renewed delight back to literary work, carrying on the
' Blake' towards completion."

Intercourse with Samuel Palmer, William Linnell
(Sen.) and James Smeltham over the biography, contributed to make life pleasant at Chelsea.  Especially
delightful was talk and correspondence with the genial,
scholarly artist, Samuel Palmer : the last of the long
line of English painters to possess and to cherish poetic-
landscape art.  We give one of his letters—in which
acknowledgment is made of a copy of Ovid.  We
need not remind the reader, that the artist was a friend
and disciple of Blake's :—

"My dear Mr. Gilchrist: You really overrate my contributions to the Blake revival. If there were any labour, it was a labour of love, of love for his memory and for those who cherish it.

"Now you have broken the charm! It is no longer 'all for love and nothing for reward:' but I must say you are the most skilful of givers, for no City gourmand could more delight to see his area filled with live turtles, than I with the savour and relish of these delicious Italian morsels of the mind. As for Ovid, he is the quintessence of poetry, as your copy is the quintessence of editions. What a text! What a margin! They did not clip the book edges then to make those shreds up into paper again! Milton says somewhere, that Ovid, under happier circumstances, would have left Virgil only a second name among the Latins.

"What a wonderful thing is a good book—next to a clear conscience, the most precious thing life has to offer.

"With many thanks for your kindness, believe me dear Mr. Gilchrist, most truly yours

Post-script                                   S. Palmer."

"I forgot I think to mention that in the late Sir R. Peel's copy of the 'Europe and America,' there is a pencil drawing by Mr. Richmond, [a disciple of Blake's] done soon after Blake's decease, while the memory was fresh, and assisted by the cast of which I spoke; most probably this is the closest likeness existing.

"I called to mind the other day a definition of Bacon's, which in perhaps the fewest possible words gives Blake's art-creed,—it is for art to 'suit the shows of

things to the desires of the mind.'    Blake thought so
too, in common with Plato and Michael Angelo, who
in one of his sonnets says—speaking of the mind or
soul :—

> ' Above the visible world she soars to eek
>         Ideal form, the universal mould.'

" By the bye, if you want to see a picture bound by a
splendid imagination upon the fine firm old philosophy, do
go and look at the Julio Romano (Nursing of Jove) in
the National Gallery.    That is precisely the picture
Blake would have revelled in.    I think I hear him say,
' As fine as possible, Sir !    It is not permitted to man
to do better.' "

The progress of the ' Life' was followed with interest
by Carlyle, who possessed the ' Job,' which he praised :
" It showed the author had had real sight in his own
mind of what he painted."

" The Life of Blake " was first offered to Chapman.
Carlyle (when giving Gilchrist a letter of introduction
to the publisher) said that ' Chapman was not without
judgment of his own, but stingy ; would probably
only offer me [Alexander] half profits, which meant, as
I knew, nothing.'    Ultimately, Macmillan undertook to
publish " The Life of Blake."    Miss Muloch was
*reader* for the firm at the time.

We must not forget to chronicle the birth of a
second son—Herbert Harlakenden—March 18, 1857.

Many were the talks that Anne and Alexander Gil-
christ exchanged with Jane and Thomas Carlyle.
These conversations have been preserved by Alexander
Gilchrist's pen :—

'Called on Carlyle about half-past three p.m.

'Lady Stanley and her friend Miss Brown were there. They talked the usual small talk: about the Peace, the Naval Review, and so forth. Carlyle agreed with them in being glad of peace "on any terms." We couldn't fight. We were the handiest nation for others to fight with, except the Yankees. When he read of their blustering (Carlyle) thought to himself, 'Well, I think you, at all events, are the handiest nation to fight with I know of; you, at all events, we can tackle.' Opposition from the ladies, who thought the Americans had always beaten us; to which Carlyle dissented.

'Lady Stanley mentioned Montalembert, and his new book on England, as so good; and that he was fond of the English. What did Carlyle think?

'Oh! I think him a very stupid fellow: I believe, too, there is a good deal of abuse of me: I have not read it.' Reverting to the subject of the Naval Review, and what a muddle it had been, Lady Stanley said that it was not to be talked about except under the breath, but the Queen was the cause of the confusion, in not having chosen some other day—the previous day—and slept at the Isle of Wight.'

(Carlyle) 'Well, I suppose the Queen thought it was hard if she, of all her subjects, must choose a day which was inconvenient to her.'

(Lady Stanley) 'Oh! but the line was shut up by her going; and the greedy railway people took more passengers than they could accommodate.'

(Carlyle) 'I heard, drunken peers were seen about.'

(Lady Stanley) 'No; drunken stokers.'

(Carlyle) ' Ah ! there was a good deal of spirituous liquor going.'

Carlyle asked Miss Brown whether she was related by her ancestors to a Marshal Brown, an Irish Jacobite, and distinguished General in the Austrian service ? Carlyle mentioned that there were two Browns, Austrian generals ; Marshal Brown the more celebrated. ' A Life of him (French) in existence, which he had never seen.   Couldn't find out anything about him.'

Miss Brown didn't know ; he probably was related. One Brown (an ancestor) had offered the crown of Ireland to the '——' family ; Miss Brown thinks he had been hung.

' It was a hanging business, that.'  Carlyle ended by asking her to inquire into the history of the Browns ; it would oblige him much.

' When I first went in, the ladies were commending Carlyle's beard.   ' There is much to be said in favour of a beard ; I see them gradually appearing up and down the world ; '—' admitted, upright collars did not go well with them ; flat linen ones, which used to be worn with beards were necessary.

" The pretty lady talked much with Mrs. Carlyle, next whom she sat ; Miss Brown with Carlyle.

" On leaving, the pretty lady coaxingly said to Carlyle, ' You will come to my Saturday evening ?   Now don't screw up your mouth so ; you must say yes.  (Lady Stanley speaking imperatively) Say yes, now.'  ' Yes ' (round and full), says Carlyle ; who then conducted them to the street door.  ' These illustrious people ! ' he mutters, after they had left.

One evening at Cheyne Row 'we talked amongst other things, of rising from the ranks. Carlyle spoke of an old British officer, Colonel ——, who had saved Head, against his will, from causing a rebellion in Upper Canada. The former had been promised rewards, but received none, except a small sum of money and the being made a Poor Knight of Windsor. Buller was to have taken up the case, but died. Colonel '—— ——', had been in debt ever since he held a commission. The officer —— had fought in thirty battles ; a wonderful man; simple-minded and good. Wrote a book on the teaching of children under ten; those he considered the most important years of education. This soldier was cured of all doubts of immortality by a vision of Heaven he once had. All the Colonel could remember was a high brass pillar, on which he saw his own face ! Looked down on earth and saw his wife weeping ; but it affected him not : life seemed too short to be considered. The Colonel had had eighteen children—nearly all died.

His wife living ?

' No ; she long was gone to look on the brass column.'

Carlyle laughed heartily when telling this story.

" *October* 11*th*, 1859. Called on Carlyle about half-past eight p.m. Found him in the dining-room, sitting at the table, looking over and marking a book catalogue. Mrs. Carlyle with a number of *All the Year Round* before her, and knitting.

' Carlyle very genial. He alluded to a cheap copy of the *Monthly Magazine*, which in an unbound state, had fallen in his way—a companion had rummaged it out of a cupboard, many years ago :—'Doesn't remember any earthly pleasure equal to what he had over that.' Remembers in particular, one sentimental story in imitation of Sterne, *The Sentinel*.    A wife had lost her husband in battle, and wished to see his dead body ; the sentinel harshly refused ; the indignation of the bystanders and relater.—In the last degree vapid and watery, doubtless.  'But I (Carlyle) went altogether along with it.  Think it was the *Lady's Magazine*. But I remember no plates.'

'Recollects afterwards, reading *Roderick Random*, with utmost delight.  Remembers the day and hour ; the mossy bank on which he sat ; the golden rays of the setting sun ; and an old Irishman he met on his way home, who had been a soldier.  A remarkable man, who lived despised by his fellow-creatures, as a Papist and Irishman : recalls his appearance that day.  Only an odd volume, the first : when he returned to the shop, the man was obliged to confess he had not the other ; but never rested till he got it.

'Remembers a year later first reading Robertson's 'Preliminary Dissertation to Charles V.,' with utmost delight and wonder.  Opened to him new worlds of knowledge to be attained ; vistas in all directions. Never seen it since : doubtless weak enough ; the first book he got any good out of ; did not get any good out of the others.

"Carlyle possessed an extraordinary appetite for, love and delight in books during the first part of his life. This lasted for clever books till middle life.  Then his appetite began to get ticklish, and now no book at all can give him delight. 'Hard work the reading a book now. Much power in the hands of those who have the giving of books to young persons. Deserves thinking of.'

"Carlyle praised *All the Year Round*; worth reading. Dickens seemed to get hold of sensible, brief accounts of men's experience's out in the East Indies. Wondered where he got hold of such. I mentioned my wife's article on the Gorilla. Carlyle had read it. 'A strange, horrible beast that gorilla, clutching hold of men out of trees, and killing for mere malice.'

[*Our Poor Relation* was the essay referred to. The article pleased Dickens, who showed it to the Carlyles. A trifle that drew forth the remark from Jane Carlyle, 'and you know, my dear, you write very nicely!']

"Carlyle mentioned seeing Madame Vestris with Mathews some years ago, in a burlesque of Planchè's, after Lewes's play; declared there was 'real genius' in her, which made its impression on him despite adverse prepossessions . . .'

During one of Alexander Gilchrist and Thomas Carlyle's midnight walks together, the latter "spoke of the curious persons who came to London in Hogarth's time; William Emerson for one, who wrote books on mathematics still valuable, some of which Carlyle has. 'A strange character; living in the country on £70 a year; his wife spinning with her distaff while her husband wrote: and his treatise written, he would come up to London to sell it. Got bald; could not bear the idea of wearing other people's hair, so made a wig of

flax and clapped it on his head.—Burnt his shins with
sitting close to the fire (as Carlyle remembers seeing
many old people's shins marbled): contrived some kind
of shield, which he called *shin-covers!* The Duke of
Manchester took Emerson up; got him to come and
live with him;—offered him a seat in his carriage.
Emerson asked, what did the Duke want with that
whim-wham? He would walk. The country people
thought him a soothsayer. An old woman came to
ask what had become of her husband (long gone away),
she wishful perhaps to be free. ' He has been in hell
these three years past.'

" ' Emerson was a free-thinker, who looked on his
neighbour the parson as a humbug. He seemed to have
defended himself in silence the best way he could against
the noisy clamour and unreal stuff going on around ;
retreating to his mechanics and fluxions, which he knew
to be real.'

" Carlyle spoke of Arkwright as worthy a biography
or essay. ' None good hitherto. A wonderful man—
rather of wonderful results to England. A poor barber,
who bethought himself of the loom, the threads then
shifted by hand. This great invention so simple, a
wonder no one had thought of it before.' Carlyle
minutely described the loom, using his hands freely to
do so. He also told how the weavers set upon Arkwright, " You son of Belial! will you not let us live?"
and drove him out of the village :—how his wife destroyed his model one night when he was asleep, thinking he ought to attend to his razors and suds, as the
more profitable ; how he told her to be off and sent her

adrift out of his house, for fear of a worse thing; probably giving her a licking first.

" Strutt,—a neighbouring yeoman, found money for the first weaving mill : he was grandfather of the present Lord Belper.   Carlyle had seen the mill—deserted and not at work then.   Strutt showed the ability of a Frederick in ordering his men and economising their labour; his descendants immensely wealthy, worth millions . . .' "

Anne Gilchrist, encouraged by her husband, began to ply her pen.   " A Glance at the Vegetable Kingdom," a short paper printed in *Chambers* (1857), was soon followed by " Electricity," an essay which was accepted by the editor of *Once a Week*.   She also wrote to Alexander's dictation, which together with housewifely duties fully occupied her time.

Mrs. Watson (Gillman's grand - daughter) ' spent many happy afternoons and evenings at Chelsea.   Mrs. Gilchrist was one of those wonderful women one reads of, for she combined high intellectual attainments with careful attention to domestic duties.   As a girl I used to be struck with the charm of her manner and conversation—the result of a cultivated mind and varied reading; her ready sympathy with the studies or occupations of others; and a persistent kindness in endeavours to be useful to her friends.   I remember Mr. Gilchrist saying to me, " I can rarely persuade Annie to take a holiday or to go into society ; "—the wife's bright smile is before me as she replied, "Oh, yes! I do go out as much as I wish ; but I do not need rest as some do; a change of work or occupation is rest for me."'

On the 16th of January, 1859, Anne Gilchrist brought into the world her youngest child, Grace. The mother experienced a serious (though temporary) relapse, as we shall see from Jane Carlyle's letter :—

"DEAR MR. GILCHRIST : Your note has shocked and grieved us both extremely. We hadn't a notion of this ! Every time I have sent to ask for your wife, the answer has been that she was 'doing nicely' or that she was 'better' or had had 'a better night,' except *once*, when Charlotte brought back word of her '*having been* very poorly the day before, but that she had had a better night.'

"I trust in God you will soon be out of anxiety about her ; nature doing for her restoration what the Drs. don't know to do !

"Meanwhile, depend on my taking all possible pains to keep things quiet. I have *tied up* our knocker, and the dog shall be *carried* out and in—Indeed it is only his master that has no authority over him to stop his barking. I had been fearing that he might annoy your wife ; without knowing how ill she was, and have several times run down to pick him up—*after* the mischief was done—But he shall be *carried* quite out of the street.

"If I can be of the least use to you in any way— Taking charge of the children—when the servants are busy—going to shops—or anything—I should really take it kind of you to tell me. I have, you know, a great debt of gratitude to your poor wife for very much kindness and help to myself in sickness.

Yours very sincerely

JANE W. CARLYLE "

# CHAPTER VII.

## LETTER FROM JANE WELSH CARLYLE.

### 1859.—AGE 31.

*Humber—Aberdour, Fife.    Summer of* 1859.

" MY DEAR MRS. GILCHRIST: I don't remember whether I engaged to write to you or not ; but anyhow the spirit moves me to write—and exactly at the wrong moment ! when I have the softest pen and the thickest ink that has fallen in my way since I left home !

" I suppose you are long  removed  to  your  country quarters  and  have  derived  I hope, more benefit from ' the change' than I have done as yet.    I suppose the dreadfully fatiguing journey knocked me up to such an extent, that it has taken all this time of ' pure air,' ' quiet ' and ' new milk and rum ' to overcome the bad consequences.    Certainly,  between  ourselves,  I  am  not sensible of having gained an atom of strength, either bodily or mental, since I left Chelsea !   And yet ; what a difference between the dead-wall one looks out on in Cheyne Row, and the ' view ' from our windows here, unsurpassed I am sure by the Bay of Naples or any other  view  on  Earth !  and  between  the  ' exhalations

from the Thames,' complicated with the vitriol Factory
and Chancellor's dung-hill; and these airs from the
Atlantic blowing on our hill-top! One *ought* to be *well*
here—and now that one has a ' *cuddy*' (donkey) ' all to
oneself' (as the children say) to *walk* about on the four
legs of; one's two own legs being *no go*, one ought to
admit one has everything needed for happiness—except
indeed *one* thing, the *faculty of being happy!*

" Mr. Carlyle is much pleased with the place and the
' soft food' it yields for himself—and horse—and, as
he hardly *works* at all, he would be much better—*if* he
didn't, as he always does in ' the country,' take health *by
the throat* (as it were) *Bathing* as if he were a little
boy in the Serpentine, *walking* as if he had seven-league
Boots, and riding like the Wild Huntsman!—the consequence of all which is that he keeps up in him a
continual fever of biliousness—

" Charlotte [the housemaid] is the happiest of created
girls—everything so *new* to her, everything delightful!
especially the open admiration of Aberdour Lads; who
call her ' *Bonnie wee Lassie*' in the public highway!
' So kind of them!' she says ' when they never saw
her before and don't so much as know her name!!'
Mr. Carlyle remarked justly that ' the compliments
to *herself*, were the only words of Scotch she could
manage to understand! and these she understood at
once, by instinct!'

" Nero is a much improved dog, by sea-bathing
with his master, he snores less, scratches less, and is less
selfish. And '*the* Horse'—Oh, Mr. Carlyle declares 'It
is in *perfect raptures* over its *soft food*—but incapable of

recovering from its astonishment at the badness of the Fyfe roads ! '

"So we shall do very well at the Farm House for as long as we have it—till the 6th of August, after that our plans are still in the vague. Good·bye dear woman I do hope Mr. Gilchrist will find some work in winter to keep you still our neighbours.

Yours most truly,

JANE CARLYLE."

Anne Gilchrist received the letter which we have read when staying with her mother (Mrs. Burrows), at Earls Colne. In the summer of 1859 she wrote a short article, "Whales and Whalemen," which appeared in the April number of *Chambers*, 1860.

Upon returning to Great Cheyne Row, neighbourly intercourse was resumed with the Carlyles; we will call with Alexander Gilchrist, and hear the gossip :—

Talking of the now well-known destruction of the first volume of the ' French Revolution,' Jane Carlyle thought that " the MS. was not lost in Mill's, but in Mrs. Taylor's house, whom Mill was then much with, and afterwards married ; ' and much more likely to have happened in a wholesale druggist's house, as her husband's was, than in a literary man's. The name kept secret for a long while ; but ultimately the Mills themselves let it out. Very uncomfortable affair for Mill before the name was known. Mrs. Austin, for instance, said in his presence, there seemed to her only one plan open to the man—to have gone home and shot himself. Carlyle almost wild at the time: with great difficulty re-wrote it.

It never seemed to him as good as the first copy ; and yet he could not remember what that first was.'

Carlyle " asked me how long I had been at work to-day ? ' From the time I got up till tea-time.' How many hours ? ' Eight clear.' ' Too long.' He never got more than six at the best of times. ' Only three or four clear now. Over the *French Revolution*, six hours a day. Used to go out about two or three in the after-noon ; read in the evening.' Carlyle said that ' people in England had an interest in the *Cromwell*; in the *Frederick*, he had to create it all ; do everything for his readers.'

Carlyle " spoke of a small French volume (1685) on ' Ziska,' he had had from Palmer, and returned. Two things in it new to him, and amused him. One, in besieging a town, Tabor, which the Hussites built for themselves, which Frederick once took and was often in ; the other side threw over into the town waggon-loads of carrion. The other incident, how ' Ziska ' in a battle when he was sore beset, got the women of his side to strew their veils, laces and other light garments ; he then provoked the opposite cavalry to advance into them. They got entangled—their spurs and so forth, in these things ; then 'Ziska' attacked and cut them up. Carlyle laughed much at this . . .

" Talking of the *Leader* to George Henry Lewes, Carlyle asked ' When will those papers on Positivism come to an end ? '

' I can assure you they are making a great impression at Oxford,' says Lewes.

' Ah ! I never look at them, it's so much blank paper

to me. I looked into Comte once; found him to be one of those men who go up in a balloon, and take a lighted candle to look at the stars.'

" Lewes mentioned that he had given up literature for Natural Science.

" Carlyle likes Lewes, and was so pleased with him that in the evening he said to his wife, ' Well, I don't know why you shouldn't call on Miss Evans . . .'

" Mrs. Carlyle alluded to the sudden death of Lady Clementina, who ' was very beautiful but getting *passé*. At a party at which that brute, the Duke of Malakoff was present, conversation turned on our regrets for the past. Lady Jersey foolishly boasted she did not understand them; she had no regrets. ' Ce n'est pas vrai, Madame: you regret your youth, and you regret the fading beauty of your daughter.' "

[The Duc de Malakoff was the Maréchal Pelissier, who commanded the French troops during the Crimean War, and who not only beat the Russians, but got on well with the English, which no doubt influenced the Emperor in giving him the exalted civil appointment which he afterwards held—that of Ambassador to the Court of St. James.]

" He affects the brutal and brusque in his style. The Duke of Malakoff and ' Skittles ' [the courtezan] ' a lady I hope you do not know, Mr. Gilchrist ? '

" I had heard of her.

" ' A very pretty and very wicked lady who rides about the Park——'

" Here Carlyle entered at last, and stopped the anecdote about ' Skittles,' to my regret."

26 *November*, 1859. " Carlyle gave an explanation of Gilchrist : from a place ' near a church ; ' Christ = Kirk Mrs. Carlyle gave a curious account of Dr. Gilchrist who lived in Edinburgh when an old man ; married a beautiful young girl. Madly jealous of her ; suspecting every man about her : once picked up a card in her drawing-room, of a gentleman ; taxed her with it. She knew nothing about it. Dr. Gilchrist challenged the man ; who denied all knowledge of Mrs. Gilchrist. It turned out he had left a card of his in a circulating library book, which had passed on to Mrs. Gilchrist. The friends on both sides interfered and would not allow the duel ! "

28 *December*, 1859. " Carlyle again asked me about the *Blake ;* what I was doing with it. I stated that I had delivered his letter to Chapman, but was giving my MS. a last revisal before sending it in. He talked of the difficulties of a book, of getting it done, of reducing chaos to order. The whole world seems against you ; but it is not so. Other men knock against you who are simply thinking of themselves, not of you at all. Carlyle's difficulties lately as to maps,—sent for some to Germany ; certain towns, battle-fields of Frederick's he wanted ; reads maps very ill now to what he used to ; obliged to use spectacles for them, though then cannot see quickly.

" I mentioned Bradbury and Evans having given a hundred guineas for Tennyson's poem—a guinea a line.

' Ah ! they won't go on paying Alfred at that rate ; ust to say he wrote for it.' Like Barnum's story (as

Barnum told Carlyle) of a Yankee newspaper at a low
ebb, bribing Everett, a man much respected in the
States, with a fabulous sum of dollars, first offering 100,
then 200, at last 2,000; he in an evil moment consent-
ing; and then their advertising throughout the length
and breadth of the Union that the great Everett had
been paid 2,000 dollars to write an article in it; and
the newspaper went up to a great circulation . . .'

"Carlyle took his seat on the footstool by the fire as
usual to smoke.    Talk fell on the dog Nero, now very
ailing.    Mrs. Carlyle has had it ten and a half years;
six months old when Nero was brought to her.    Carlyle
said, 'Never dog had given trouble more dispropor-
tionate to its use and worth than Nero had to him.'
(Mrs. Carlyle) 'It had been worth it all.'    He denied
it, and reiterated the absurdity of its existence.    It
would be a kindness to kill it.

(Mrs. Carlyle) 'If he is to be believed, he shouldn't
make affectionate speeches to Nero in the garden when
he thought no one heard.'

"Carlyle regretted not to have been taught music or
at least singing.

" When a boy at school, the class was singing once,
the master remarked on the beautiful voice of that boy
(Carlyle), which boy was destined never to turn his
voice to any account.    Liked Scotch tunes much:
'Robin Adair,' 'Gilderoy' very plaintive and melodious.
Carlyle was also fond of Irish airs.

" *Gilderoy* showed a soul bathed in melancholy.
'Rude music, probably first performed, as Burns said,
on cow-horns, these old Scottish airs; but came from

the heart. That old tune to which Bruce led his men at Bannockburn, for instance. Carlyle recited 'Scots wha hae wi' Wallace bled'; the whole poem, with measured emphasis, the right stress on each word. Recited it with great fervour, repeated some passages, in particular the

> 'Lay the proud usurpers low!

and

> 'Liberty's in every blow!
> 'Forward!—let us do or die!

"Remarked on the practical character of the song. Burns hit the nail on the head at each blow; not a blow lost. Rude, but not a word too much or little, or to be altered.

"'Burns sat down and strummed the air for an hour, and then, possessed of the spirit of it, wrote, 'Scots wha hae wi' Wallace bled.' No such song-writer as Burns. Some of the songs in Shakespeare alone equal to them. Beranger not to be compared. Whatever theme Burns took, the same qualities shown.' Carlyle recited—

> 'Had we never lov'd sae kindly,
> Had we never lov'd sae blindly,
>     Never met—
> Oh, had we never met,
> Oh, had we never met and never parted,
>     Never parted,
> We had ne'er been broken-hearted.'

"'This Jessie, a very nice girl, the daughter of a neighbouring exciseman: Burns married at the time. No princess had ever had such a song written of her. Some of the Jacobite songs fine, about a dozen genuine.

' Bonnie Prince Charlie ' the finest, breathing devotion and love.'    Carlyle recited this also :—' Quite carries you along with it into readiness for the time to join the cause '; expatiated on the swing and lilt and picturesqueness of it.    Another humorous one, ' *There was a German laddie*,' breathing entire contempt of the German laddie, but hoping the world would have justice on him yet, ' through the sow's tail he had caught hold of,' meaning fat Kilmansegge (?), his mistress. . . . One of the coarsest of songs.'

"At parting Carlyle again kindly asked about the book, and wished me a happy deliverance of it.  Manner kind throughout, and his face looked kind."

# CHAPTER VIII.

## LETTER FROM JANE WELSH CARLYLE.

### 1860—1861. AGE, 32—33.

"*13th June*, 1860, 5, *Cheyne Row*.

" M Y DEAR! Behold a cap! Fresh from India— a delicate attention to Mr. Carlyle on the part of a Lady! But the cap fits Mr. C.'s large head like an inverted tumbler! so I laid it aside to give you when you came as a delicate attention to Percy on the part of *me!*

" Now you have come so seldom lately and staid so short a time, that I have never got subsided into recollection of the cap—so I transmit it by Charlotte—who is much obliged to you for sending her tea all in a heap *instead* of *in quarters*, as it insures her *better weight*, measured out by *me !*

Affectionately yours, JANE CARLYLE "

" DEAR MRS. GILCHRIST: Here is a letter I have had to-day from that dear little Mrs. Hawkins, so amusing that it seems a shame to keep it all to myself when there is another intelligent reader otherside the wall. Let me have it back to-morrow.

Yours affectionately, JANE W. CARLYLE."

Anne Gilchrist was an excellent housewife: Carlyle liked her home-made bread so much, that his wife took lessons in the art of bread-making. Jane Carlyle did not prove an apt pupil; to knead well, plump hands and patience are the necessary qualifications.

"DEAR MRS. GILCHRIST: I would go in to *speak*, but that I should probably bring you away from something. So I write to ask can you conveniently come in and *stand over me* while I make the bread myself to-day? My cousins are *not* coming to-day and *are* coming to-morrow; so perhaps I had best avail myself of the present opportunity. If to-day; tell me what hour—and tell me where Emma gets the yeast. And *when* Charlotte shall come for the flour? A precious Bother I am to be sure to you! But if I can never reward you on earth you are pretty certain to have two little additional wings for it in heaven!

Yours most gratefully<br>JANE CARLYLE."

With what are termed amusements, Anne Gilchrist had little to do; but she enjoyed a chat with lively Jane Carlyle, who possessed charming audacity and winning gaiety of manner; for instance, she would greet Monckton Milnes and Forster with a kiss; given in so natural and unaffected a manner as to cause no surprise.

"*Friday*, 17*th*. Annie called upon Mrs. Carlyle, who mentioned that her husband had received, two days ago, a parcel inscribed, ' to be delivered on the fourth'. On opening it, was disclosed an expensive Prayer-Book, one of Pickering's, with ornamental borders, texts on the fly-leaf, and pasted in :—

' For dear Carlyle a Valentine :
May God's glory on him shine.'

" The other day, Mrs. Carlyle, in company with Barlow, met Dickens coming out of Burlington Arcade. 'God bless my soul, you here!' says Dickens, in such a droll way as has made Mrs. Carlyle laugh ever since; such an arch face and tone of voice he has, sharp as a needle. She asked Dickens to come and see them; Dickens said he would, one day next week. 'And bring'— the girls, Mrs. Carlyle was going to say; then, thinking that would be too formal, said: ' one of the girls.' ' Yes! I'll bring *one* of the girls'! responds Dickens."

' " Mr. Carlyle likes Dickens personally very much, though he never reads his books."

" Speaking of Thackeray and his wife, Mrs. Carlyle alluded to his want of means when an artist; but Sterling found him employment in reviewing books in the *Times*. 'Married Miss Shawe in part to take her away from a disagreeable mother. She, far too small a thing for a great riotous, energetic man like Thackeray, —sunk under the anxieties; went silly after her third confinement.'

" The day that *The Cornhill* was first published, Thackeray set up a pair of handsome greys to his carriage. A lady met him; Thackeray said he was going to look at, and buy if he could, Lord Macaulay's house. She told him that Lady Airlie had bought it, and added, What a good thing it was to be so rich.' ' Shall I tell you the secret to be rich?' answered the novelist; 'set up a Magazine!'

G

" Mrs. Carlyle mentioned having had a letter from
Ruskin, who had returned from the Continent, very
out of humour with the Munich doings in Art.
Had made up his mind to give up writing and painting, and everything, except *reading*. Mrs. Carlyle
said, ' No one managed Carlyle so well as Ruskin ; it was
quite beautiful to see him. Carlyle would say outrageous
things, running counter to all Ruskin valued and cared
for. Ruskin would treat Mr. Carlyle like a naughty
child, lay his arms round him, and say, ' Now, this is
too bad ! . . .' "

" Talk fell on the two Scottish books that I left for
Carlyle on New Year's Day : ' James the First's Poems '
and ' Pennycuick's Poem ' ; pleased with both, especially
with James the First's *Christ's Kirk on the Green*,
which was on the model of Chaucer.

Carlyle read the first few stanzas, entering into the
humour and picturesqueness with much gusto. Pennycuick very scarce ; ' did not know before a copy was to
be had, only having seen parts extracted in Burns.' I
said he was a Scottish Cleveland, which Carlyle assented
to ; and then read a satirical poem on one Captain ' ——,'
a noted Border robber of horses, from whom Mrs.
Carlyle claims collateral descent with some pride, as from
a remarkable man, a kind of eighteenth century Rob Roy.
Carlyle read the poem with some sly satisfaction over
his wife.

" I asked Mrs. Carlyle about Lady Ashburton ? ' Oh,
she had been completely vanquished ; ' resolved not to
like her, but had been obliged to ; ' stood out five
days.' It was not her fascinations in the drawing-room,

but when on ' the fifth day she came up into my room, and spoke like an unaffected Highland girl, that Lady Ashburton won my heart; she spoke so freely and unguardedly about persons and things; most people in that station so guarded and careful.' "

*January*, 1860. " Annie called on Mrs. Carlyle, whose husband was in great misery over his proofs; always is; alters and re-alters always, and won't let them alone. Mrs. Carlyle reads them, and suggests alterations. Carlyle begins by calling her a fool, and so on, and ends often, after a few days, by saying ' he thinks he shall strike out so and so.' This time the proofs seemed to Mrs. Carlyle to hang fire; the story not to progress. ' A great deal about ' our melancholy friend' which impeded the progress. One passage in particular, justifying ' torture.' The world has ceased to care for 'justice.' ' If Mr. Carlyle had had space to go more into it, he might have made good his position; but as it was, the impression would simply be : ' Mr. Carlyle regrets the abolition of torture.' He at first angry with her. ' She, like the rest of the world, did not care about justice, did not see the distinction between the guilty and the innocent. ' The first day Mr. Carlyle came down very cross, in the evening, saying that he had done nothing all day; hang it ! had spent all the afternoon trying to alter that paragraph of her's, and he couldn't. The second day uneasy, the third day more so; the fourth sent L. in post-haste to recall the proofs, that he might strike out the whole of ' our melancholy friend's ' remarks.' Mrs. Carlyle sorry to find fault, and not to seem pleased,

as he is always dispirited himself at first, and wants
encouraging.

"Carlyle writes best when he is obliged to write fast.
One of his best things (in Mrs. Carlyle's opinion), the
'Johnson,' so written.  A commission, and he tied to
time.  Notwithstanding all Carlyle has written, he still
writes with difficulty, with labour, as he always has
written.  'A mistake, Carlyle's writing such long
works; gets tired out before he has done; the end gets
feeble.'

"Annie asked what Mrs. Carlyle thought her husband's best work?  'The French Revolution' her
favourite, though perhaps *Cromwell* the best written
book.'

'Mr. Carlyle never complains of serious things;
but if his finger cut, the house turned upside down; one
must hold it and another get plaster.'

"When staying at the Grange, Monckton Milnes read
aloud in an impressive dramatic way, Tennyson's Poem
in *Macmillan*.  [Sea Dreams.]  Mr. and Mrs. Carlyle
kept laughing: Monckton would say, 'Now do listen;
you *should* listen; it's beautiful.'

"Annie called upon Mrs. Carlyle, who has been in
great trouble.  Her dog Nero killed by the doctor, last
week, who had kindly offered some days before to
administer poison, and put him out of his misery
'old age.'  'Has been quite upset.'  Carlyle that
evening cried like a child.  On Sunday evening
told her he could not rebuke her; he felt so wretched
himself.

"Some time ago Mrs. Carlyle read aloud the account

of the Italian's execution—Buranelli's. The tears rolled down Carlyle's cheeks—he, who talks of shooting Irishmen who will not work.

"Mrs. Carlyle asked Annie various questions as to how she first met *me*, etc., etc., to all of which Annie naïvely replied in full. *Mem :*—This is how Mrs. Carlyle gets possessed of the private biographies of half London."

When staying away from six Great Cheyne Row, Alexander Gilchrist received a lively letter from Jane Carlyle :—

"31*st July*, 1861, 5, *Cheyne Row, Chelsea.*

"MY DEAR MR. GILCHRIST : A thousand thanks for your kind thought about us !—tho' fated to remain 'a devout imagination' on your part ! We are no longer on the Farm-House quest,—'anything BUT !' (as my maid says.) In fact Mr. Carlyle is become so enamoured of the retirement he enjoys—beside the water-barrel, under that ten shillingsworth of calico— that I don't think a farm-house even within a stone cast of *the sea*, warranted free from cocks, dogs, and donkies, would tempt his imagination ! And certainly on the principle of '*letting* WELL *be*'—'*letting sleeping Dogs lie*' —and that sort of thing, for nothing in the world would I unsettle him, when he is so peaceable !—Just come and *see ;* the next time you are up ! For myself the back-court is by no means *country*. . . . I am speculating about going with Geraldine Jewsbury for three days to Ramsgate ! I do so need a change?

"Your house seems to be taken most perfect care of — but ! Oh the noise of that stumping wooden leg !—it gets up so early too ! [An old soldier acting as care-taker at number six.]

" My kind love to your wife when you see her or write to her I miss her dreadfully.

" I went to see Fechter the other night and found myself between Lewes and Miss Evans !—by Destiny and *not* by my own Deserving. At least Destiny in the shape of Frederick Chapman who arranged the thing. Poor soul ! there never was a more absurd mis-calculation than *her* constituting herself an improper *woman*. She looks Propriety personified ! Oh so *slow !*

Yours very truly,

JANE CARLYLE."

# CHAPTER IX.

## DANTE GABRIEL ROSSETTI.

### [1861. AGE 33.]

ALEXANDER GILCHRIST met D. G. Rossetti in the spring of 1861 ; correspondence began over the " Life of William Blake."

The poet-artist took a keen interest in the illustrations for the Life ; he writes about them April 20.

" MY DEAR GILCHRIST : I have been thinking that if you are still unprovided with a satisfactory copyist (or a sufficiency of such) for the Blakes,— Mrs. Edward [Burne] Jones would be very likely to succeed. This occurred to me shortly after seeing you the other day, but I did not see her till to-day, when I mentioned the matter to her. I hope I did not do wrong, but she is too intimate a friend to make it awkward for me if you and Linton cannot entertain the idea. She says she would be happy to try—is very diffident, but I believe in her capabilities fully, as she really draws heads with feeling, and could give the expression—besides, Jones would be there to give help without trouble to himself.

" My great anxiety about my wife lasts still. She has

a doctor in whom I have confidence, and an excellent nurse, and we have also seen Dr. Babington, head of the Lying-in Hospital, so I feel sure all is being done for the best.   She has too much courage to be in the least downcast herself ; and this is one great point, nor is her strength unusually low.   So we can but wait, and trust for a happy termination.

" With kind remembrances to Mrs. Gilchrist . . ."

On the second of May, D. G. Rossetti says :—

" Swinburne and I will be with you on Saturday.

" This morning my wife was confined—Our fears were correct in one respect, as the child was still-born—In all other respects she fares as yet, thank God, better than we had ventured to hope.   Still of course anxiety cannot be at an end yet.

" I will try and come to the ' Cheese ' on Thursday, though perhaps rather later than six, but I dare say I should find you till nearly seven."   [The " Cheshire Cheese," a well-known tavern in Wine Office Court, out of Fleet-street.]

" I believe I am going to Macmillan's afterwards and perhaps you will bear me company.   I send him the book to-day, and when I see him shall add your salutary stipulation, as to a fortnight's grace for decision. Patmore has written me most encouragingly concerning opinion of the book."   [The book in question was " *The* Early *Italian Poets*, from Ciullo D'Alcamo to Dante Alighieri."]   " I shall lend you a copy, if you have time to look at it.   Of course I mean to beg your acceptance of one as soon as it has the etchings and is otherwise completed."

" My wife goes on well, and gets out daily."

In a letter (June 18, 1861), Gabriel Rossetti speaks of being troubled with " an ulcerated sore throat, with fever, to which I am subject. I used a remedy I have used before, and am now better. I wish I were with you to get the benefit of some sun, and should much better even like it for my wife, but we must see ; she has been working very hard these few days, and made a beautiful water-colour sketch, but is none the better for it . . ."

" Smith and Elder have made me the offer of taking all expenses, but will not give a halfpenny, furnishing a calculation similar to Macmillan's, proving that the speculation would not in that way be a convenient one at all. I think I shall close with them now (though I deferred my answer), as I should only hear the same from Chapman's, and perhaps unaccompanied by so decent an offer ; I see Ruskin has much influenced S. and E. in my favour. They propose, as the only way, to sell the book for 12s. in one vol., and without the etchings, if I do not think them worth making, unpaid ; but I almost think I shall make them for the book's sake. What say you ? Have you any suggestion ? "

" P.S.—Weigall brought me (when he came to sit for my *Boswell* yesterday !) another plate he is doing for your book, a *Job* border with the *America* head-piece in the middle. I have asked him for the future to let me see his first drawing."

In a long letter, describing his late friend Woodward, Rossetti speaks of a visit to Oxford with the architect : —" Going there one day in his company to see the progress of the Museum, in 1857, at the outset of the long vacation, I was greatly struck with the beauty of the building he showed me, one on which he was then engaged—the new debating room of the Union Debating Club. Thinking of it only as his beautiful work, and without taking into consideration the purpose it was intended for, (indeed hardly knowing of the latter) I offered to paint figures of some kind on the blank spaces of one of the gallery window bays; and another friend who was with us, William Morris, offered to do the same for a second bay. Woodward was greatly delighted with the idea, as his principle was that of the mediæval builders, to avail himself in any building of as much decoration as circumstances permitted at the time, and not prefer uniform bareness to partial beauty. He had never before had a decided opportunity of introducing picture work in a building, and grasped at the idea.

"In the course of that long vacation, six other friends of ours—Edward Burne Jones, Arthur Hughes, V. C. Prinsep, John Pollen (the painter of the lovely roof of Merton Chapel), R. S. Stanhope, and Alexander Munro, joined in the project, which was a labour of love on all our parts—the expenses of materials alone being defrayed from the building fund. Each of the five painters took one window-bay, and the sculptor the stone shield above the porch, and the work proceeded merrily in concert for several months.

" The subject taken for illustration throughout was the ancient romance of the *Morte d'Arthur*, and the pictures were painted on a large scale in distemper. The roof was also covered with a vast pattern-work of grotesque

creatures by Morris, assisted by amateur workmen, who
offered on all hands, chiefly University men who stayed
n Oxford that 'Long' for the purpose.

" The work was, as I said, done for its own sake, and
therefore, after that long vacation spent on it, could only
be resumed when other business on the part of its various
members rendered it possible. All were however bent
on completing it,—a perfect scheme having been drawn
out for the whole series, of which several bays still
remained untouched, though I had myself made designs
for two, besides the one I in great measure carried out.
However, the owners of the building, a set of youths,
among whom some had taste and feeling, but these not
the majority, and with whom of course we had held no
sort of council on the matter,—grew impatient in 1859,
two years later, and applied to me to suggest that some
one of us should consent to complete the series from my
existing designs, for which (*i.e.* for the carrying out) I
must say they stated themselves willing to pay. We
held a counsel on the matter, and one or two among us
agreed to go down and fill the empty bays at a stated
period, charging only a sum sufficient to cover the price
of materials. We could not however agree on all
points, and they then requested me to lend my designs
to another artist of their own to work from. This I
refused, and they employed this person to fill the
remaining spaces from his own designs : which I have
never seen, but hear are wonderful exceedingly.

" Thus ended this jovial campaign on which I might
give you more details but have said too much already ;
my business being with Woodward. . . ."

" Woodward built the new Crown Insurance Office, in New Bridge Street, Blackfriars, close to my studio. It seems to me the most perfect piece of civil architecture of the new school that I have seen in London. I never cease to look at it with delight; and the decoration designed by Pollen and executed by Woodward's excellent trained workmen, the Brothers Shae, is worthy of the building. . . ."

Dante G. Rossetti, who was furnishing Alexander Gilchrist with biographical details of the young architect Woodward, for an (obituary) notice—goes on to say :—" I must have been the last friend who saw Woodward in England, as he called here, after we had long been unseen by each other, on his way to the station, going this last time to Paris. I am sitting now in the place, and I think in the chair, he sat in, to write this. If I am ever found worthy to meet him again, it will be where the dejection is unneeded which I cannot but feel at this moment; for the power of further and better work must be the reward bestowed on the deserts and checked aspirations of such a sincere soul as his. . . .

" No doubt the work by which his name must at any rate be preserved, is the Oxford Museum. I know how much there is in this building with which he himself was greatly dissatisfied—the influences at work in its direction being in great measure inartistic, not only to the extent of indifference, but of antagonism. Carping and opposition had wearied him partially of a work on which he entered with the warmest enthusiasm; but still, it is in the main a very noble one, and worthy of its purpose. Many faults in it, were things traced to their sources, are not his at all; but committed in his absence by the presumptuous interference of Oxford Dons, to suit each man's fancies for his own department. . . ."

D. G. Rossetti, in the next letter, speaks of his own affairs, especially alluding to one—Plint, a Leeds stockbroker, and purchaser of Rossetti's pictures, who died suddenly, after having just paid a big sum of money in advance for pictures not executed. His death therefore, and the demands of his executors, caused harass to the artist in his money affairs. D. G. Rossetti had, however, a knack of keeping duns and the importunate at a distance. He writes :—" That Plint business has become the plague of my life. . . . G. talks about law. I shut him out as yet; but don't know what will happen. I should like to consult with you; could you look in Monday morning and see my daub, which gets on fast now? Of course it *is* of the genus daub strictly; but not so bad now, I hope, as before, and sure to improve with the last touches.

"It seems there is some stir in the *Times* about Llandaff, which I have not seen. . . ."

In response to an invitation from Alexander Gilchrist to go into the country, Gabriel Rossetti writes :—

" 10*th July*, 1861.

" My wife is staying with the Morrises for a little— so such ' outs ' as I am able to make are made there. But I really must manage one with you, and will write again soon. I could not get to the ' Cheese ' the two days you named, and had no idea you had made a stay in London. My own work seems to drag on as usual.

I have just finished the water-colour of *Johnson*, and have nearly finished the large head which I have made into ' Fair Rosamond,' and have been doing some cartoons for glass, for the shop." [This was the name Rossetti and the other sleeping partners constantly applied to the firm Morris and Company.]

" P.S.—My wife is about the same and has not got into the country again yet, I'm sorry to say, as she's had to sit to me a good deal. I hope you have good news of Mrs. Gilchrist and the little ones. I can't make out whether Munro is ' one of us' yet. The last time I saw him, he told me his intended had been very ill, and I don't know whether this may have put off the wedding, but hear no further news.

" Both Wells and Boyce have told me to thank you most warmly for your excellent notice of Mrs. Wells, which also gave me the greatest pleasure."

Mrs. Wells—wife of the Academician, and sister of G. P. Boyce—was a gifted designer, who died in 1861.

Talking of the ' Life of Blake,' Gabriel Rossetti says:—" I am glad you approve of my rather unceremonious shaking up of Blake's rhymes [the editing of Blake's poems, *i.e.*, the correction of Blake's grammar]. I really believe that is what ought to be done—perhaps with a word of general explanation.

" I would like much to show you my picture finished, as it will not be fit to see till then—great alterations going on to the last.

" On the tenth I send it to the architects, Pritchard and Seddon, 6, Whitehall, and I should think they would have it on view there for a day or two, before setting it up at Llandaff. But perhaps I will see you again here before the tenth."

The following is the last letter that Alexander Gilchrist perused from his friend, and is endorsed by the former 19 November, 1861.

" *Tuesday evening*.

" My DEAR GILCHRIST: Two or three [friends] are coming here on Friday evening at eight or so—George Meredith I hope for one. Can you look in? I hope so—nothing but oysters, and of course the seediest of clothes.

" I trust your family anxieties are less every day now, and that your poor little Beatrice is more and more herself again.

" I have been reading with great pleasure (and corresponding impatience to go on) the two first sheets of Blake, which I return herewith.

" I thought ' —— ' was more meteoric even than usual the other night—a point on which some light was eventually thrown by the geometrical curves which he described from time to time on the pavement as we walked home. With kind remembrances to Mrs. Gilchrist,

I am yours sincerely

D. G. ROSSETTI."

# CHAPTER X.

## LAST YEAR OF LIFE AT GREAT CHEYNE ROW.

### 1861. AGE 33.

THE "Life of Blake" was nearing completion, the Memoir practically finished; though still a good deal to do as to arrangement and editing of poems.

"Many were the projects to be realised after the *Blake*. For a life of Wordsworth Alexander had already begun to make preparation: and lighter enterprises were to come in between whiles. Countess D'Aulnois, whose sprightly genius has been a good fairy of the nursery for a couple of hundred years, Lord Herbert of Cherbury, Sir Kenelm Digby, old Howell (first and most respectable of book-makers)—of these, and many another, it was my husband's cherished hope to revive the faded and forgotten lineaments: to create a small gallery of portraits in which the lover of literature should linger with as curious an interest as does the antiquary amid the relics of the external life of the past. But it was not to be. Life was opening out fair prospects around; the steepest pitch of the hill was climbed; men of rare genius, among them the poet-artist, Dante Gabriel and his brother William Michael Rossetti, Ford Madox Brown, and others, were stretching out to him the hand of friendship."

" In the autumn of 1861 our eldest girl, Beatrice, took scarlet fever of a malignant type. . . ." Jane Carlyle writes to her neighbour 25th of October, 1861:—

" MY DEAR : I am very sorry for your anxiety— but, it is the price one has to pay for the joy of such nice children !—Mr. Gilchrist said you were always in Beatrice's room.—If you ever come down stairs, and have time, I should like to see you—I *believe* I have had the scarlet fever.   I don't forget that I owe you the price of the first detachment of brown flour—and will pay it with transport when you tell me what it is—Also I would like to have *half a sack* of *white* from the same man—if he would send the quantity.   Would he ?   I got some of the German flour I told you of and it is surpassingly beautiful but Mr. Carlyle can't endure to eat it !—it is so tasteless he says.   Perhaps he is right ; and the flour like women and Birds and many other things can't be pre-eminently *beautiful* and pre-eminently anything else at the same time.

" *Would* you write the address on the envelope and the order on the paper ?   What a nuisance I am to you.

" Do you want any books ?   Mr. Carlyle stupidly forgot *again* about *All the Year Round* and sent it off the day after it came—but I have scolded him and he will mind next day—J. W. C."

The dark thunder-clouds were gathering around the family, rather than dispersing.

" MY DEAR MRS. GILCHRIST : I am most sincerely

sorry for you in this long solitary confinement. I am sure both your health and spirits must be suffering from it. Do you see any near prospect of getting away with the dear little girl? or do you never think of sending away the other children to your mother's; and so delivering yourself from the tantalizing wretchedness of being so near them and yet separated from them?

" What a pity about that new woman! [servant]: if you were to gain nothing but *flesh* in compensation for *cleverness* as well to have gone on with the other! If you had only your feet and hands and heart free again; however, you will be able to remodel your new arrangement one way or other. But it *is* particularly vexatious to have such a complication, with sickness in the house! I am feeling the cold severely— off my sleep and all that sort of thing!

" When lying awake in the dark night I think of you and your troubles on the other side of the wall!

" I have no news to tell you but that I was in a room the other day with Miss Frederica Johnstone! a large, fair, *goodish* looking woman, over forty. She didn't seem in low spirits on account of her lover in penal servitude, and her own egregious folly in the newspapers!

" I send a letter from Madame Venturie in case it might amuse you to read it—if not, have no *delicacy* as to returning it unread. Tell me if you have any leisure or *spirits* to read an amusing novel. I have one on hand—Give poor little Beatrice a kiss for me,

Yours affectionately,

JANE CARLYLE."

Beatrice continued ill; " at the end of six weeks,

while she was struggling back to convalescence, our eldest boy [Percy], and then the father sickened with it."

"Oh God help you, poor afflicted soul !—What can any human being say to comfort you? Nothing—nothing !—- But is there anything I can do? or Mr. Carlyle do? Can I write any letters for you?—you would only need to give me the addresses. Can I send anywhere? Get anything?—Have you money at hand? Oh do use me in some way !—Affectionately yours, J. W. CARLYLE."

Dante Gabriel Rossetti wrote on the thirtieth—

"MY DEAR GILCHRIST: I have only just heard from Macmillan that you yourself have been attacked by the Scarlatina ; and cannot say how concerned I feel for you and for Mrs. Gilchrist's increased anxiety—I feel by no means safe about troubling you and her with a note, as you may be too ill and she too busy for a word of reply ; but it occurred to me as possible that I or my brother (for whom I know I can speak as for myself) might be of some use in transacting literary business which may require immediate attention, till you are better again. Is there anything we can do in this way for the *Critic* or other work? If so, pray let me know. If there is nothing to say on this head, do not let anyone be troubled to answer my note, as I shall learn how you get on by calling to inquire. . . ."

The letter which we have read, was one that Rossetti's friend never opened.

Alexander Gilchrist dissatisfied with the slow progress of his little daughter, had unfortunately just changed his medical man : one who was at least conscientious, and as Carlyle said " had stood at many death-beds."

At a critical time, one of the five nights that Alexander lay wrestling with the fever, Carlyle fetched the new doctor. The fashionable physician looked in, he timidly kept his distance from the patient—remarked that there was ' enough fever at number six to stock the parish,' and vanished, leaving the wife alone in the house, save a drunken nurse (the servant ill at the hospital), worn with six weeks' previous night watching, to struggle against approaching death.

In the tragedies of life there seem to be among our fellow beings always one or two with a dash of heroism in their natures. Mrs. Madox Brown offered to come and help. Anne Gilchrist, even then, remembered that Mrs. Brown possessed children ; a thought which made her decline the noble offer. Mrs. Ireland in like manner tendered assistance, when news reached her of the dire need of such ; which was not until Alexander Gilchrist had succumbed.

" The brain was tired with stress of work ; the fever burned and devastated like a flaming fire : to four days of delirium succeeded one of exhaustion, of stupor ; and then the end ; without a word, but not without a look of loving recognition. It was on a wild and stormy night, November 30, 1861, that his spirit took flight. If life be measured not by years, but by what it contains, this life of thirty-three summers was not short. With a sweetness of disposition, a tenderness of heart that gave and took the utmost of happiness in domestic life; a sturdy enjoyment of work ; fair, though not strong, health; a fineness of perception and an ardent love for all that is genuine or great in literature, in art,

in nature, in humanity, and a silent faith in immortality,
I think he knew no moments of tedium or *ennui*,
though of sorrow, toil, pain and privation he had his
share.    To such a nature the cup of life is full of fine
flavours."

# CHAPTER XI.

## JANE WELSH CARLYLE WRITES TO HER NEIGHBOUR.

### 1861—1862.   AGE 33—34.

" M Y DEAR FRIEND : Will you be brave and
good, and come to *me ?*  You might wait till
*after dark,* when you would only have to throw a shawl
over your head—and I would send you the latch-key,
and you could let yourself in, and come straight up to my
bedroom without having to see or speak to anybody.  I
have been on the drawing-room sofa most part of the
last two days.  I am *much* better—and please God I shall
soon be able to go to *you*—I mean to ask Mr. Barnes
if I may go out in a carriage to-morrow."  So wrote
Jane Carlyle.

Dante Gabriel Rossetti writes :—

" 14, *Chatham Place, Blackfriars, Dec.* 5, 1861.

" MY DEAR MRS. GILCHRIST : I have doubted
hitherto whether it could be pardonable to address you
at such a terrible time ; but the pain of this still almost
inconceivable loss has so pervaded everything for me
since the news reached me on Tuesday, that I cannot

forbear venturing to say to you that, even for me, no greater shock has ever occurred in my life than this.

" I truly valued and loved your husband, more I think than I had ever felt towards anyone on the same length of acquaintance or, I should say friendship, for such I believe it was on both sides. And I know that, since this appalling calamity, the very room I sit in, to which no one brought more welcome cheerful friendship than he did, seems like a ghost to me, and I feel like a ghost myself. The awful mystery of such an event is beyond all words, when I think of him as I saw him in his own house so few days before.

" Neither I, nor any of the various friends of his who feel as I do now, could have a right to speak of comfort to you. Yet comfort and compensation there must be somewhere, sooner or later, when so good and gifted a man is snatched suddenly from all whose love he deserved. This can hardly be thought or said now, yet surely so it must be.

" I had not the heart to be present yesterday ; [the funeral] but believe me, none who were there could well have been more possessed by the thought of the terrible time than I was then.

" Whenever you are able again to think of other matters, I will rely on you to permit my brother and myself, if there is any opportunity of doing so, to assist you in the management of such works as he may have left in progress. From this point of view also,—as a far-sighted and nobly honest writer on subjects of which few indeed are able to treat worthily,—his loss is I believe an irreparable one.

" Mr. Macmillan has begged me to express to you, on his part all the deep concern which he feels—

" At such a moment it seems almost intrusive for one friend even to venture on the expression of what all feel. I must ask you again to pardon this attempt to convey a grief and sympathy which I know are at least truly heartfelt.

" I hope and pray that your anxiety on your children's account may now be lessened, as well as that which all friends must feel for your own health,

And remain most sincerely yours,

D. G. ROSSETTI."

Jane Welsh Carlyle says :—

" MY DEAR MRS. GILCHRIST : Are we still to go on not seeing each other,—you in sorrow, I in sickness ; with just a partition between us,—of no comfort to each other at all ?

" For more than three months now, I have been ill and confined to the house—Three times I have seemed to be recovering, and made an attempt at getting about ; but after one drive in a Fly, there was always a relapse ; and since New Year's Day I have had the worst bout of all !

" The visit to the Grange which has lain so long a-head of me, and to which I looked for some freshening-up, is finally thrown over altogether as far as I am concerned.    Mr. Carlyle will go on Monday by himself for two or three days.

" Since the mild weather came, I have been so much better, however, that I am again projecting a drive ;

being heartily sick of my two rooms.    But for the rain
I should have tried it to-day.

"  *Will* you come here ?  or must I wait  till  I can *go*
to you ? that is till it is quite dry ; for I should be
foolish to expose myself to the damp, after such long
shutting up.

Yours affectionately, JANE CARLYLE."

And again on Monday :—

" DEAR MRS. GILCHRIST : I am puzzled to understand why you send me back these miserable debts without a word of answer to my Saturday's note about seeing
you.    I must take for granted from your silence that
you would still rather be left alone—at  least so far as
*I* am concerned.

"You sent me a sovereign, of which I spent only
five and ninepence halfpenny—so there is owing you
out of that 14s.  2½d.—and long ago you paid a
bushel of brown flour for me—as the last was ten
shillings, I suppose *that* would be the same.    Which
makes a balanc e due to you of one pound four shillings and 2½d.    What wretched particulars to write
about, after so long as a separation.

Yours ever truly, JANE W. CARLYLE."

No sooner was the funeral over, than scarlet fever
attacked the younger son, who, some few days prior to
taking it, had been conveyed to Colne.

The following letter of Jane Carlyle's was received
by Anne Gilchrist when nursing him :—

" 5, *Cheyne Row, Friday, Dec.* 7, 1861.

"MY DEAR MRS. GILCHRIST : I was glad and thankful to get your letter this morning.    I knew thro' the

nurse that the little Boy was going on favourably; but I needed some token from yourself, that you were not dwelling quite shut up within the black circle of your own great sorrow; without a thought for anything beyond it, or any of us who care for you, and sympathize with you so sincerely.

" It is a strange thing to say; but I was *glad* when I heard your little Boy had taken the fever, and that you had gone off to him ! I felt sure—perhaps because so much had been taken from you already—that *he* would be spared; and in the meantime, the anxiety on his account would recall you to a sense of what you had still left—to lose !—and the very movement, and change of scene, and of air, would rouse you out of that blackness of despair in which your last lines to me were written, poor dear soul !

" Things seem to go on very well in your house. That nurse, from all my girls say of her, seems to be a most anxious painstaking woman. I have had good accounts of the children every day. . . . I sent in this evening to ask if she [the nurse] wished anything told you as I was going to write, and she said she had already mentioned everything to Mrs. [Edwin] Ireland, who would write. Anne has been much better the last two days—it was announced to me quite radiantly by Maria that 'Anne had eaten a chop!'—The nurse thinks that by next week Anne will be quite up to her work. . . . I do hope you will tell me if there be *anything* you want done, that I can do, either directly or indirectly. Yours affectionately,

JANE CARLYLE."

Anne Gilchrist speaks of her sorrow to her old school friend :—

"6, *Great Cheyne Row, Chelsea.*

"MY DEAR JULIA : The sight of your hand-writing, and still more the unchanged tone of affection it conveys, are very welcome to me: But you must for the present forgive my being unable to do more than send you a few words. It tears me to pieces so, to go through the terrible history—It was scarlet fever that carried him off in the prime of life and health and strength. It has laid all my children prostrate, and since the grave closed over him, I had almost lost my youngest boy—But thank God, he and all our four children are spared to me. He is slowly recovering.

"I *do* feel it an imperishable and inestimable blessing to have had his love and been his wife for eleven years, but how can I help its making the anguish greater too—in proportion to the blessedness of that lot ? . . ."

Amongst letters of sympathy received, appear two worthy of note, (besides D. G. Rossetti's)—from Madox Brown and Samuel Palmer. The latter writes :—

"MY DEAR MRS. GILCHRIST: We are out of suspense! Thank God the children are saved ! . . .

"I venture to write, and *may* venture again, in the confidence that you will treat me as you would a friend o much longer standing—that is, read or not read as you feel disposed, and clearly understand that I expect *no answer*—otherwise I shall be vexing you with a tax, instead of, perhaps for a moment, diverting your attention from an unspeakable sorrow—or at least claiming my humble share of companionship in it. That house in Cheyne Row, and that family, so happily and so lovingly compacted within it—will not flit in and out of memory, with those who knew it, but will remain a present and almost tangible image of the past. I see it as it *was* and as it *is*.—I see too, my own once happy and hopeful home before the destroying angel poured forth upon it calamity only just less than yours,—the seventh plague of Egypt—the destruction of the first-*born* ; and now, thrust out from *home*, it is ours, dear Mrs. Gilchrist, to be wanderers—dwellers in tents— explorers—for a time at least, of a wilderness so flat and beaconless that like Arab nomads, we must lift our eyes from these shifting sands beneath our feet and guide ourselves by the lights of Heaven. . . .

" It is a strange thing to be glad of—but I *am* glad —yes *glad to* find that you look your great sorrow in the face ; that you have not suffered yourself in the tender-ness of grief to underrate its bitterness ; it is as you say ' anguish ' and there is no other word in our language to express it. One of my kindest friends, whose ministra-tions gave me the most real comfort, began at once with this—almost *dwelling* on the intensity of the sor-row ; and *then*, on those true promises, finding topics of *real* comfort, which the heart could cordially receive because the understanding was not hoodwinked.

" You have now known the worst— —in returning to your *home the worst*. Thank God *that* is past ! I was glad you did not write to me till *that* was over. Well ! midnight has struck, and the hours, however slowly, creep towards dawn—Yes, *slowly— slowly :*—we are both of us in the thick darkness as we converse a little by the way. . . ."

The following letter is from Ford Madox Brown :—

" I can now no longer defer the expression of the deep sympathy we have for you and your dear children.

" The loss, you must be well aware, is a great one to the arts generally in this country—and as an artist is a personal loss to myself—quite independent of the disappointment of the hope of many years pleasant intercourse and gradually increasing friendship—. . .

" We are most anxious to hear how your children are progressing and beg you to let us know by the bearer of this ? . . ."

Dante Gabriel Rossetti writes again :—

" *Blackfriars*, 15 *January*, 1862.

" My Dear Mrs. Gilchrist : Your dear husband's death has been so much on my mind at all times and in spite of all other occupation, that your letter falls in with what is still and will long remain in the current of all my thoughts. I am glad more than I can say to think that there is reasonable hope of your troubles— or rather the actual presence of trouble to you—being now soon at an end, from what you tell me of your children's progress to restored health. On your own account I have felt the greatest anxiety, but I now trust in God that this may prove unnecessary.

" I need hardly say that I have heard on all hands expressions of the sincerest sympathy with you, and of real grief for your dreadful loss, both from those who knew your husband personally and from others. One of these especially, from Mr. Wells [the Academician]

the widower of the gifted lady who died this past year,
was couched in a letter of so much deep feeling that I
had put it aside to send to you, and am sorry I cannot
now succeed in laying my hand on it, having lost it I
suppose through too much care.   Mr. Wells had felt
extremely the sincere and generous tone of an obituary
notice of his wife which your husband wrote at the time
—having indeed meant ever since to seek him and thank
him for it; and the association of two such deaths
struck him as forcibly as it had already done me.

" But this is only one instance of the sorrow felt on
all hands more deeply than it can ever be expressed.

" I shall see Mr. Madox Brown this evening, and
shall take the liberty of showing him your letter, for no
one better deserves to see it.   It was only the other day
that we were saying, when he and I were met with
other friends, that it almost seemed shameful to be even
cheerful or occupied as usual in friendly intercourse so
shortly after so valued a friend has left us.   But in these
feelings, as in all other respects, what can be done except
to trust to what is surely at least a natural instinct in all
—though as you say, one which it seems almost impious
to offer at the moment in the form of direct consolation,—that is, that such terrible partings from love and
work must be, unless all things are a mere empty husk
of nothing,—a guide to belief in a new field of effort
and a second communion with those loved and lost ?

" I have already made one or two utter failures in
attempts to recall his features on paper, but if you
would send me the daguerreotype you speak of (however different it may be from ·what I knew of him), it

would doubtless help me to something slightly less unsuccessful; but I shall never cease to regret that I
omitted what I was always meaning to ask of him at
odd moments—that is, the getting him to sit for a drawing of his face—I should like much now as a last
resource to try what I could do with the help of the
daguerreotype, but shall never succeed I know in doing
anything worth doing. I remember so well now speaking to him of my regret at the same omission on my
part in respect of Mrs. Wells, of whom no good
portrait, I then thought, existed, but have since found
that there is one in profile by her husband. . . .

" When I have made such a sketch as I find possible
with the help of the one you speak of, I have thought
of another use to which, if at all tolerable, it might well
be put :—that is, to head a prefatory notice of him
which should surely now be prefixed to the Life of Blake.
That work will no doubt do much to keep his name,
and something ought to be said of him in connection
with it.

" Perhaps you yourself have thought of this and
intend carrying out the idea. If, on the other hand,
you would prefer its being attempted by a third person,
it would be a melancholy pleasure to me to speak of him
publicly as I think he ought to be spoken of; always
supposing Mr. Macmillan fell in with the idea, which I
should think from the feeling he has expressed on many
occasions there would be no doubt of his doing. I
know that my friendship with your husband was a short
one ; but what you so kindly and warmly tell me, con-
firms the belief I entertained that his sympathy with me

was as strong as mine, I assure you, was with him from the very first. Indeed I never met a man whom I could call my friend in so full a sense on no longer personal knowledge. But indeed I, as well as others who met him afterwards through me, had already felt that he was a man to seek out and know, from the time when we read his 'Life of Etty.' Thus, if such facts could be furnished by yourself, as you would wish to be included in a memoir of him, I think I might rely on my own knowledge of and sympathy with, his views and powers, to convey a true idea of these.

"Whenever you are ready to claim such assistance as my brother and I are not only ready but most anxious to render in bringing out the book, [Blake] conjointly with yourself, you may rely on our not delaying the publication by any neglect on our part. I have not a perfect idea in what state the MS. remains, but I know enough of his plans to be able perhaps to recognize where anything remains to be done. From what he last told me, however, I trust his work on it was almost complete if not quite so.

"I hope you will let me know therefore as soon as you are quite ready to enter on this task, and shall hope also, either now or when I see you, to receive the daguerreotype.

"With warmest wishes and remembrances, I remain, dear Mrs. Gilchrist, ever yours sincerely,

D. G. R."

The following letter was the last that Anne Gilchrist received from Dante Gabriel Rossetti before her departure from Chelsea :—

I

"14 *Chatham Place*, 31 *January*, 1862.

MY DEAR MRS. GILCHRIST: I am convinced you are quite right in purposing to return to the country for the present. Indeed I am sure all your friends would feel the greatest increase of anxiety on your account were you to remain at Chelsea. The associations there must indeed be quite overwhelming, when even to his friends elsewhere the reality of such a loss still seems bewildering.

"Mr. Ireland spent an evening with me and kindly brought the photograph, which is indeed as you say a record of him ten years ago, but not as I knew him— his face having gained latterly no less in power, I should think, than in what are commonly called good looks. . . .

"I was very glad to hear from Mr. Ireland of the continued improvement in your little invalid [Herbert Harlakenden], and trust that recovery is now quite ensured."

Jane Carlyle endeavoured to persuade her neighbour to continue to live at number six; even suggesting that Anne Gilchrist and Geraldine Jewsbury should unite forces and live together. After a good deal of anxious consideration, Anne Gilchrist commenced house hunting in the country, and unassisted, one pouring wet night, lighted upon ' dear little Brookbank,' Shottermill: a wiser choice was hardly possible, as will be seen.

When the time drew near for leaving Chelsea, Jane Carlyle wrote: "Feb. 1862. . . . Since you *are* to go, I wish to Heaven you were out of all this! I know how dreadful these details must be! how little chance of calm there is for you, till you have gathered yourself together in a new scene.

" Don't write, but tell Maria how the little girl is ? and how your own head is ? "

The day of departure soon came. " I remember," says Isabella Ireland, " watching from the windows (Mrs. Carlyle's drawing-room) the loading of the vans. When the third waggon, heavily laden with pretty old carved furniture, started for Haslemere, Mrs. Carlyle shrugged her shoulders and avouched a belief that Mrs. Gilchrist would ' skin, and bury herself alive for the benefit of her children.' "

BROOKBANK.

# CHAPTER XII.

## SHOTTERMILL.

### 1862.   Age 34.

BROOKBANK Cottage stands upon the summit of a steep little Surrey hill, at the base of which flows a brook; crossing it, the pedestrian must imagine himself in Sussex, or if he linger upon the bridge and look to the right he faces Hampshire, and half a mile of the stream's course will bring him into that county.

Shottermill is a mile from Haslemere, once a coaching town, *en route* for Portsmouth and London; and also one of the rotten boroughs.   In 1862 Haslemere was still a cosy little town, at whose principal shop might have been bought most commodities ranging from a watering-pot to a ham!   This was a shop managed by one Clarke; a barber, who, when tugging at a customer's hair, would give advice as to what not to do in gardening; for instance, not to dig snow into the ground as he had once done to his cost, how nothing throve that year owing to the lowered temperature of the earth.

Clarke had a word to say about the famous Hind Head murder—of his conversation with *the barber* who met the two murderers at the Devil's Punch Bowl—

how that barber sidled near the ditch as the two men approached, and was asked roughly, 'What are you afraid of, man?' to which he replied with show of effrontery, 'I aint a-fear'd,' adding to his listener, 'If ever I told a lie in my life, that was one.'"

The murder happened in this manner. Three sailors were making their way to London from Portsmouth, but at Liphook, E. Cafey and J. Marshall spent their last shilling in drink, and at night on reaching Hind Head just where the grass sloped smoothly into the middle of the 'Bowl,' these two sailors fell upon their companion, robbed and then dragged his body some way down the green sward into the Bowl. E. Cafey and J. Marshall were caught, sentenced, and hanged; their bones gleam on the gibbet in Turner's print of *Hind Head Hill*.

How often Dickens must have walked and 'posted' along the Portsmouth road, is known by his description of it in *Nicholas Nickleby*:—"They walked upon the rim of the Devil's Punch Bowl; and Smike listened with greedy interest as Nicholas read the inscription upon the stone, which, reared upon that wild spot, tells of a murder committed there by night. The grass on which they stood, had once been dyed with gore; and the blood of the murdered man had run down drop by drop, into the hollow which gives the place its name. 'The Devil's Bowl,' thought Nicholas, as he looked into the void, 'never held fitter liquor than that!'"

The inimitable Dickens hits off the character of this part of the county with a touch: we quote again from *Nicholas*:—

"Onward they kept [Nicholas and Smike], with

steady purpose, and entered at length upon a wide and spacious tract of downs, with every variety of little hill and plain to change their verdant surface. Here, there shot up, almost perpendicularly, into the sky, a height so steep as to be hardly accessible to any but the sheep and goats that fed upon its sides; and there, stood a mound of green, sloping and tapering off so delicately, and merging so gently into the level ground, that you could scarce define its limits. Hills swelling above each other; and undulations, shapely and uncouth, smooth and rugged, graceful and grotesque, thrown negligently side by side, bounded the view in each direction; while frequently, with unexpected noise, there uprose from the ground a flight of crows, which cawing and wheeling round the nearest hills, as if uncertain of their course, suddenly poised themselves upon the wing and skimmed down the long vista of some opening valley, with the speed of light itself."

Portsmouth-road, in coaching days, must have been a pretty sight at one o'clock, at which time the coaches crossed each other at the Bowl—post-chaises, horsemen, horns winding, vendors crying, and numbers of little children running barefooted alongside the coaches, throwing nosegays, made of purple and white heather, broom and whortle-berries, at the passengers, and catching coppers in return.

Now and again, at night, a portmanteau would be stolen; one containing a quantity of gold was so cut off a post-chaise by a man named Pimm, who invested his ill-gotten coin in purchasing land; he built two paper-mills at Barford, a beautiful steep valley; but the mills never prospered, one reason being their inaccessibility.

There is no such country as the borders of Surrey, Sussex and Hampshire, for long varied country rambles. In 1862, Shottermill was quite primitive, a time when the pedestrian after tramping to the bottom of the Bowl was rewarded by a sight of the *Osmunda* growing gloriously.

And who so well qualified to enjoy these walks as the subject of our Memoir ? An old friend, Walter White, speaks of these rambles with Anne Gilchrist. She " was very fond of walking. The movement, the air and sunshine, the aspects of nature, brought out her bright points, and animated her conversation. Many a walk have I had with her across the breezy heaths, and into the deep lanes of Guildford and Haslemere. She liked to linger where a gate opened a prospect, and there talk our subject out.

" Heartiness, that made you at once feel at home, was the prevailing characteristic of her hospitality, especially when illumined by a crackling wood fire. And she seemed never better pleased than when a visitor took her by surprise."

# CHAPTER XIII.

## LETTER FROM DANTE GABRIEL ROSSETTI.

### 1862—1863. AGE 34—35.

MRS. GABRIEL ROSSETTI died in February, 1862. Dante Rossetti writes about his loss March 2nd, from 45, Upper Albany Street:—

"My dear Mrs. Gilchrist: I thank you sincerely in my turn for the words of sorrow and sympathy, which, coming from you, seem more terribly real than any I have received. I remember clearly the mistrustful feeling of insufficiency with which I sat down to write to you so short a time ago, and know now what it is both to write and to receive even the sincerest words at such a time.

" I have now to be thankful for obligations connected with my work which were a source of anxiety before ; for without them it seems to me that I could never work again. But I already begin to find the inactive moments the most unbearable, and must hope for the power, as I feel most surely the necessity, of working steadily without delay. Of my dear wife I do not dare to speak now, nor to attempt any vain conjecture whether it may ever be possible for me, or I be found worthy, to meet her again.

"I am staying at my mother's just now, and hope that some of my family, if not all, may join with me in seeking a new home together, as in any case I cannot any longer bear to remain in the old one. I have thoughts of coming if possible to Chelsea, and have already, in the impossibility I find of remaining inactive, been seeking for fresh quarters in that and other directions. Your photograph I still have, and still hope to send you some result from it, if I find such possible. [Gabriel Rossetti wished to construct some kind of posthumous portrait of Alexander Gilchrist.]

"Whenever it may be necessary to be thinking about the ' Life of Blake,' I hope you will let me know ; as my brother is equally anxious with myself, and perhaps at the present moment better able to be of any service in his power. While writing this, I have just read your letter again, and again feel forcibly the bond of misery which exists between us ; and the unhappy right we have of saying to each other what we both know to be fruitless. Pray believe that I am not the less grateful to you, at least, for the heartfelt warmth with which it is said.—I remain my dear Mrs. Gilchrist, yours ever sincerely,

D. G. Rossetti."

Shortly before going to Brookbank, Anne Gilchrist wrote to William Rossetti about the completion of *The Life of Blake* :—

"My Dear Sir : Mr. [Gabriel] Rossetti has so earnestly assured me you are willing to render help in my sorrowful task, that I venture at once to trouble

you.    I have not at present found, and much fear I
shall not find, any memoranda respecting the 'Selections'
from Blake's writings, which were to form an important
part of the volume.    I would by no means trust my own
judgment in making these selections.    Will you therefore, in those cases in which I did not know my dear
husband's intentions, help my choice? . . . .

"I have been obliged to return Mr. Monckton Milnes's
' *Jerusalem*,' in which also were many markers, but I
took a note of the pages at which these occurred, and I
feel sure the British Museum possesses a copy of that.
I send also Mr. Denman's ' *Gates of Paradise*,' because I
found written on a little slip, ' Look in the Gates of
Paradise for headings to Chapters.'    This of course must
refer to illustrations, as there is little or no letter-press."

On the twenty-eighth of April, 1862, Anne Gilchrist
wrote for the first time from Brookbank to William
Michael Rossetti :—

" The *French Revolution* was not engraved by Blake,
but printed and published in the ordinary manner, though
it had no circulation at all.    Mr. Linnell has a copy,
but we shall not need to borrow it, as I distinctly remember copying either the whole or such portions as my
husband thought he might want, and shall doubtless
come upon this copy.

"Mr. Denman's must certainly have been an imperfect
copy of the ' *Gates of Paradise*,' for I find it spoken of
as ' one of Blake's most beautiful and characteristic books
. . . a little foolscap octavo containing sixteen plates of
emblems *accompanied* by verse, with a title or motto to
each plate.'    My Husband's old and dear friend, almost

brother, William Haines, had copied out for him the
entire contents of your Manuscript book. . . . . . .
Whether the work of selection is already done or no,
Mr. Haines, who is shortly coming here, will be able to
tell me. . . . I find that ' *Thel* ' was to be given entire.
. . . In regard to the additional chapter, I earnestly
thank Mr. Rossetti and yourself. If it ought to be
done, assuredly his and yours are the hands to which I
would gratefully intrust the task.    But I think you
will not find it hard to forgive me a little reluctance that
*any* living tones should blend with that voice which
here speaks for the last time on earth.    I will not however, sacrifice the interests of the book to this feeling.
Perhaps, we are not yet in a position to decide with
certainty what is best.    When I have incorporated all
the additional matter contained in the notes, we shall be
better able to do so.    With renewed thanks, and with
kind regards to Mr. [Gabriel] Rossetti, believe me,
Dear Sir, yours very truly,      ANNE GILCHRIST.

" This place is a bona fide Cottage, and would stand
comfortably in your drawing-room in Tudor House.
Hence I found myself on first arrival in a dense wilderness of furniture.    But having stowed a good deal into
the attic we are now tolerably comfortable, and as there
is plenty of scope for the children out of doors, I think
it will do well enough.    The scenery round is of sur-
passing loveliness."

" *Brookbank, May 22nd*, 1862. . . . . I trust Mr.
[Gabriel] Rossetti is well in health, and able to throw
himself into work with sufficient earnestness to beguile
that ' up hill all the way,' which for both of us the

journey of life has with terrible reality become." ["Up hill all the way," is a phrase from a poem by Christina Rossetti.] . . . I am glad to say I find the Manuscript even more complete than I anticipated, and that a large mass of notes which I thought contained new matter, were merely for reference and verification."

They commenced printing the Life in the summer of '62, and Anne Gilchrist, in a letter to her sister-in-law *Mrs. Burnie,* speaks of literary and domestic life at Brookbank; though at the time staying with her mother at " Colne, near Halstead in Essex : *August* 25, 1862.

" Reluctant letter-writer as I am, I have in truth, *longed* impatiently for a spare hour in which to write to you—without being able to find it—so harassingly busy and anxious a life has mine been of late. Ever since we resumed printing, in fact—for not till then did I get *in* to my work enough, get sufficient command of it, to see what really needed doing. I found that the only grave omission in the book—the only place where dear Alec had left an absolute blank that *must* be filled in—was for some account of Blake's mystic writings, or ' Prophetic Books,' as he called them. And then to begin with, was the grand difficulty of how to get sight of these, some not even at the British Museum. At length after much letter writing, I got Mr. Monckton Milnes to lend me, down at Shottermill, his magnificent copies of some of these; but they were to be fetched and returned by hand, and only to be lent for a week ; so, as they are far too difficult to understand or to give any intelligible account of in a hurry, William Haines and I copied them all out. Then there was to write the account of them and to keep the printer going, and correct proofs, and to prepare Percy for school, and the children for coming here, and so that you will see it is not exaggeration to say I have literally not had breathing time. . . .

"I am thankful to see my dear mother and to find her tolerably well, always excepting her malady, which increases. But Colne is intolerably painful to me, and I quite pine to get back to my quiet cottage among the dear Surrey Hills; for there Alec's spirit is with me ever—presides in my home, speaks to me in every sweet scene; broods over the peaceful valleys; haunts the grand wild hill tops; shines gloriously forth in setting sun, and moon and stars. But here bitter memories almost crush me : thank God for the hard work, that like harness to an overtired horse, keeps me up. . . ."

It will be remembered that as long ago as February, Gabriel Rossetti offered to write a memoir of Alexander Gilchrist; but eventually the idea was abandoned, owing chiefly to the amount of other literary matter which it was found necessary to include in the two volumes. Gabriel Rossetti speaks of this subject in a letter: "*August*, 1862, 59, *Lincoln's Inn Fields*:—You ask me exactly *what* particulars I need respecting Mr. Gilchrist for the notice? All such dates as concerned his life would of course be necessary, but besides this I would like any account that could be furnished me of the causes which led to his decided tendency towards the study though not the practice of art—a point I have often thought over as very curious in a man who was more really cognisant of Art than any one I have known

that was not practically an artist—and rendered more
curious by the declaration I have heard him make, that
he not only never had drawn—but never *could* draw in
the least. Was this strictly and literally the case ? . . .
Of the mysterious *Oothocn* I never heard, nor did
even Mr. Swinburne, who has made, next to your husband, the most diligent researches of anyone into the
more recondite side of Blake.

"I shall be only too glad if I find a moment to run
down to you, but am just now in the very act of moving,
and cannot call my time, or indeed hardly my soul—my
own. [Dante Gabriel Rossetti moved to Cheyne Walk,
Michaelmas, 1862.] Some day I hope to show you my
new house at Chelsea. What a much greater good fortune it would have been a year ago ! For one thing it
would have made us neighbours."

William Michael Rossetti writes:—"The pervading
idea of the 'Daughters of Albion' is one which was continually seething in Blake's mind, and flustering Propriety in his writings; or rather *would have* flustered
Propriety, if she had either troubled herself to read the
oracles, or succeeded in understanding them. It is the
idea of the unnatural and terrible result in which, in
modern society, ascetic doctrines in theology and morals
have involved the relation of the sexes. A great deal
of his most powerful, appealing, incisive, odd, provok-
ing, and enigmatic writing is expended upon this formidable question ; in whose cause he is never tired of
uprearing the banner of heresy and nonconformity."

Replying to William Rossetti, *October 3rd*, 1862,
she says :—"I am afraid you will be vexed with me that

I was afraid to adopt entirely that most vigorous and admirable little bit apropos of the ‘Daughters of Albion.’   But it was no use to put in what I was perfectly certain Macmillan (who reads all the Proofs) would take out again.   I am certain of this from past experiences—but I would have *tried it* at an earlier stage; but as that sheet has been twice set up—and has now kept us at a standstill for three weeks, I did not think it right to do so :  I therefore ‘ reduced the subject ’ to still less—to a very shadowy condition indeed—but left enough, I trust, for the cause of truth and honesty.   It might be well perhaps to mention to Mr. Swinburne, if he is so kind as to do what was proposed, that it would be perfectly useless to attempt to handle this side of Blake’s writings—that Mr. Macmillan is far more inexorable against any shade of heterodoxy in morals than in religion—and that in fact, poor ‘ flustered propriety ’ would have to be most tenderly and indulgently dealt with. . . .”

To edit Blake’s Prophetic books, to hold a publisher in hand, and to keep everybody going, was anxious work, responsibilities that drew forth Anne Gilchrist’s judgment and tact.

She writes on November the ninth, about Frederick Tatham, the sculptor :—

“ MY DEAR MR. ROSSETTI : I should be so sorry on the one hand to throw hindrance in the way of one who is, I believe, a man of considerable talent struggling with great adversity ; and on the other to be the means of leading you to do what you might have cause to regret—that I think the best thing I can do is to tell you all I know about Tatham, and then leave you to decide the *Fraser* question.

[The *Fraser* question means this—F. Tatham sent W. M. Rossetti various MSS. of his own, " forcible and striking work in their peculiar way," Mr. Rossetti tells us, " and I was willing to offer them to *Fraser's Magazine,* with which I had then a slight literary connexion. Finally they were either not offered or not accepted."]

" He is the actual Tatham who knew Blake and enacted the holocaust of Blake manuscripts—not designs, I think, as I have heard from his own lips.   He is the son of an architect of some repute I fancy ; and was himself originally a sculptor.   He abandoned that early, and took to portraits in crayons by which he earned (chiefly in the Provinces I believe) a very sufficient income—but when the evil days (for this class of artist) of daguerreotype and photograph began, gradually lost all his practice : and has since been striving ineffectually, I fear, to succeed with Oil Painting.   I remember when he first came to see us at Chelsea his bringing a picture under his arm to show my Husband, who was interested by it—in which Dr. Johnson was one of the figures. Now as to his (Tatham's) relations with Blake—of course it could only have been during the last year or so of Blake's life that Tatham, then a very young man, knew him.   His acquaintance was mainly with Mrs. Blake when a widow.   And it is an inexplicable, and take it how you will, an ugly circumstance that while Miss Blake, the sole surviving relative and natural heiress to what was left of Blake's possessions after the widow's death—while Miss Blake I say, lived in such

penury, such absolute want, that I have heard a rumour
she died by her own hand rather than continue in life on
such terms of misery—Tatham came into possession of
so large a stock of Designs and engraved Books,
that he has, by his own confession, been selling them
'for thirty years' and at 'good prices.' It is quite
possible that Mrs. Blake may have bequeathed them to
him however—for she and Miss Blake got on very ill
together ; and latterly never met at all. Even this,
however, would not wholly acquit Tatham, I think.

"There was another matter of which it is more difficult
to get at the rights :—Linnell, as I daresay you know,
during the last few years of Blake's life when nearly all
other buyers failed him, took all Blake did (though himself a struggling man then, with large family) at fair
though not high prices, paid in the way most convenient
to Blake—so much a week.   After his death Linnell
fetched away the Dante Drawings as his own, having
been paid for in this way.   But Mrs. Blake—who appears to have always much disliked Linnell—said that a
considerable sum was still due on them ; which Tatham
claimed on her behalf (and afterwards on his own) : hence
arose a quarrel ; and Tatham and Linnell have never
spoken since.   Now my Husband, who had sifted the
matter, and knew both parties, thought Linnell an upright
truthful, if somewhat hard man, and that towards Blake
his conduct had been throughout admirable.   He also
inclined to think, that Mrs. Blake retained one trait of an
uneducated mind—an unreasonable suspiciousness.   But
Tatham would of course be disposed to give an entirely
different account of the affair.   You know I believe the

reason he assigns for the destruction of the manuscripts ?
Tatham was at that time a zealous Irvingite and says
he was instigated to it by some very influential members
of the Sect on the ground that Blake was inspired ; but
quite from a wrong quarter—by Satan himself—and was
to be cast out as an ' unclean spirit.' Carlyle says he is
quite certain Irving himself never had anything at all to
do with this.

"I sincerely hope the 'Essay on Sculpture' may
be of such quality as to warrant your giving Mr.
Tatham some kind of introduction for art criticism.    I

WILLIAM BLAKE.

Sketched from memory by FREDERICK TATHAM in 1860.

believe there is a great deal to like and admire in him. His letters are interesting, and have afforded some excellent material. . . ."

" *Brookbank, Nov. 22nd*, 1862. . . . . I am afraid we shall have to abandon the hope of tracing Mrs. Aders's collection. . . . It seems a pity that Miss Kearsley's Blakes cannot be investigated, seeing that she lives in Bedford Square, but it would be quite too impudent I suppose, as she was a friend of the ' predacious Yorkshireman's ' [Cromek]. Tatham speaks of there being one design at the British Museum shown as Blake's which was not his : I remember Mr. Haines saying he felt very certain of the same thing. . . .

" I have read your descriptive catalogue with extreme interest. What a notion one gets of Blake's powers of invention ! or rather, seeing the high qualities of his inventions, one should say of his creative imagination. I am afraid I have not a single suggestion to make. . . .

" Only think of Mr. Disraeli's collection turning out such a mare's nest, and Dibdin's whole account a mere fabrication. [The antiquarian said that Disraeli (Beaconsfield) possessed original drawings by Blake; so W. M. Rossetti wrote to Disraeli, and he replied in the most courteous spirit, showing that he possessed only some of the published books.]

" Mr. Linnell did offer, I well remember, to read the proofs or the MS. for my Husband, the bare notion of which filled him with horror : I do not think he ever showed proof or manuscript to the most congenial friend even. He had made most minute notes of all that Linnell told him ; and there is a good deal in the shape of letters in Linnell's own handwriting, all of which have been most carefully used. In the mode of viewing the facts, I fancy there would often be considerable divergency between Linnell and my Husband. Besides a biographer's duty often is to balance the evidence of conflicting witnesses. When Linnell made the same offer to me, I hesitated, for the case was different. No—I do not think I did hesitate—for he frankly said 'that he might put in or take out what he did not agree with,' or words to that effect—and I felt sure it would be a most imprudent, and indeed treacherous thing on my part to accede to."

*December* 13 William Rossetti replies :—"I think the view you have acted upon in your answer to Linnell the most scrupulously fair and honourable one, and considering that Tatham *is* one of the persons concerned, probably the most prudent and satisfactory to carry out in all regards. I therefore post the letter at once.

" Blake's favourite personage, ' the Giant Albion,' had been hitherto a mere name to me. But, in reading the old Chronicler Holinshed, I find that the Giant Albion is, in history books of that class, the reputed aboriginal founder of the British nation, long and long before ' Brute the Trojan.' My copy of Holinshed is imperfect, containing only an allusion to a foregoing account of the Giant Albion."

Apropos of Linnell, Anne Gilchrist writes :—

" My dear Mr. Rossetti : See now what an unreasonable man ! If I had sent him the proofs, he would have struck out as false every fact he had not communicated himself. I had *an instinct* of this, though I have never

seen him nor read half a dozen of his letters. You see
also (I hope I am not unjust) that the real ground of
his anxiety to see the proofs, was lest my Husband had
taken the Mrs. Blake and Tatham side in the Dante
[drawings] controversy."

Dante Gabriel Rossetti writes:—"I am working
closely this morning at the concluding chapter, in hope
of sending it off to-night, or if not, certainly to-morrow.
I was delayed by the necessity I found of going to the
Print Room to study Blake's coloured works there, as all
I could think of was to dwell on some of these. Facts
and descriptions of facts are in my line, but to talk
*about* a thing merely is what I could never well manage.

"I have worked in all your matter. . . What a
herculean labour that catalogue is ! [*i.e.*, the Catalogue
Raisonné, compiled by W. M. Rossetti, of Blake's
pictures and drawings]. I was quite astonished on
seeing it for the first time last night. . . . . .
Last night I saw Capt. Butts's collection of Blakes. He
has four or five large coloured ones, the same size as
your *Elijah*, which are of the same value, and constitute
with it the finest class of Blake's larger sized works I
know : they are truly glorious."

Shortly after receiving the last letter, Anne Gilchrist
wrote to William Rossetti:—" Mr. [D. G.] Rossetti's
*Supplementary Chapter* has come, and is a most glorious
and imaginative treatment of the subject. . . .

". . . I have had a gruffish, but not altogether
unfriendly, answer from Linnell. Cannot, however,
extract any further information from him, and as he
persists in it that Tatham's account of the oil-printing

process is inaccurate, I think it had best be left out."
Tatham's account was eventually printed in the Book,
as it was found to be the true description of Blake's
method of oil-colour printing.

Anne Gilchrist writes again to William Rossetti from
Brookbank:—" I send you with this Blake's *Descriptive
Catalogue*, and if you have never read it, you have a treat
in store."

Alluding to a water-colour drawing of *Ferdinand and
Miranda* she says: "Surely the 'baby' is Ariel? a very
quaint and Blake-like Ariel, certainly; but it would be
quite as original and startling a way of treating a little
baby to make it balance itself bolt upright on its mother's
hand in that way, as it is of a fairy. I only remember
the foremost of the figures below, and surely that is very
Caliban-like, and certainly not human? [At the time
this was written, she had lent this water-colour drawing
to a friend in London.] However, having always looked
at the picture with a strong preconception, I am not a fair
judge: but my husband shared this; nor did any one we
ever showed it to, seem to doubt. I almost fancy, as it
never entered our heads to start a doubt, that you will find
*Ferdinand and Miranda* written on it somewhere, for your
view of it is certainly a very possible one. . ."

" *Jan. 29th, '63.*—Dear Mr. [William] Rossetti:
Absence from home prevented my acknowledging by
return of post the safe arrival of the catalogue. Well
might your Brother call it 'a herculean labour'! Even I
who have seen it in previous stages of growth and order,
am astounded. How would my husband rejoice in so
exhaustive and harmonious a complement to the bio-

graphy ! . . . I have all but finished copying Blake's letters ; a task of real enjoyment, for they are indeed supremely interesting, admitting one as far as anything he ever wrote into the 'inner precincts' of his mind. Really Mr. Butts must have been a remarkable man in his way to have had such letters addressed to him—to have been chosen by Blake as the recipient of such soul's confidences."

On the third of January, 1863, Dante Gabriel Rossetti wrote:—" I am sure you will say with me, that each of us may well wish the other a happier year than the last. I do so most warmly on my side, and am ever yours sincerely,    D. G. R."

And on the fifth of January:—" Pray do make a stand for the passage from the 'Everlasting Gospel' about the Woman taken in Adultery. It is one of the finest things Blake ever wrote, and if there is anything to shock ordinary readers, it is merely in the opening, which could be omitted, and the poem made to begin with ' Jesus sat in Moses' chair,' etc. . . ."  Soon after, the poet-artist wrote :—

" My dear Mrs. Gilchrist : To-night at last I send the *Chapter*.  I really found it impossible to know what to say more of the poems, individually, but am sincerely of the opinion I express in the text as to the uselessness of doing so.  The truth is that as regards such a poem as ' My Spectre ' I do not understand it a bit better than anybody else, only I know better than some may know that it has claims as poetry apart from the question of understanding it, and is therefore worth printing. . . .

"I, on my side, hardly know how to thank you for so many kind expressions about the little I could do for the book, or rather the arrangement of it. However, such as it is, I would have done it gladly for Blake's or gladly for your husband's or gladly for your sake, and moreover, had always a great wish of my own to do something in this direction, so have much more to be thankful for the opportunity myself, than any one can have to me for the little done.—Yours very sincerely, D. G. Rossetti.

"*Postscript:* By the bye, I have been a martyr to unsatisfactory servants here, and have been asking all my friends if they know any desirable ones. Our household consists of four men, two of whom only, myself and Mr. Swinburne, are at all constant inmates. [The other two were George Meredith and William Rossetti]. Our plan, hitherto, has been to get a married couple. The first couple was recommended by an aunt of mine from the country, and would have done well, but London air knocked the man up. The second couple were people I knew well, who did famously, but were conditionally pre-engaged when I took them, and being wanted had to leave me. The third couple I got by advertisement, and are just going to rid me of themselves after driving me half crazy with their stupidity. . . .

". . . These nightmares of mine leave now in a few days. Is it possible that you could suggest better people for the place? Pardon my troubling you. . . ."

The long and anxious task of editing the 'Book' was drawing to a close. The next letter to William

Rossetti concludes the correspondence over the production of the ' Life and Works of William Blake.'

*"Brookbank ; May 2nd,* 1863.

" I had a little note from Miss Rossetti yesterday, which gave me much pleasure, for it responded very kindly and cordially to my hope of her coming here with you.   About the middle of May would suit me quite as well as now.

" I have received since I last wrote to you proofs of the poetical portion of Volume II., and indeed I hardly know how to speak adequately of the satisfaction and delight with which I read them ; never, I think, was the task of editorship so admirably performed, if the aim of editorship be to quicken the reader's insight and enjoyment. I need not tell you I read your explanation of the ' Mental Traveller ' with wide open eyes.

" Certainly that ' Idea ' binds the most chaotic, disjointed, obscure looking poem that ever was written into a harmonious, connected, nobly pregnant whole.   My husband would have been beyond measure pleased with it. . . ."

Now we can leave the book with the publishers : they waited till the autumn of 1863 before launching *The Life of William Blake.*

# CHAPTER XIV.

## LETTER FROM JANE WELSH CARLYLE.

### 1863. AGE 35.

AS soon as ' The Life of Blake ' was finished, Anne Gilchrist wrote to Jane Carlyle (after a lapse of two years) placing Brookbank at Carlyle's disposal, and was answered by a letter which at first sight seems a little *gauche*, but, we take it to be merely the honest indignation that one clever woman entertains for another of her sex, who is also clever, but who, in addition, is immersed in maternal cares, silently grappling with literary work, with what appears to Jane Carlyle, unreasonable energy and devotion! In this impatient mood the apparently neglected friend writes from *Cheyne Row*, *June* 15:—

"My dear Mrs. Gilchrist: It is indeed long since we exchanged words, we two! So long that when I received your letter this morning I did not recognise the handwriting; but had to look for the signature; and when I found your name I was struck with astonishment, thinking the letter was from a *Catherine* Gilchrist whom I used to correspond with 45 years ago!! And yet I have often thought of you and often talked of you in the past year—and have not thought of *Catherine* Gilchrist the least in the world! What a thorough belief in *your* total forgetfulness of me did this little fact indicate, that my mind should have leapt back forty-five years for the writer of that letter!

" I answer it in a hurry, having to go up to town for groceries, etc.—before dinner time, which is now *half-past* three with us!

" I should like much to go and see you in your country home—not with any view to our own convenience—but just to *see you* and talk with you—and refresh our friendship which seemed in the way of fading out *like a photograph!*

" But *I cannot* go just at present. I have been to St. Leonards on a visit for a week—am just come home, and have a great many things to see after before I could leave Mr. Carlyle again. I was to have gone with a lady [Miss Davenport Bromley] to Folkestone on Wednesday, for a few days, and broke off my engagement, on account of Mr. Carlyle not liking I should go away again just when I had come home. So I could not go in another direction on Wednesday.

" Tell me when you return from Essex, and there is a little time to choose a day out of, and I shall be only too glad to go!

" Mr. Carlyle is getting on very peaceably with his work, suffering nothing from heat as yet—and it would be most imprudent, *while that is the case,* to not let well alone. Shifting his quarters for more than a day or two, is always for him a most dangerous measure! I want him to go to the sea for a few days—and I think he will—

there being a dear old friend [Dr. Black] at St. Leonards who would receive him at any time and keep him all right.    But even *that* he will not do till he is *burnt out*. A thousand thanks to *you* all the same—I will write at more leisure—but I would not keep you in suspense about the house.—Affectionately, J. W. CARLYLE."

*The Life of Blake* is now fairly afloat, and Anne Gilchrist speaks of the book in a letter to William Rossetti :—" I was very pleased with the *Spectator's* review—have not yet seen Mr. Scott's. . . . Macmillan issued 2,000 copies of the Blake : I wonder how soon it is reasonable to expect such an edition as that to run out."    And to Mrs. Burnie she writes :—" I know you will much like to see Carlyle's letter to me, therefore I enclose it. You must bear in mind in reading it, that he is a man very sparing of praise, stern in his requirements, inflexibly sincere, both in forming and in expressing his judgment. To me its effect was almost overpowering—knowing the man as I do.    Knowing the depth of meaning and feeling conveyed in those brief words. . . ."    Carlyle wrote from Chelsea, thirty-first of October, 1863 :—

"DEAR MRS. GILCHRIST: I receive with many feelings the *Book* you send me, after these long delays.    Thankfulness is one clear feeling ;—not only to you from myself, but to you for the sake of Another who is not now here.    Sorrowful remembrance, I need not say, is a background to the whole :—very curious to me as I read on.    For the *better* the Book is, the *shadier* grow those dark tints of memory ; the shadier, but also the more beautiful, and in a sort, the less painful !—

" I have been upon the book these three evenings,

with all the leisure I could amass for it; and find every-where that it is right well done,—minute knowledge well arranged, lively utterance, brevity, cheerful lucidity; —and, in fact, that it is a Book likely to prove extensively acceptable, and have the many fine merits that are in it recognised by the Public. Your own little Preface is all that is proper:—could but the Queen of these realms have been as *Queen*-like in her widowhood!—

"I send you many thanks and regards, dear Mrs. Gil-christ; and shall wish you and yours always well.

Yours sincerely, T. CARLYLE."

In a letter, to a relative, written from Brookbank, *Nov.* 12th, 1863, Anne Gilchrist says:—" That beloved task (the Blake) kept my head above water in the deep sea of affliction, and now that it is ended I sometimes feel like to sink—to sink, that is, into pining discontent —and a relaxing of the hold upon all high aims. I find it so *hard* to get on at anything beyond the inevit-able daily routine, deprived of that beloved and genial Presence, which so benignantly and tenderly fostered all good, strengthening the hands, cheering the heart, quickening the intellect even."

Anne Gilchrist goes on to speak of the Carlyles, upon whom she called, while on a visit to London:—

" Poor Mrs. Carlyle I did not see; and received the saddest news of her, but I spent a delightful two hours with Carlyle himself on Monday evening. He again spoke most warmly of the Blake; called it a ' beautiful delineation of character;' spoke of the ' acuteness and thoroughness with which the slightest clues had been followed out in gathering the materials, and with all this toil and minute accuracy on the writer's part, nothing but pleasure for the reader—no tediousness;' and many more things had I but time to write them. I had a beautiful and enthusiastic letter from Mr. Palmer, and one full of feeling from Browning," about the Blake.

Samuel Palmer's letter is characteristic; we give nearly the whole of it:—"*Furze Hill House, Red Hill, Nov.*

"MY DEAR MRS. GILCHRIST: How shall I thank you enough for such a treasure as this dear delightful book— how keep it so long out of my hands as will suffice to let me fill this paper? I could not wait for the paper-knife but fell upon it, reading all in between:—now, I have cut the first volume, and read wildly everywhere:— and now again I begin at the beginning, and mean-while write to tell you how it has delighted me; raising, however, a strange ferment of distressing and delicious thought.

" Surely never book has been put forth more lovingly: the dear Author and the Editor,—Mr. Linton, the Pub-lisher, and Printer, seem all to have laboured at a labour of love:—and instead of being sparingly illustrated, as I understood it was to be, it is, both in quantity and un-rivalled quality, the richest Book of all illustrated ones that I have ever seen. It is not a pearl thrown to the swinish many, but a tiara of jewels.—What will they do? turn again and rend, or take kindly to this new and costly diet?

" Hitherto the English people have shown themselves inflexibly obtuse to high art,—making the very words a favourite bye-word.

" There is an evident preciousness (if there be such

a word) about the book,—as we read, and look at the illustrations, and read on again,—which can hardly fail to strike every one ;—and to those who are too callous even to feel this, it must at least commend itself as the most curious and extraordinary thing they ever handled. And then, the ' respectable ' who keep gigs, and ' by sweet reserve and modesty grow fat,' will be enraged at it—an excellent symptom ;—grasping it like an electric eel—the more the pain the tighter the grasp. So, with one thing and another I cannot help thinking it will have a great run, edition after edition ;—and as already it is certain to be an *imperishable monument* of the dear Biographer,—it seems to me likely to bear his name far beyond the bounds of his native land, perhaps by way of translations. The fancies however of the piggy populace are beyond calculation,—or anything more than vague conjecture. Akenside said he would be willing to stake the value of his judgment on the success of *Dyer's Fleece*—but it did not ' take.'

" I rather thought there would have been an engraving from the cast of Blake's head taken during his lifetime,—as Mr. W. B. Richmond told me he had made a very careful drawing on purpose ;—perhaps it might be worth considering for a future edition ; but it seems ungracious even to hint an addition to so profuse a banquet.

" I do hope it may provoke a lively art-controversy in the periodicals, unless people have gone quite to sleep —and ceased to care for anything but their cheque books and arm chairs. . . . How often I think of your sweet house on the ' L' Allegro ' upland among the green hills.—How your book,—so doubly and dearly your own book, will delight your eyes—as you sit within those enriched walls !—And your dear children will grow familiar with every page of it—  . . . And now, my dear Mrs. Gilchrist, I have two requests to make, one is that you will not write a line to me when you could be otherwise better employed.   Secondly, that when you exist in a vacuum and want something to do,—you will tell me any little doings of the little people ;—any particulars you have time for, which will bring all before my mind's eye, as you are already within my heart.—Believe me, Dear Mrs. Gilchrist,

Ever faithfully yours,    S. PALMER."

" P.S.   Now I am going to begin the Book at the beginning even before the ink is dry."

About this time the family at Brookbank made the acquaintance of Christina Rossetti ; mention is made of her by Anne Gilchrist in a letter to Mrs. Burnie :— " The week before I left [Brookbank] Mr. William Rossetti brought down his sister, Christina, to spend a few days with me, and Mr. William Haines came over to meet them.   We were both altogether charmed with Miss Rossetti—there is a sweetness, an unaffected simplicity and gentleness, with all her gifts that is very winning—and I hope to see more of her.   She was so kind to the children and so easy to please and make comfortable that though a stranger to me, she was not at all a formidable guest."

# CHAPTER XV.

## LETTER FROM CHRISTINA G. ROSSETTI.

### 1864—1867. AGE 36—39.

" MY acquaintance with Jean Ingelow's *Poems* to which you kindly introduced me, has been followed by a very slight acquaintance with herself. She appears as unaffected as her verses, though not their equal in regular beauty : however I fancy hers is one of those variable faces in which the variety is not the least charm.

" Have you noticed the advertisement appearing from time to time of William's blank verse translation of Dante's *Inferno?* I hope it will soon be published, but Mr. Macmillan does not send proofs with all the speed we could wish. Next year promises—or threatens—to bear an unwonted crop of Dantesque literature: however, I think that on its own ground and within its own confessed limits, William's work will be well able to hold its own.

"Since my pleasant days at Brookbank last summer, I have paid a visit to Cheltenham and made a short stay at Malvern. The latter place is very delightful with its grand old Priory church and view-commanding hills. . . ."

From Hastings, in the same year, Christina Rossetti writes :—" My dear Mrs. Gilchrist : Thank you for one of those truly kind letters which ought to live (and I hope will live) in my affectionate memory. You are indeed good to offer me change of air at pleasant Brookbank, but my date will show you that something less *genially* cold has been advised. Not that there is much the matter with me ; but a cold caught several weeks ago has not added to my bloom or strength, and as my Uncle and Cousin are wintering down here there is every convenience for my staying with them. . . . We have seen Gabriel two or three times since he returned from Paris ; and thought him looking perhaps less stout, and so far better.

" Can you think yourself strong enough to face a second winter in sole charge of your children ? I hope, specially for their sake, that you will not run rash risks ; and cannot but fear that you are over-taxing your powers. My love to them, please. The Burne Joneses are down here with their little boy; and some of the De Morgans, but I don't know whether the abstruse Professor himself.

" I have just received a present of Jean Ingelow's 8th edition : imagine my feelings of envy and humiliation ! "

Brookbank was originally one of two cottages : " Finding no other chance of a suitable house in the neighbourhood," writes Anne Gilchrist, "and already the prospect of going through another winter in the same discomfort as last, I have at length made up my mind to have my cottage enlarged.

"My neighbour here, Mr. Simmons, who is a magistrate, was telling me of a case that came before him at Farnham the other day. An itinerant showman with a 'ghost' on the principle of the Polytechnic Ghost, finding himself very 'hard up' indeed, was obliged to pawn his Ghost. The clumsy pawnbroker broke the large glass reflector which is the most important part of the apparatus. So the unhappy showman went up to London to get another. But not having money enough to pay for the whole journey back, he took a ticket for a short distance only. When he got out at Farnham the railway people took him up for the deficit in his fare : and he summoned the pawnbroker. But being unable to redeem his Ghost or himself he could not enforce his claim on the pawnbroker, so Ghost and Ghost proprietor remain in [pawn].

"By the by I saw my Cousin John Carwardine a few days ago. He has been two years in the army of the Potomac under Generals M'Clellan and Burnside : has fought in ten battles, one of which lasted seven days ; and was never wounded but once and that only with a bullet in the leg. He left because he had a return of the Panama fever, to which he has been subject ever since he originally took it, in crossing the Isthmus. . . . He tells me the accounts of the miseries and hardships endured by the army of the Potomac are exaggerated, and that in fact they have not at all exceeded what are inevitable in a military campaign : that the commissariat was well managed and they never suffered from want of

provisions, except, occasionally during forced marches.
He also speaks very favourably of his comrades in arms;
though it took him some time to get to like them. . . ."

On the first of July the family at Brookbank
migrate to Earls Colne, to pay their annual visit to
Henrietta Burrows; and on the twenty-fourth of July,
1864, a letter is written to William Haines from the
Priory Cottage :—

"The Colne people have finished their church to
everybody's satisfaction; and really I think justly so.
Knowledge and taste have, I suppose, now so far advanced
that even small county architects know what they ought
to imitate. And where there is nothing to spoil in the
way of genuine ancient work—where they merely undo
hideous churchwardenisms—they are real benefactors.
They have, here, thrown open the oak roof, carried
away the pews, built an aisle and put a tessellated floor,
and really the church looks quite noble within. The
lovely Tower, with staircase turret and flint work round
the top; which I daresay you remember, as forming
with the glorious avenue of elms, the beauty of Colne,
they of course did not meddle with.

"I have had a parcel from the London. *Hallam's
Remains* one reads with some eagerness for the
sake of *In Memoriam*. But except the love poems addressed to Tennyson's sister, which I like much from
their sweetness and earnestness of feeling, there is not
much that strikes one—at least I do not fancy there
is any vigorous thinking or originality, though much
scholarship and fineness of perception. In the prose, he
has such a provokingly *metaphysical* tendency, the most

barren of all tendencies I believe.   By the by, the last essay in the volume is a controversial one about one of Professor Rossetti's works—very antagonistic to his views of Dante's hidden meanings.

" I have been trying to get together (Walter White's advice) materials for an article on Dr. Carpenter's writings.   Chiefly on his very remarkable and philosophical views of life and the ' vital force,' but I have not succeeded—seem to have got together every book he has ever written but the right one.   " Nothing but minute descriptions of *foraminifera*, and so forth, but no general views.   However, I must hunt further.   The worst of it is, the best thoughts of our scientific men are buried alive in *Philosophical Transactions*, Proceedings of the Royal Institution and the like, and arduous and inconvenient is the fishing them out.   It seems odd and unreasonable perhaps to you that in the teeth of all my difficulties and limitations within and without, of time and opportunity and ability, I should still persevere in trying to write,—but I feel that I must do it, for this reason : that else I should slowly gravitate downwards into entire absorption in busy, bustling, contriving working-day material life—weakly and basely giving up all attempts to fulfil dear Alec's hopes of me.   For after all, when youth and growing time are left behind and *ripening* time comes—if there be anything to ripen—reading is not enough.   Prose reading becomes either oppressive or useless unless the mind rouses itself to take a more active part than that of the being the bucket pumped into."

Soon after returning to Brookbank, Anne Gilchrist,

on November the twentieth, writes to the same friend :—

"The Madox Browns and William Rossetti ran down for a Saturday to Monday visit in the latter part of October. How you will like Madox Brown. He seems to me to have a wider range of thought and of sympathy and more geniality than any other of dear Alec's delightful artist friends. I do not mean that they are deficient in these qualities, only that he is pre-eminent. Madox Brown will be working especially hard for the next five months, as he contemplates getting up an exhibition of his works in the spring.

"There has been some talk of Tennyson's coming to look at that little estate near Churt which Mr. Simmons showed Mr. White [Walter White, for many years assistant Secretary at the Royal Society] : Tennyson seems much taken with White's description, and has made many inquiries through the latter. I therefore wrote a note to Mrs. Tennyson containing all the particulars I could gather, and have received two such kind little notes from her in return. Mrs. Tennyson seems much attached to their present residence, but I think the Laureate is rather tired of that Cockney's Paradise, the Isle of Wight : *She* would like to retain Farringford, and add some room to a farmhouse in this neighbourhood, but *he* has an idea of giving Farringford up, and building a large house on one of these 'Devil's Jumps' just a little beyond the Cross.

"I am glad Christmas is over ; it is a trying time—a time that cannot but bring up vividly what was and what might have been."

And from Brookbank, Jan. 21, 1865, the same writer in a letter to her sister-in-law :—" Masson has accepted the article I wrote last spring : [' The Indestructibility of Force :' *Macmillan's Magazine*.] And *that* will be the last thing I shall attempt for many a long day, as I have fully made up my mind to give myself up wholly to educating the children : I find it such a harassing strain to attempt *two* things—bad for me—because to be hard at work from the time you step out of bed in the morning till you step into it at night is not good for any one—it leaves no time either for general culture—for drinking at the refreshing fountain of standard literature and of music. Bad for the children because it made me grudge them my time of an evening, when so much indirect good may be done to them by reading aloud and showing them prints. And after all they will not always be children ; and if I have it in me to do anything worth doing with my pen, why, I can do it ten years hence, if I live— when I shall have completed my task so far as direct instruction of the children goes—I shall only be forty-six, then—not in my dotage. Do you think I am right ? A *divided* aim is not only most harassing to a conscientious disposition but quite fatal to success—to doing one's very best in either. . . . I quite enjoyed Sid's visit—he is a dear fellow I think." Sidney Gilchrist Thomas, since famous as the inventor or co-inventor of the *Thomas-Gilchrist process*, the Gilchrist being Percy Carlyle Gilchrist, Anne Gilchrist's eldest son : S. G. Thomas, her nephew.

" Do you remember how dear Alec used to talk of

Thursly? as one of the wildest, loneliest, loveliest
villages in England : so that the name was as familiar
to me at Guildford ten years ago as it is now. I prize
inexpressibly these fine subtle links of association that,
subtle as they are, seem tangibly to link my present
here with that happy past. They give me far more
pleasure than pain."

Talking of associations, curiously enough, the Rev.
Thomas Carwardine with his daughter, Henrietta,
[Anne Gilchrist's mother] visited Hayley at *Eartham*
in 1790. We have the sonnets by us, which the
' Hermit' composed on this occasion to Henrietta Carwardine [Mrs. Burrows] : Hayley would present, with
a gallant flourish, a sonnet to his fair guest every
morning at breakfast!

In the summer of 1865, Madox Brown opens an
Exhibition : William Haines is advised to go and see
Brown's works [191 Piccadilly, opposite Sackville-
street]. "And the catalogue of which he kindly sent
me a copy is as interesting in its way as the famous
Descriptive Catalogue [Blake's] we know so well.

" I ran up for a few hours some weeks ago and
managed to accomplish a glimpse at his pictures as well
as some business : I must say I was never more impressed with the sense of intellectual power from pictures
than before some of his canvases."

Christina Rossetti also mentions the Exhibition :—

" My dear Mrs. Gilchrist : Your letter reached me
at Hastings, but well content I sit down to answer it
from home. Delightful home, whatever its aspect to
outsiders : was there ever yet a snail who preferred the

*Drawn by Herbert H. Gilchrist, from a Sketch in Oil-Colour by George Romney
at Colne Priory.*

WILLIAM HAYLEY.

bravest nautilus floating to his own convenient shell?
. . . By the by, I hope your shell is rapidly becoming
more and more convenient and comely: one really
needs some compensation for universal upset.

"What a long bitter winter it has been: at Hastings
the cold was searching; what must it have been at
Shottermill? But how pleasant this spring weather is.
. . . I am better too than I was, though my looks
don't earn me many compliments. Better indeed, yet
not so well but that kind William talks of taking
me in his holiday to enjoy my first glimpse of Italy.
Our plans are unsettled: but if we go, I hope our
Mother will accompany us and obtain her first glimpse
also; and perhaps we may start in the course of next
month, not to return I suppose for about five weeks.
For one reason however, I could almost like the whole
lovely scheme to miscarry: if William went alone he
would be able to travel further south than he has ever
yet been, or than could be managed with us; and he
had already indeed, I fear, been actually looking forwards to possible Naples; as yet he has not gone
beyond Rome.

"Thank you for taking an interest in my prospective Volume II. I am receiving proofs of it now,
and hope it may see the light before so very long: but
doubtless you are aware of the nature of publishing
delays, and know that weeks and months may slip away
before the counted-on literary chick hatches. William's
*Dante*, having actually left the nest, seems accounted a
vigorous bird enough by the reviewers: I hesitate to
say how much I like and admire it, just because I am

his sister; otherwise I should have somewhat to say on the point.

"To-day we went to see Mr. Madox Brown's Exhibition; and interesting and very full of matter it is: I had not been before. Some of the works were familiar, some of course new to me: I particularly admired two of the three compositions designed to illustrate Dalziel's Bible ; indeed one of these, *Elijah restoring the resuscitated child to his mother,* is I think the work which to please myself I should select from the entire room full.—No, I don't know anything of Gabriel projecting a similar exhibition.

"Funny little Grace: I daresay various of your correspondents don't omit 'love' to her. Please present mine with all due gravity, and to Herbert, and to Beatrice. Beatrice comes last, because I have to add my request that she will give me pleasure by accepting a little book I send her with this : [Poems by Gerda Fay—Mrs. Gemmer] accept it, that is, unless (as I fear she may) she scouts it as too childish; in that case I hope Grace will not consider she has outgrown such lore, but will graciously accept it as befits one of her name. William desires very kind regards.— Always, very truly yours,

CHRISTINA G. ROSSETTI."

The letter we have read, dated from 166, Albany-street, is soon followed by a second from the same writer :—

" My dear Mrs. Gilchrist : Thank you for such a delightfully kind letter received this morning. Please give my love to your three young people. I am truly pleased if they remember me, but suspect Grace's reminiscence of being somewhat shadowy.   You do not tell me how your house alterations have prospered : well, I hope, they looked so promising in theory.

"Our small continental tour proved enjoyable beyond words ; a pleasure in one's life never to be forgotten. My mother throve abroad, and not one drawback worth dwelling upon occurred to mar our contentment.   Such unimaginable beauties and grandeur of nature as we beheld no pen could put on paper ; so I obviously need not exert myself to tell you what Lucerne was like, or what the lovely majesty of Mount St. Gothard, or what the Lake of Como, with its nightingale accompaniment, or what as much of Italy as we saw to our half-Italian hearts.   Its people is a noble people, and its very cattle are of high-born aspect; I am glad of my Italian blood. I don't say a word about art treasures : the truth being that I far prefer nature treasures, but we saw glorious specimens of both classes.   Our longest stay was at Milan; where we witnessed a rather interesting ceremony, the unveiling by Prince Omberto of a statue of Cavour. At Milan, too, we went over a most interesting in-stitution, the Ospedale Maggiore ; the children's ward was quite a pretty sight with its population of poor little patients.   Of course I could run on indefinitely with disjointed scraps and facts, but this sample may suffice.

" Gabriel dined with us to-day ; and that is worth saying, because we have so few acquaintances in common. Do you recollect how I battened on your Plato last time I was at Brookbank ?   I have since become possessed of an own private Plato, my mother having given him me for my last birthday. On the same occasion I was enriched with Jean Ingelow's Poems, with which my first thorough acquaintance was made at your house.

" May I offer you my mother's and sister's kind regards, though they have not yet the pleasure of knowing you ? Anyone who is kind to me has a claim on them. Till our next meeting, whenever that may be, and not the less after it, pray believe me—

Affectionately yours, CHRISTINA G. ROSSETTI."

On the ninth of July of the same year Anne Gilchrist takes up the pen again, to William Haines :—

" Did I tell you that I had a very narrow [escape] on the top of Hind Head a few weeks ago ? Mrs. Simmons was driving another lady and myself when somehow or other the reins got under the horse's tail, and he set off at a furious pace, began to kick, and of course was perfectly unmanageable, because the more you pulled the reins the worse he was ; we were just coming to a tremendous pitch down hill when happily he plunged into the ditch and threw us all out into the hedge. I felt the chaise draw along over my head and knock my hat off. Yet we all jumped up unhurt.

" It seems to me the thing to do if your horse runs away *is* to make for the ditch, for it is certainly more advantageous to be thrown out into the hedge, even if it be a *holly* hedge, than on to the hard high road. There is generally a comic element in these affairs—there certainly was in ours—for the friend behind was a stout old lady who had charge of the provisions (we were to have picniced at Churt.) So she was landed in the

hedge with the bottles and baskets all on her stomach,
and the tenacity with which she afterwards clung to the
same—called vehemently for corkscrews and insisted on
our immediately beginning to eat bread and cheese—
which after the excitement of being pitched out, one was
of all things least inclined for—tickled me immensely."

" Earls Colne ; July sixteenth, 1865.

" How famously the Liberals are getting on. It is a
thing worth rejoicing at, that John Stuart Mill has got
in, is it not? I am to meet at dinner on Tuesday a
Mr. Abel, a barrister who has been attacking Peto
furiously and trying to spoil his chance with the Bristol
electors.

" Is it not remarkable how the latest views of science
corroborate Blake and the mystics in regarding everything as Force Power ! All substance melts into that
under the experimentalist's hands ; and power force of
every kind he finds wholly indestructible. Is it reasonable, is it *possible* to believe then that the noblest and
most potent of all forces, the vital or soul, should be
the one exception—the one destructible Power ? It is
quite as irrational as it is faint-hearted to believe so."

Apropos of an invitation from Brookbank, William
Michael Rossetti writes, November the twenty-sixth:—
" I am to be Holman Hunt's 'best man' at his
approaching marriage—to come off some earlyish day
in December, but not as yet fixed to my knowledge, and
till that important function is discharged I don't quite
know which days to call my own."

The visit (one of many) is only deferred ; in the
meantime the inmate of Brookbank speaks of domestic

life and of "teaching as real hard work, and I spend
five hours a day at it, and then the amount of industry
that goes to making two hundred a year do the
work of four or five is not small. However my
prime rest, pleasure, society all in one—what keeps me
going in a tolerably unflagging way,—are the glorious
walks. Hind Head is as fresh to me as the day I first
set eyes on it. And if I go out feeling ever so jaded,
irritable, dispirited, when I find myself up there alone
(for unless I have perfect stillness and quietness and my
thoughts are as free as a bird, the walk does not seem to
do me a bit of good) care and fatigue are all shaken off
and life seems as grand and sweet and noble a thing as
the scene my bodily eyes rest on—and if sad thoughts
come they have hope and sweetness so blended with them
that I hardly know them to be sad—and I return to my
little chicks quite bright and rested, and fully alive to
the fact that they are the sweetest, loveliest chicks in the
whole world—and Giddy says, 'Mamma has shut up
her box of sighs.'"

Christina Rossetti sends her friend a copy of *The
Prince's Progress:* after exchanging a letter, Christina
Rossetti writes :—" Thank you for so very kind a welcome of my poor offering. *Songs in a Cornfield* seems
one of the most successful pieces in the volume, and
somewhat disappointingly I must ask you to correct a
mispunctuation in it (p. 71). There should be no stop
whatever after *coil* (' The green snake hid her coil '),
but a colon after *thickest* in the next line.

" My more than seven weeks in Scotland proved a
thorough success, and have sent me home to receive

friendly congratulations on my looks and *fat*.  I think my dear hostess at Penkill Castle, Miss Boyd, might charm you if you knew her : perhaps she is the prettiest handsome woman I ever met, both styles being combined in her fine face; and Mr. and Mrs. Scott, who shared the long visit with me, are tried old friends . . . and now I am well content to be at home again, and to take my turn at housekeeping. . . .

"Gabriel and William charge me with messages of friendly remembrance and interest in you and yours. My mother and sister and myself dined with them at Chelsea last Thursday, and found plenty to admire in the old house and its curious contents. . . . William is likely soon to be leaving for Italy, towards the end of this month it may be; his special aim being Naples, which he has not yet seen, and where much of our Father's early life was passed.

"Do you know that Mrs. Madox Brown has lately recovered from a somewhat alarming attack of illness ? She and her family have left Kentish Town, and now occupy a large handsome house in Fitzroy Square.  I went there the other day to see Mr. Brown's fine picture of the *Coat of many Colours;* a very noble work. . . . What a deal of satisfaction one can command with a penny postage stamp well bestowed!  Please don't arrive at precisely the opposite conclusion."

In a letter dated *Brookbank, Haslemere, September* 16, 1866, Anne Gilchrist writes to William Haines of a visit from the Tennysons :—

"I was sitting under the yew tree yesterday, when Fanny [the maidservant] came to me and put a card into my hand. And whose name do you think was on that card ? If I were talking instead of writing, I should make you guess and keep you in suspense a long while, but that is no use in a letter, because you can peep forward. It was,—' Mr. Alfred Tennyson.' He looks older than I expected, because of course the portraits one was early familiar with have stood still in one's mind as the image to be associated with that great name. But he is to my thinking far nobler looking now; every inch a king; features are massive, eyes very grave and penetrating, hair long, still very dark and, though getting thin, falls in such a way as to give a peculiar beauty to the mystic head. Mrs. Tennyson a sweet graceful woman with singularly winning gentle manners, but she looks *painfully* fragile and wan.

"They said they should like to see the 'Jumps,' the 90 acres to be sold for £1,400 ; beyond the Punch Bowl, if I could tell their driver the exact spot. I felt the most useful thing to do would be to introduce Mr. Simmons, and sent over for him ; but, alas ! he was just gone to Churt, so then I ran over and had a consultation with Mrs. Simmons, and she proposed having the pony put to and driving me over with them (accompanying their fly), that we might find Mr. Simmons and then proceed to the 'Jumps,' and that we did.

"But what you will be most anxious to hear is all that he said. Mrs. Tennyson having mentioned that they had just come over from Petersfield, and that they had been there to see a clergyman who takes pupils with an idea of placing their boys with him.    When Giddy [a child of seven] came into the room [Tennyson] called her to him, asked her her name, kissed her, stroked her sturdy legs, made Mrs. Tennyson feel them, and then set her on his knee, and talked to her all the while I was over at the Simmons' arranging matters.    Afterwards when we were walking up a hill together he said, ' I admire that little girl of yours.    It isn't everyone that admires that kind of very solid development of flesh and blood. But I do.    Old Tom Campbell used to say that children should be like bulbs—plenty of substance in them for the flower to grow out of by-and-by.'    Tennyson asked me how many children I had ; and when I said ' four,' answered hastily, ' quite enough ! quite enough!' At which I was not a little amused.

" By the time we reached Churt a heavy shower came on, so we all took shelter in Mr. Simmons' little farm-house there.

"In course of conversation, Tennyson repeated a good story, which a Southern American had recently told him—apropos of the extensive heath burning we some-times have on our hills here.    ' Two Yankee lawyers were travelling across a prairie, and in a mischievous frolic (being the worse for drink) set fire to it.    Just before doing so they had passed a gang of very poor miserable-looking people—miners migrating to some new opening.    The fire proved so frightfully extensive and destructive that the authorities at the nearest town took the matter up, and the poor miners were arrested for it.    The two lawyers were actually engaged, one as counsel for the defence and the other for the prosecution. The case was going entirely against the miners, when *their* counsel said, "If my learned brother the counsel for the prosecution can lay his hand on his heart and say that he solemnly believes these poor men did the deed I give up my cause." The learned counsel being not entirely without conscience declined to do this, and the poor miners were acquitted.'

"As soon as the shower cleared off we (fly, pony-chaise and Mr. Simmons on horse-back) went to the piece of ground in question—the Jumps. Tennyson was by no means favourably impressed with it, and indeed it struck me as one of the barest, most desolate looking spots to be found hereabouts, though not without a certain wild bleak grandeur ; but it is just outside and beyond all the beauty : 'Very dear at the money,' he said emphatically, and 'what is the use of a number of acres if they will not grow anything?' I should tell you that there was a tremendous fire on this very spot last year (something like a mile of flame) : and therefore the ground looked deceptively barren and black.

"Tennyson then said he should like to see the Punch Bowl : while we were driving thither, one of the most tremendous rain storms I ever saw swallowed up the country behind us, a magnificent effect it was. I think Tennyson was much impressed with the grandeur of the views from the top of Hind-head, though he saw them under decidedly unfavourable circumstances.

"I must complete my narrative another time, having already kept the letter by me a week for lack of opportunity to finish my long story. I will only add, that when we parted he thanked the Simmonses and myself very cordially and pleasantly — said he should like another day here when he could find the opportunity. And though we certainly saw nothing to suit him this time I do not despair of our doing so by and by.    It *was* a happy day ! though the weather and the spot we went to see proved unpropitious.    One feels, somehow singularly happy and free from constraint in his presence—a sense of a beneficent, generous, nobly humane nature being combined with his intellectual greatness."

In a month's time the poet returned to Haslemere: " The Tennysons have been here for ten days—two with me and a week in lodgings—and have taken a house in Greyshot that will serve their purpose for a time, enabling them to judge how the climate suits, and to be on the watch for any land that may be in the market.

" He is very anxious all this should *not* be known . . . a paragraph in the *Athenæum* would disgust him with the whole project.

" I have undertaken to see to the repairs and the furnishing of the house." . . . And on the eighteenth of March (1867) Anne Gilchrist writes again to William Haines about the same subject :—" I have put my hero worship into a very practical shape this winter and done some real hard work for Tennyson.    Just as the day was fixed for their coming, these two were plunged into trouble by the dangerous illness of their eldest boy (Hallam) at Marlborough, where they now are with him —I rejoice to add he is recovering rapidly.

" In such chance moments as I could snatch ' as

from a conflagration' I have not failed to try and carry forward an inch or two my literary scheme, but have not much to show for it—the separate bricks have such a sorry aspect one's faith in anything of an architectural result sometimes fails. But on the other hand I feel increased confidence in my power of work. Anything that hard work will do I may hope to achieve by and by.

" I have just been reading two essays of Herbert Spencer's, one on the Nebular Hypothesis, the other on ' Illogical Geology,' which are masterly; subtle; convincing beyond anything of the kind I have ever read."

Writing to the same friend a month later she says : " I am still busy furnishing Greyshot and hence of course very frequent letters from Mrs. Tennyson.— I do hope it will turn out well—but there are drawbacks. I think they are eager to try it, and will come as soon as ever it is ready.

" When shall we have a friendly chat ?

" The horizon looks somewhat dark to me this winter.

" Thank God the children are all well, but one cannot help being full of cares and misgivings as to whether one is doing all one ought and might in the rearing of them—and of course the older they grow, the greater one's anxieties on this head."

Anne Gilchrist worked too hard for her friends; the long walks to Greyshot, the anxiety always to do the very best economically for her friends : this, in addition to her own cares ; for it is only six years since the tragic

and admires the Queen personally much,
ion with her. Mrs. Tennyson generally
ays the Queen's manner towards him is
harming, and they both give their opinions
hen these differ from the Queen's, which
perfect good humour, and is very ani-

est part of the day was the walk home
e); he accompanied me as far as the top
ollow; he talked gloriously, I wish I
it all.—Likes much Spencer's ' Nebular
had himself had that idea about the
an intermediate stage between nebula and
ke of materialism. I ventured to say that
of reproach chiefly because people had so
and false an idea of matter, that matter was
nifestation of force and power; he agreed,
ng I căn't exactly remember, and then added,
that we have a little bit of God in the
us ; ' to which I cordially assented. Spoke
ity of mere argument about immortality and
, it being wholly a matter of instinct and un-
I said conservation of Force went a great
ds actual proof.
Tennyson said that notwithstanding the draw-
Greyshot she regarded the coming here as a
cess ; [Tennyson] likes the country and the
d enjoys his walks, and is anxious to buy. She
ly said that he liked me to show him the way—
he would often come down after my early
hat we might thoroughly explore those places

winter of 1861—made inroads upon her naturally
strong constitution, which, alas! was to culminate in
serious illness in the autumn of 1870.

Truly we may say of her, as Bassanio said of his
" dearest friend," that she showed an " unwearied spirit
in doing courtesies."

Here is a descriptive touch of the walk to Greyshot,
taken from a letter to her eldest daughter Beatrice :—
" I walked to Greyshot yesterday.—Waggoner's Wells
was not frozen in spite of the intense cold, so rapid are the
brooks that feed it. All the trees round were feathered
with hoar frost more beautifully than I ever saw before,
in fact it was the loveliest winter picture you can
imagine there."

" We went to the Cross on Sunday : [Feb. 19, 1867]
and saw a lovely effect—there was a thick hill mist
while we were going, but when there the sun broke
through and drew up the mist visibly into a wreath of
white cloud : it melted from off the landscape—first a
hill here, then a single field in another direction, then a
wood or two emerged till the whole grand stretch of
landscape was laid bare and stood out brightly in the
sunshine where a few minutes before there had been a
blank wall of fog."

" Yesterday [April 7] Herby had *his* donkey ride.
We went to Hurt Hill. Do you remember the coppic
*below* the footpath which Tennyson said he must have
too if he bought Hurt Hill ? I thought from the slope
of the ground it looked as if there must be what he so
much desires—a little brook down there. So we explored thoroughly and found one—and a great many

springs which if they had a free channel cleared for them would form into a broad beautiful brook. I was so pleased."

Tennyson though short-sighted was most observant: in one of their Haslemere rambles, Anne Gilchrist pointed out to him a number of springs bubbling and dancing their way up through the sand (probably Spring Head in the hamlet of Shottermill). The poet could only see their tiny movements by lying down near the edge of the brook, with his face almost touching the water.

We remember Tennyson staying at Brookbank, indeed can see him now (wearing a dark cloak, big hat in hand) as he shuffled across the long unequally shaped drawing-room, to stand before and examine a glorious water colour by Blake of " Elijah mounted in the Fiery Chariot ; " he would ask in his deep voice " what is it ? " William Rossetti can answer that question best. We quote from his Descriptive Catalogue. " Elijah lays hold of the rein with his right hand : his left is upon a book placed on his knees. He is draped—but Elisha, who stands before him, with joined hands, lost in a flood of beard, is perfectly naked, and looks as ancient as Elijah. The Horses seem compact of fire ; fire flows out in place of chariot-wheels ; behind Elijah, a sphere of rolling red flame ; for sky, a blaze of yellow. A magnificent work—awful and preterhuman in its impression, even to the length of the Prophets' beards."

We recollect being impressed by the Poet's tall, gaunt figure, and felt vaguely conscious of the propriety in the fact of Tennyson's confronting such a poet's picture.

Callin
tected t
lawn to t
a pipe, I
The Po
trailing ov
(Κληματίς, -ι
was exactin
against *quan*
One trait
never criticise
In a letter
Tennyson env
which the Ten
". . . You
went off. *W*
was comfortable
at dinner—says
shall start the
Mrs. T.'s which
Spoke of his visit
Bell thinks the ter
end here, is a corru
as a quack and im
was merely quoting
Landseer's lions a f
flank—great poverty
repeat him in different
to have had a distinct
" After the lunch M
smoke, and Mrs. Tenn

Tennyson likes
enjoys conversa
goes too, and
child-like and c
freely, even w
she takes with
mated herself.
" But the b
(the rest drov
of High H
could repeat
Hypothesis ;
comets being
planet. Sp
it was a ter
inadequate
wholly a m
said someth
' You mea
middle of
of the futi
such topics
provable ;
way towa
" Mrs.
backs of
great suc
people ar
also kind
and tha
dinner,

where there was any chance of buying.   I have seen an agent for them.   He is coming to-morrow to go to 'Mead Fields,' and one or two places the other side of Hazlemere."

In a letter to William Haines (July 7, 1867), we are told about the purchase of Greenhill:—"Yes, we succeeded at last in finding land to suit, and Mr. Simmons is buying it for him at a very moderate price. There will be no more land in this neighbourhood sold so low again, I think.   It is a wooded hollow in Blackdown (south side near the top) at once very sheltered, for the hill curves round on either side and rises sheer behind it to the north, so that it is like a little bay ; yet elevated, very near the top of Blackdown, and commanding the view you know well, Surrey, Sussex and parts of Hampshire and I suppose part of Kent, South Downs.   Surrey Hills spread out before you : I saw the sea distinctly from what will be their lawn and three ships on it through the gap in the downs by Little Hampton.   Chanctonbury Ring was conspicuous, too, last time I was there.

"I do think if ever there was a place made for a poet to live in this Green Hill, as it is called [now changed to Aldworth] is the spot.   Thirty-six acres— half coppice above, three large fields and little old farmhouse below. . . . Tennyson was so pleased ; a sort of child-like glee that is beautiful ; contrasting curiously enough with his saturnine moods."

# CHAPTER XVI.

## LETTER FROM CHRISTINA ROSSETTI.

### 1868—1870. AGE 40—42.

IN response to an invitation from the family at Brookbank, Christina Rossetti writes from Scotland :—" If the end of my Penkill sojourn deprives me of seeing you, its beginning mulcts me of a visit to the Isle of Wight in which I was promised to meet Tennyson—poor me! This invitation was only given me yesterday, too late to be closed with: however I am not certain that in any case I should have screwed myself up to accept it, as I am shy amongst strangers and think things formidable.

" Please give my love to the young people, whose recollection of me I must try to revive some day in person if opportunity offers. . . ."

In 1868, Anne Gilchrist was studying Victor Hugo. Some lines of his are quoted in a letter to William Haines :—" I subjoin a translation of one or two things that struck me as fine and extractable, but it is the whole that you must read and judge by :—

" ' What power is there in a grave and kindly examination ; let us not bring flame where light will suffice.'

" ' Morals are the blossomings of truth.'

" ' It is one of the fatalities of the human race to be eternally condemned to make war against phantoms : a phantom is hard to get by the throat and trample on.'

" I met Mr. Hutchinson (the eminent surgeon) at a friend's here in the autumn, and found him one of the most delightful men I ever saw—of course, a master in science and with an almost equally great enthusiasm for literature.    As they lodge at Stoatly all the summer I hope to see more of them."

" You know perhaps William Morris the poet, is the Morris of whom we have heard William Rossetti often speak, whose energies are such, that he doubles up a table fork in two sometimes, to emphasize his remarks ! "

To the same friend :—

" I dined with the Rossettis on Thursday (April 19, 1869).    William is in Italy just now, but Gabriel was there, also Madox Brown and his daughter Lucy : also a gifted man of the name of Cayley, of whom you may have heard dear Alec speak—a brother of Cayley the mathematician and a translator of Dante.    Madox Brown and Gabriel Rossetti seemed to agree that George Watts's picture of *Endymion* would be the finest thing in the coming Exhibition, especially dwelling on the subtle and imaginative way in which the woman's figure floating over him seemed to suggest the moon.

" Gabriel Rossetti told a good story which Carlyle I believe tells of himself,—how he met Browning and *meant* to say something to please about the *The Ring and the Book*, but somehow ultimately found himself landed in the reverse of a compliment:—'It is a wonderful book, one of the most wonderful poems ever written.    I re-read it all through—all made out of an Old Bailey story, that might have been told in ten lines and only wants forgetting!'   G. R. seemed himself to lean a little to this view, and to think there was perversity in the choice of the subject, though of course redeemed by superb treatment."

A few months after 'the dinner-party' Christina Rossetti wrote from Scotland, [*Miss Boyd, Penkill Castle*]:—"The home budget informs me that William is at home again, fresh from all the glories and beauties of most beautiful Naples.    However, even Naples in imagination cannot efface the quiet fertile comeliness of Penkill in reality : and when, beyond the immediate greenness, a gorgeous sunset glorifies the sea distance one scarcely need desire aught more exquisite in this world. . . . I hope you know that my laggard book [*Commonplace and other Stories*] is out at last—and now I am in the thick of reviewing.   As yet I don't know of any very severe handling of me and mine.   And my health at present is so very tolerable that I may be all the braver to undergo the lash.

"What delightful plans yours are for dividing your home between Earls Colne and London : Beatrice must be coming into bloom now, though rather like a lily than like a rose as I recollect her ;—but can Grace be as funny as she used to be ? . . .

"When you are in London please don't forget 56 Euston Square : we are more central than we used to be, and proportionately more accessible."

In 1869 Anne Gilchrist decided to let Brookbank for a time—to divide her home between Earls Colne and London; in order that her children might enjoy the educational advantages which London alone possesses :—
" And yet I am very fond of the place. It was the kindest, friendliest, health and strength restoring refuge for me after the storm ; and I shall always think of it with affection and thankfulness : but I feel as if life here were a chapter ended for me. However it may not be so. Certainly, if I had no call to be anywhere else, I should come back here."

An exchange of photographs with Christina Rossetti, brought a letter from the poetess :—" Thank you cordially for the *cartes*, which I like to possess. What a great girl the little Grace of my admiring memory has become. Pray ask your 'nurse' and your 'sunshine' to accept my love. As to a stand in their education surely they may gain more by tending a beloved mother than by a great many books ; though for all your sakes it will indeed be a joyful day when you can take your old place amongst those who love you.

" My Mother and sister and William join me in all the affectionate good wishes which this season calls out. William also joins me in a return-offering of photographs, though you will notice that what represents myself is not taken from me direct but from a great drawing Gabriel did of me in 1866. This must account to you for its unblemished smoothness and finish.

" We spoke of you the other evening at the Madox Browns', where I dined and met the gentleman who is engaged to Cathy,—a learned German, Dr. Hüffer ;

but despite his learning only 25, so appropriately young for his fiancée of 20. I do not know how soon or how late the wedding is to be expected; certainly they have time to wait a little. Pray believe me

Affectionately yours, CHRISTINA G. ROSSETTI."

Sixty-nine was a memorable year to Anne Gilchrist, for in the June of that year she made the acquaintance of William Rossetti's *Selection from Whitman*; which led to a deep study of Walt Whitman as a poet:—

"*June* 22, 1869.

" Dear Mr. Rossetti: I was calling on Madox Brown a fortnight ago, and he put into my hands your edition of Walt Whitman's Poems. I shall not cease to thank him for that. Since I have had it, I can read no other book; it holds me entirely spell-bound, and I go through it again and again with deepening delight and wonder. How can one refrain from expressing gratitude to you for what you have so admirably done? . . ."

William Michael Rossetti replies:—

" My dear Mrs. Gilchrist: Your letter has given me keen pleasure this morning. That glorious man Whitman will one day be known as one of the greatest sons of Earth, a few steps below Shakspeare on the throne of immortality. What a tearing-away of the obscuring veil of use and wont from the visage of man and of life!

" I am doing myself the pleasure of at once ordering a copy of the *Selection* to you, which you will be so kind as to accept. Genuine—i.e. *enthusiastic*—appreciators are not so common, and must be cultivated when they appear.

N

" I am obstinate enough to think I was right in missing out the whole poem, wherever a necessity arose of
missing out so much as a word : indeed in one sense I
*know* I was right, for, after some semi-misapprehension
on the point, it turned out that any other course would
be revolting to Whitman himself.   It is also to be
remembered that mine is confessedly and intentionally
(this is the publisher's affair) a mere *selection*, and the
volume even as it stands is rather beyond the size proposed ; and, as everything in it is excellent, to substitute
other excellent things involving any complication of
whatever sort might hardly have been well-judged.
The sort of thing that people object to in Whitman's
writings is not so easily surmised until one sees them.
It might be expressed thus—that he puts into print
physical matters with the same bluntness and directness
almost as that with which they present themselves to the
eye and mind, or are half worded in the thought.

" From one point of view this is even blameless ; but
from another, the modern reader's point of view, it is
quite intolerable.   On the abstract question also I
think I was more right than wrong.   If Shakspeare
were a new author requiring to form his public, and if
one or two of his plays (suppose Measure for Measure
and Pericles) were practically unacceptable, I should
consider it pardonable to print *other* plays, avowedly
missing out these : the volume would then consist of a
certain (though not the whole) number of complete
dramas.   But I should condemn and abhor the plan
(Bowdler's) of cutting out every startling phrase that
can be found throughout the whole number of plays—

equally the two above-named and such severe works as
Macbeth or King John.

"Anybody who values Whitman as you do ought to
read the whole of him.   If I have the pleasure of seeing
you before you leave for Colne, I will proffer you his
book.   My own complete copy is already lent out;
but I have the unbound copy which Whitman himself
sent over for possible English republication, with his
own last corrections, also the separate original editions.
I should like also to show you a letter he wrote me,
when the question of excision rather than total omission
was mooted : it is manly and kind in the highest
degree."

Mr. Rossetti has kindly placed the letter by Walt
Whitman in our hands : we print nearly the whole of
it, for the letter is one which throws light upon his
purpose in poetry, and illustrates the dignity of character and loftiness of aim characteristic of the great
American : —

*"Washington, December* 3, 1867.

"My dear Mr. Rossetti : I have just received, and
have considered your letter of November 17.   In
order that there be the frankest understanding with
respect to my position, I hasten to write you that the
authorization in my letter of November 1 to Mr.
Conway, for you, to make verbal alterations, substitute words, &c., was meant to be construed as an
answer to the case presented in Mr. Conway's letter
of October 12.   Mr. Conway stated the case of a
volume of selections in which it had been decided that
the poems reprinted in London should appear verba-

tim, and asking my authority to change certain words in the Preface to first edition of poems, &c.

"I will be candid with you, and say I had not the slightest idea of applying my authorization to a reprint of the full volume of my poems. As such a volume was not proposed, and as your courteous and honorable course and attitude called and call for no niggardly or hesitating response from me, I penned that authorization, and did not feel to set limits to it.    But abstractly and standing alone, and not read in connection with Mr. C.'s letter of October 12, I see now it is far too loose, and needs distinct guarding.

"I cannot and will not consent of my own volition, to countenance an expurgated edition of my pieces.    I have steadily refused to do so under seductive offers, here in my own country, and must not do so in another country.

"I feel it due tomyself to write you explicitly thus, my dear Mr. Rossetti, though it may seem harsh and perhaps ungenerous.    Yet I rely on you to absolve me, sooner or later.    Could you see Mr. Conway's letter of October 12, you would, I think, more fully comprehend the integrity of my explanation.

"I have to add that the points made in that letter in relation to the proposed reprint, as originally designed, exactly correspond with those, on the same subject, in your own late letter—and that the kind and appreciative tone of both letters is in the highest degree gratifying, and is most cordially and affectionately responded to by me, and that the fault of sending so loose an authorization has surely been to a large degree, my own.

"And now, my friend, having set myself right on that matter, I proceed to say, on the other hand, for you, and for Mr. Hotten, that if, before the arrival of this letter, you have practically invested in, and accomplished, or partially accomplished, any plan, even contrary to this letter, I do not expect you to abandon it, at loss of outlay; but shall *bona fide* consider you blameless if you let it go on, and be carried out, as you may have arranged. It is the question of the authorization of an expurgated edition proceeding from me, that deepest engages me. The facts of the different ways, one way or another way, in which the book may appear in England, out of influences not under the shelter of my umbrage, are of much less importance to me.

"After making the foregoing explanation, I shall, I think, accept kindly whatever happens. For I feel, indeed know, that I am in the hands of a friend, and that my pieces will receive that truest, brightest of light and perception coming from love. In that, all other and lesser requisites become pale. . . .

"I have to add that I only wish you could know how deeply the beautiful personal tone and passages of your letter of November 17, have penetrated and touched me. It is such things that go to our hearts, and reward us, and make up for all else, for years. Permit me to offer you my friendship. . . .

"Let me know how the work goes on, what shape it takes. Finally I charge you to construe all I have written, through my declared and fervid realization of your goodness toward me, nobleness of intention, and,

I am fain to hope, personal, as, surely, literary and moral sympathy and attachment.   And so, for the present, Farewell.           WALT WHITMAN."

Reverting to the subject of William M. Rossetti's last letter, Anne Gilchrist writes, June 23, acknowledging 'the unbound copy' of *Leaves of Grass* :—

" Dear Mr. Rossetti : This gift of yours I have not any words to tell you how priceless it will be to me. You know I am but a poor critic—indeed averse to criticism ; what I like I grasp firmly but silently ; what I do not like I prefer to let go silently, too. . . ." The rest of her letter will be found incorporated in *An Englishwoman's Estimate of Walt Whitman ;* an essay which is represented at the end of this volume.

William Michael Rossetti, in answer to the complete letter, writes, July 13, 1869 :—

" My dear Mrs. Gilchrist : All you say about Whitman delights me beyond measure : it is the earnest of the boundless enthusiasm he will one day excite, and continue exciting for ages—though where to find the other woman who would be true-hearted and brave enough to express herself with the decision and perfectness of perception which I find in your letter I know not for yet awhile.   I quite agree with you about the glorious music that Whitman commands.   Considered abstractly and as a whole, the sound of the entire book is like a portentous roll of chorus—such as ' The Lord God omnipotent reigneth ' in Handel ; and more perfect musical chords than are to be found *passim* in particular things of Whitman's do not exist in literature.   What a line, for instance, that is—following others just as grand :—

> 'No more on the mountains roam, nor sail the stormy sea.'

" I wish you could find it practicable to print something about Whitman.   The very words of your letters would be the best you or anyone could find to express what claims to be said.   Do you know anything of a Mr. Symonds, living in or near Bristol ? [John Addington Symonds].   Soon after my Whitman Selection appeared, he wrote me two or three very enthusiastic letters, being an *old* admirer of the poet ; and he was thinking of doing something substantial in print—but since that period I have heard no more about it.   Also do you know Mr. Charles Kent, editor of the *Sun ?*   The Selection (he knew nothing of Whitman before) put him into a wonderful state of enthusiasm, which he expressed in his paper, not with great literary force, but still most genuinely.   He is the only reviewer of the Selection that has done Whitman justice in point of fervent outburst of feeling—though some others have recognized his greatness partially.

" Is not that second letter which Whitman addressed to me enough to make one love him—worthy of himself in short ? "

Answering William Rossetti's letter from Earls Colne, July 14, 1869, she says:—" It would rejoice my heart to be able to write anything that should help to clear away the clouds of mis-apprehension that now hide Walt Whitman from men's eyes.   I will revolve it in my mind ; but I shall be terribly slow, because I have

scarcely a moment I can call my own, and shall not have
at least all the summer.    Meanwhile, since my letters
please you, do you think there is any way in which you
could make use of them to serve the cause ?    The firm
conviction I have that these poems are the seeds of such
immeasurably grand results for the world that any delay
in the successful planting of them is grievous ;  the pain
and indignation I feel at the thought of how that great
name, the mere sound of which will hereafter stir in men's
hearts a very passion of gratitude and love, has at the
outset been saluted chiefly with injurious epithets and
hateful imputations ;  my belief that none  but a woman
can be the decisive judge of the question involved in
these attacks (she being supplied with finer subtler tests);
the clear and  sweet consciousness I  have that men and
women may trust me to the uttermost in this, even if
they cannot at present see the matter at all as I do :—all
these things combine to make me absolutely fearless for
myself.

"It seems to  me that it would  be wise in the future
editions to  divide  the poems into two entirely distinct,
not consecutive volumes ;  the one very large (and
certainly including that noble prelude the original Preface to the ' Leaves of Grass ') ;  the other very small :
and to put a few words before this one that should, if
possible, guide it into the right hands—the hands of
those who can think greatly or love greatly, either or
both.    Thus a stumbling-block would be removed from
those who might, to their own infinite joy, receive a
great part, but not yet all that Walt Whitman has given
them.

"One day, when the truth that other men have dreamed of and grasped at, but that this one has laid hold of and brought alive and full of power in the midst of us, that there is no particle of matter in the universe but ' has reference to Soul,' nay, that body is entirely a manifestation of Soul—*is* Soul—when this is seen to be the most vital and practical of facts—then we shall understand all and love all and fear nothing. And then, I am persuaded the little book will be dear to the hearts of many women, and that the husbands of those women will be the happiest husbands."

In another letter to William Rossetti, she says :—
"If you decide to do anything with my letters there are one or two sentences I should like to add, that would, I think, complete all I feel a wish to say."

The above was written in response to a suggestion from William Rossetti that her letters about "Leaves of Grass" should be published. In the meantime another letter is received from him, in which this subject is still under debate ; and this is her answer :—

"My dear Mr. Rossetti: Your letter is very good and kind, and I thank you heartily for it. I feel a persuasion, the strength and persistency of which astonishes even myself, that it is possible for a woman so to treat this difficult subject as to command respect (and if she do not succeed in this she will do no good, to speak of, to the cause) and to win, not indeed *acceptance* for these poems specially in question—that I believe is not at present possible to more than a dozen people in the world—but a consent to lay them silently aside and no longer to look at the Poet through the distorting medium bred by an utter misconception of them : but to open their hearts and minds to all the rest of his teaching, and then the other will follow in good time."

The essay in question is at length tackled ; and many literary details are discussed with William Rossetti. In a letter dated July 23, 1869, he says:—"No literary matter that I could well name has given me deeper or more unmixed delight than your resplendent enthusiasm for Whitman consequent (originally) on the Selection I was concerned in—and as I say expressly in that selection, I long to see the complete book diffused and appreciated here."

A sketch of the proposed article on *Leaves of Grass* is finished, and despatched to W. D. O'Connor by William Rossetti, who writes :—

" At last, this morning, came the enclosed letter from Mr. O'Connor. It gratifies me extremely, and I trust will not produce any very different impression on you. . . . You see he starts no faint suggestion even of *publishing* what I sent him of yours. Any move in that direction lies solely with you.

" Like other people he falls foul of poor Mrs. Stowe. For my part, I am on that subject in the very small minority of people who think that Mrs. Stowe, being deeply convinced of the truth of what she has written, felt justified and called upon to publish it, and was by no means wrong in so feeling. This I say without professing belief in · what Lady Byron told Mrs. Stowe : I think it open to serious question, but certainly not to be dismissed on any mere *a priori* ground of unlikelihood. Strict inquiry into evidences is now wanted, and *may* result in establishing or refuting the allegations."

We give that part of the letter from W. D. O'Connor, which refers to " An Englishwoman's Estimate of Walt Whitman :—

" *Washington*, *D.C.*, 1869.

" My dear Mr. Rossetti : Your letter of the 20th November, enclosing the precious manuscript, is to hand, and we are of course immensely gratified and thankful. The lady's contribution is simply superb, which is all that *can* be said, and we shall use every effort to have it fitly given to the world, and as soon as possible. . . . I don't say much about the dear lady's article, but it is in my thoughts a great deal nevertheless.    Unquestionably, it is the finest and fullest appreciation yet uttered."

It is thought advisable to preface the Essay with a few words ;  Anne Gilchrist writes :—

" My dear Mr. Rossetti : Have you any objection, or should you think it inexpedient, to prefix a few words yourself, as the friend to whom the letters were addressed : not, of course, to praise them in any way, nor yet to take upon yourself the responsibility of their being printed, but just to say the simple truth, that when you received them it seemed to you that they expressed something that ' claimed to be said,' and that you had therefore expressed a wish I could find it practicable to print them or something to the same purport as the letters ?  I feel as if this would make it easier for me somehow. For though I have a deep conviction that some of these poems never will be rightly apprehended by men, not if they have to wait a hundred years, till some woman

takes courage to speak : I do not see how any could
without the help of a friend like yourself. I know I
could not have written so except to a friend who I felt
sure would understand me aright. But with that help,
and believing as I do that the first that sees and knows
the truth is bound to speak, I should for ever despise
myself as a coward if I shrunk back. Though whether
I am the right one or no—have put it in the right way,
only the result can prove."

William M. Rossetti answers, *October* 12 :—" It will
be a pride and delight to me to add a few prefatory
words ; I would submit them to you when written."

To the same friend (October 17th) when comparing
Walt Whitman to modern leaders of thought Anne Gilchrist says :—" I say *leaders* of thought ; but I believe
it is almost exclusively Carlyle that I have in my mind,
for I really think he is (apart from our poets, who can
none of them be called leaders of thought, whatever their
greatness in other ways) the only man with enough of
the fire of genius in him to deserve that name. And it
seems very curious to myself that owing so much to him
as I do and having been ever since I was a very young
girl an enthusiastic admirer of him, the first thing I
should ever write (that can be called writing) should be
almost a bitter protest against his teaching. But he has
pressed that ' stone of contempt ' down so very hard
and fast on our hearts of late !

" Asceticism has always seemed to me a sort of mad
attempt of man's to do better for himself than God has
done for him. To supersede His scheme by trying
one that shall produce higher results.

" Also it appears to me that Judaism has been more in fault in this particular point than Christianity, especially that astounding invention of the Jews that the having children was the result not of man's greatness but of his guilt ; that Adam and Eve never dreamt of such a thing till they were turned out of Paradise. And that most pernicious invention of a Fall of Man ! the belief in which, has really accomplished itself—and really been a Fall of Man : such a sneaking invention too, ' She did it ' !

" And now, my friend, when this [An Englishwoman's Estimate of Walt Whitman] is on its way to America I shall not feel the least bit afraid of what I have done. I have unshakable faith in its being truth that needed uttering, and that will prevail.  And if you say, why then has not Whitman's grand utterance of it prevailed, I say, as I have said before : that I believe it needed corroboration, acceptance from a woman (as closely concerned as man in this question and approaching it from entirely distinct stånding ground) before it could be accepted by men.   I think they will take from a woman's lips, what they seem as though they could not from a man's.   I have hopes even of the ' titmen and mannikins,' Rhinoceros and all.  But then my ' disposition is of hopeful green stuff woven.'   Yet how can any be angry with me for thinking of them as men, more nobly and tenderly than they think of themselves : that is all I have done—that is what this divine book teaches a woman."

William Michael Rossetti writes, *October* 25 :—" You raise (I mean in your letter of 17 October), the contrast

between the personal quality of Whitman's poems, and
the impersonal of (for instance) Homer and Shakspeare.
Now certainly it would be both stupid and perverse in
me to eat so many of my own words for the mere sake
of opposition, and say I don't agree with you to a great
extent.    I do to a great extent, but not wholly.    I think
even in Shakspeare's plays one can discern pretty well the
general outlines of his character, and his sonnets (unless
one gratuitously assumes them to be mere fantasies) are
full of himself : Homer seems quite equally transparent,
and indeed I take it that one chief argument against the
critics who reject an individual Homer is the great one-
ness of personality throughout Iliad and Odyssey.   Then
what shall we say of such poets as Dante, Petrarch,
Michael Angelo, Byron, Shelley, Wordsworth—who
surely write an immense amount *about* as well as *out of*
themselves ?    I think then it is most true that Whitman is prëeminently personal among poets, but not that,
in being so, he differs in kind from all his predecessors.
His electric influence on the reader is dependent partly,
I apprehend, on this great personality, and partly on
another quality which is perhaps his more peculiar
differentia (as the schoolmen say), his boundless fellowship : he will arrogate nothing to himself exclusively,
but will have all men and women sharers with himself.
He insists that you shall be good enough for the
Universe because he knows himself good enough : if
you know yourself despicable in some things, he proclaims or even vaunts himself the same.    This is the
sublime of Democracy. . . . I enjoy your manifesto on
Whitman more and more as I go closer into it."

William Rossetti prefaced " An Englishwoman's Estimate of Walt Whitman " with a few lines : anent this, the author of the Essay writes :—" My dear Mr. Rossetti : I would not have a line otherwise in the beautiful sustaining words you have prefixed for me. I have indeed good cause to be grateful : for I do not see how I could have accomplished this which (whatever the immediate consequences to me) I shall never cease to rejoice in having accomplished, without your aid. Certainly I could not otherwise have had such favouring helpful circumstances.

" I often feel as if my enterprise were very like Lady Godiva's—as if hers indeed were typical of mine. For she stripped the veil from woman's body for a good cause and I from a woman's soul for a great cause. And no man has ever dared to find any fault with her."

She goes on to speak of Shelley, and apropos of the poet, William Rossetti replies :—" Very glad to find you take such interest in Shelley's life as well as works. If a past promise is kept, I shall soon be receiving twenty extra copies of my Memoir of Shelley (apart from the poems) and will offer you one—though I confess to do this is something like the old joke of Hamlet with the Prince of Denmark omitted. . . .

" I received yesterday (Jan. 4, '70) a letter from Stillman, who had re-encountered Whitman in Washington. They had a long talk ' principally about me.' He is ' as like his poetry as a man can be like his work : full of life and blood, and the red in his cheek is that of a man whose health never knew disturbance. He

begged me to give you [W. M. R.] his love, and say
that if you came out next summer (which I have some
sort of idea of doing) you must come to Washington
and 'we would have a good time.'' This is a considerable hash of you's and me's, but perhaps you can pick
out its drift. . . . ."

Anne Gilchrist says in answer:—" My dear Mr.
Rossetti: I have found the 'Memoir' of absorbing
interest; it makes me full of impatience to turn to
Shelley's works again.

" The pain one feels at realization of the adverse, and
indeed baleful circumstances of Shelley's birth and
youthful environments (how far more essentially adverse
than those of Burns for instance) subsides in the second
half of the narrative under a sense of his triumphantly
maturing greatness.

"I like much the few words in which you discriminate
the characteristics of each of his great poems. They
make me feel my own knowledge of them so immature
that I cannot open my lips to say a word to you that is
worth saying about Shelley.

" For it is certainly true of Shelley, if not of all Poets,
that it is the Poetry which teaches us to interpret aright
the life, rather than the life the works. Section 32
headed 'Shelley's Opinions' (altogether a chapter of
peculiar interest to me) contains some words of the
Poet's in answer to Trelawny's question, 'why do you
call yourself an atheist?' which seem to me more significant than they do to you, and indeed to furnish the
clue to the so-called atheism of a nature as incapable of
real dismal purblind atheism as of moral baseness or

calculating selfishness. It was that dark Image, the creation of the oriental mind with its intuitive subservience to despotism made more and more repulsive as it passed through and was projected from the minds of generations of men-despising, power-loving priests—which great dark Image, casting a black shadow over the world, is still the popular idea of God, that Shelley so fiercely hated.

"Had he lived a few years later he would have seen, as clearly as Goethe did, that the few born to be Architects of imperishable monuments may leave to ordinary hands the task of attacking and destroying. Every truth they utter, devours some lie or other to perish off the face of the earth in due time."

And from Earls Colne, April 20, 1870, she writes to the same friend :—"I put my hand by a lucky chance the other day on a little book I have long wished to see (your Criticism of Mr. Swinburne), a very interesting and indeed pregnant essay, I think. Though I cannot feel with you as to his Poems . . . It seems to me impossible for a man so destitute of human sympathy to conceive humanity grandly or truly in his poems. Was there ever before a gifted man so barren of great thoughts or deep feelings ? His emotions seem all the effluence of a heated brain, not of a strong beating heart. Even those aspects of nature which he paints with such power and pomp of sound are to him I verily believe not realities, only splendid similes, glorious epithets.

"When I read such a poem as that 'Ballad of Burdens,' the trite, dreary, sickly conceptions of life, that have already been uttered *ad nauseam*, though never so musically uttered before, it gives me a kind of physical oppression on the chest; a vehement longing to get out into the sweet fresh air to breathe; and the extreme sweetness of the flow of the words, makes it the worse, because it holds me, obliges me to go on. . . .

" I can go with you any length in admiration of Victor Hugo, ' cet héros au doux sourire ' as I always think of him."

William Michael Rossetti replies on the twenty-fourth of April, 1870 :—" What you say about my criticism on Swinburne pleases me, of course : but I am sure you underrate *him*. . . . The Ballad of Burdens should be taken, I think, as a study from a particular point of view, both of conception and of art. It seems to be about as true as Ecclesiastes—which is to me one of the most moving and powerful books in existence, and true too in its own sphere of thought : but, even if the Ballad of Burdens can't be allowed to pair off with Ecclesiastes, I think it has a fair right (as a matter of art and optional selection of emotional mood) to say what it does say, over-enforced though no doubt it is. It takes one side, and refuses to know anything of the other side. This is the privilege of a passionate lyric : besides which the poem is obviously of the *reproductive* class to a great extent. It is what a Mediæval Troubadour, very fond of the enjoyments of sense, and very sure that he would be damned to all eternity for indulging in them, might have found to say."

In reply she says:—" Yes, it is too certain I do not rightly appreciate Mr. Swinburne. . . . But

'Whitmanism' is not only 'another sort of thing' but an absolutely destructive—capable of swallowing up all that, as light swallows darkness. When once the world has got well hold of it—incorporated that teaching into its life—both the Poetry and the Philosophy of despair, disgust, satiety, ennui, and scepticism will dissolve into unreality, like evil dreams at dawn :—do not you think so?

". . . I fancy too, you would find in all women, whatever their bent of mind, a sort of averseness or at any rate an absence of enthusiasm towards literature that transports itself into the Past in that absolute way, quite disconnecting it from the present ; owing to the subtle but deep and real sense they have of the starved and barren heritage in life of woman in that old world ; excepting for the fleeting year or two when they were man's delight.

" To-day is but the dawning time for them, I am persuaded—hints of a future of undreamed of beauty and greatness just beginning to disclose themselves, by and by to unfold into a Life Poem that will beggar all words.

" The similarity between Swinburne and Landor I judge to be deep."

Her friend replies on the first of May :—" My dear Mrs. Gilchrist : I agree with you that 'when the world has incorporated Whitman's teaching into its life, the poetry and philosophy of despair, &c., will dissolve into unreality.' Only I would substitute *if* for *when*.

" I am afraid human nature, as concreted into human society, is a very tough affair, and that neither Whitman nor anyone will fully permeate it, or wrench it aside from itself. I believe Whitman will exercise a very real and a very valuable influence ; but, as long as there are men and women who prefer to 'do what they choose' at the moment to doing what the highest intuitions or the most universal interests would dictate, I am afraid there always will be wronged, aggrieved, disappointed, discontented, and misled people in ample number for keeping up the philosophy of ennui. Prometheus will have to wait a longish while before he is unbound. . . ."

# CHAPTER XVII.

## " JENNY."

### 1870—1871.   AGE 42—43.

IN the spring of 1870, Dante Gabriel Rossetti published his first volume of *Poems*.   He presented a copy to Anne Gilchrist.   After acknowledging its safe arrival, she writes a second time to the poet, and alludes to the poem, *Jenny* : —

" My dear Mr. Rossetti : Now I have read all, the wish is very strong in me to write to you again.   And please, do not make up your mind beforehand that my letter is burdensomely long, because these Poems have stirred me so deeply, will remain to me so precious, that I think you cannot help caring a little to hear the way in which this is so.   I could linger long content, absorbed, over such noble Poems as the ' Dante at Verona,' ' The Last Confession,' ' Sea Limits ' (grand !).   But I should not tell true if I did not own to you that I believe the glory, the imperishable life of the book is in the Poems which treat of Love ; including among these that dear first Poem, *The Blessed Damozel*, and one or two others, as well as the Songs and Sonnets.   So it may well be.   What material, gathered by the intellect from afar, can be wrought into life and beauty like that which grows up out of a man's own Soul, with roots in his heart that are nourished by his life blood? The very outward form of the verse takes in these a subtler beauty, so that one thinks of the lines,

> Whose speech Truth knows not from her thought,
> Nor Love her body from her Soul,'

the words seeming to flow bodily into the mind and the outward ear to catch the very pulse and breathings of the Soul.

"They make me sigh with happiness to realize that the earth did bear on its bosom such sweet life for two human creatures.  Then, Such Pity—such pity, it strains the heart too tightly, whelms it.  I wish I could convey to you a sense of the vividness and strength of my conviction of the imperishableness of all Realities. Only a little pause, in that blended life!  Only one of the two hidden for a few yards by a bend of the road, my friend!  How could God spare the sight of such happiness out of His Universe?

"There is another poem — other indeed !—which moves me even to anguish : one which comes upon a woman with appalling force after she has been standing gazing into the very Sanctuary of Love where woman-hood sits divinely enthroned.  For she knows that if, looking up joyfully, the brightness shining on her also, she may say, ' my sister,' she must also, though shame should rise up and cover her, look down and say ' O my sister,

‘ If but a woman's heart might see
    Such erring heart unerringly
    For once !   But that can never be.’

No, that cannot be.   But looking into her own, and
there seeing what that poor heart once was, she may find
a little light for this dark question that men could not,
no, not even Poets.   I think of how Jenny stood
that fatal day innocent, ignorant, (how innocent, how
ignorant of harm I do not think any but a woman
rightly understands) heedless, rash, too, and near the
edge of an abyss the very existence of which was only a
far-off ugly dream to her—only an unmeaning word
perhaps—and in one swift blind bewildered moment
was drawn by a strong ruthlessly vehement hand over
the edge—her cheerful day changed into one long black
night—he that might have led so high hurling her so
low—teaching her to take the very characters with
which she might have spelled in heavenly radiance a
word whose meaning would unfold in unutterable
beauty throughout her life, and, with them, dipped in
smoke and lurid fire from below, to write one that blasts
her with shame and ruin.

   " Then it seems to me that as God's eyes look on at
this, they grow dim with such a mist of the tears of pity
that it veils her guilt (if indeed the blind folly of yielding herself a passive victim ought to be called guilt,
just because the consequences are so terrible) even from
Him ; nay I will dare to say, blots it out.   Afterwards
with no human hand to help her up again, perhaps
pushed down from above by sisters—grasped from
below by ever more and more brutalized men, her poor

body dragged and dragged through the mire, even then
I do not believe its vileness stains through to her very
inmost self.   If I did, the pain would be more than I
could bear : these tears would burn my cheeks like
flame ; I should hate my womanhood—crave annihilation for the race.   No ! God has not cursed men with
the hideous power to wreck her soul as they can wreck
her body.   Poor soul ! it was but half awake and alert
to begin with—all its finest instincts yet undeveloped,
else it would not have let her stand for a moment within
the atmosphere of danger, but would have shed round
her a subtle atmosphere banishing, dispelling danger !
Now, crouched away, back, with face averted from the
mad riot of a body that carries but is scarce owned by
it—numb with misery, and the utter privation of all
healthful activity and sympathy ; conscious of itself
only through sullen despair ; it waits and waits, till
there comes at last the mighty rescuing friend Death—
mysterious New Birth.   Then it finds itself once more
animating a stainless body standing, not indeed among
the happy sisters, but free to climb towards them carrying no defilements with it.   Something within me—no
echo from the Past—something more deeply convincing,
more illuminating than reason or the evidence of the
senses, tells me this is so.

" You touch Jenny gently—tenderly even, and I feel
grateful to you for that ; yet I think even you are hard
on her : ' fond of guineas,' yes, for want is bitter and it
always dogs her steps, or at any rate lurks just round
the corner ; and real enjoyments all gone clean out of
life for her, she grasps at the paltriest sham ones.   But

'fond of kisses,' no, I do not believe there is ever more any sweetness in a kiss for her, only, with whatever semblance it may be given or taken—an inward loathing. I could kiss poor Jenny if that would do her any good; but I fear it would not.

"Perhaps it will not be so very long before women find out how to help one another. But it is a hard problem.

Yours always truly, ANNE GILCHRIST."

We revert to the principal subject of the foregoing chapter—*An Englishwoman's Estimate of Walt Whitman*, anent the publication of which W. D. O'Connor writes from Washington, May 18th, 1870, to William Michael Rossetti:—

". . . And here, as you will see when you receive the May number [of the *Radical*], our bird of Paradise has found a perch. It is the best thing possible, and in some respects could not be better.

"I need not add a word about the article. It is great—and better even in type than it was in manuscript. The friends of Walt Whitman are infinitely indebted, beyond words, for so broad and luminous an interpretation of his pages. It cannot fail to let in light, and to do good.

"I hope your own share in the matter will return to you in honor—in 'good fame renounné,' as Sir Thomas Malory's preface phrases it. We are all very grateful.

Faithfully yours, W. D. O'CONNOR."

*July the fourteenth*, William Rossetti writes: "I am ready for any amount of talk or writing about Whitman: but don't very much expect to be convinced out of my own present opinions—being tough. On main points you and I agree: but nothing will reconcile me to such words as Orotund or Santa Spirita : they are as bad in the poet Whitman as they would be in the Poet Bunn or the Poet Close."

Returning to the subject of Dante Gabriel Rossetti's poems he says :—" I believe heartily in Gabriel's poems. Some of those I particularly like (I name them as they occur to my mind at the moment) are Blessed Damozel, Sister Helen, Troy Town, Last Confession, Jenny, Song of Bower, First Love Remembered, the Sea (which you mentioned, I think, in a previous letter), and *several* of the sonnets. In fact there are few of the poems that I don't think highly of : and none that I think really poor. I think they are very uncommon indeed in *combined* (or aboriginal) intensity of passion, insight, and art ; and if these three qualities in high degree don't constitute good poetry, I don't particularly know what does. Some of the reviewers have objected to obscurity, and some to over-elaboration. The latter objection I agree with in a certain measure : I think some of the poems suffer somewhat by over-evidence of literary intention. As to obscurity I do not consider the poems *strictly* obscure in the ordinary sense ; but some certainly demand a degree of reflection rather beyond what one is always inclined for in poetry. . . ."

Of the Essay published in the *Radical*, Anne Gilchrist says :—" I wish they had not cut out a piece between ' out of the free air and sunshine of to-day,' and ' But this poet.' Because now the assertion ' out of the scorn of the Present came scepticism ' stands very abrupt and unsupported. What is left out was meant to show how illogical, how utterly unreasonable are, on the one hand, the theologians who think *because* there is nothing at all to their minds here and now, therefore they will have everything to their minds by and by : and on the other those artists, poets, historians, who can find nothing great, divine, august, sufficingly noble and beautiful around them or within, but credit with an indefinite amount of these qualities almost anything and everything that looms dimly through the mist of Time. For my part, if I held such views as they do of the men and women around them, of life, of themselves, of God, I should be as utter a sceptic of all good as Mephistopheles himself. For the Past was made of the same stuff as the Present ? Surely there is no other key that can unlock its true meaning but a profound insight into the present, wherein all is summed up? How piece together into coherent types of the whole, the waifs and strays that have floated down on the ocean of time, but by mastering the types and penetrating the meanings as now clothed in living flesh and blood around us ? "

" *June* 26. See, my letter has lain a whole week unfinished. I have such a stress of needlework to do just now, that what with some teaching, and time given to my mother, and a little music which I cannot live without, it leaves me not a moment. I do not fail daily to bless the inventor of the sewing machine, you may be sure.

" . . . Whitman is, I believe, far more closely akin to Christ than to either Homer or Shakspeare or any other poet. I may say this to you, because I know you hold with me, that 'the whole theory of the supernatural departs as a dream.' And this is what I meant when I said 'Poetry must accept him, &c., or stand aside.' Surely we must regard as 'greatest, divinest,' those human suns who send out their waves of light and impulse through the longest and widest stretches of time and space, vitalizing most germs; kindling and vivifying most hearts and brains? If the poet type is still to be accepted as the highest type (as I think it will) the boundaries must be enlarged to include Christ who never wrote a line: it must be entirely a question of the thing uttered and not at all of 'the mode of utterance;' and many names that have stood very high on the roll must go down to the rank of 'sweet singers only.

"What I, in my heart, believe of Whitman is, that he takes up the thread where Christ left it; that he inaugurates, in his own person, a new phase of religion; a religion which casts out utterly the abjectness of fear; sees the 'nimbus round every head,' knowing that evil, like its prototype darkness, is not a thing, an existence at all but the absence of a thing—of light; of balanced and proportionate development—activities not having found their right outlet—or not yet subordinated by the higher ones that will by and by unfold—impulses that have not yet opened their eyes to the beautiful daylight provided for them, but work in a kind of darkness as before birth, the soul remaining so much longer an embryo than the body—how often even when the hair is grey! So then is laid to rest that phantom of a Devil —of some 'power or being contending against God.'

" For you see what is called Christianity is not of Christ's making at all, but is the idea of Him, of His teaching, life and death passed to us through the darkening medium of infinitely less developed, less great and beautiful natures than His own—minds which clung with passionate tenacity to the traditions of their past—to the notions of a vindictive angry God to be propitiated by sacrifices and atonements; which seem to belong as inevitably to the early life of races as the belief in and dread of something cruel and terrible, ghost or demon lurking in the dark, does to childhood. But now I think what the keen strong honest intellect of the Voltaires and Humes could not accomplish : nor the eloquent scorn, the passionate indignation of beautiful divine Shelley—I mean the demolition of the childish and outgrown absurdities, the moral basenesses in the idea of God interwoven (shaped on the pattern of an Eastern despot) with the memories of Christ's beau·tiful life and teaching and death into a system embodying the intellectual and moral status of that time and nation by Matthew, Luke, and Paul ; and that demolition will happen now gently and quickly—now that there is once more a kindred human soul to Christ's on the earth—one filled with the same radiant glowing consciousness (it *is* a consciousness, not a belief) of the divine and immortal nature of the human soul—the same fearless, trusting, loving attitude towards God, as of a son, the same actual close embracing brothers' love of every human creature—all taking shape in what new and rich developments through the lips of this Poet ! The earth has not journeyed eighteen hundred times round the sun for nothing, since then! Now Christianity will go—and Christ be better understood and loved than He has been since those early times when His great personal influence yet vibrated in the world, and the darkness of His expounders had not begun to work adversely to the growing lights of succeeding times.

" Thus, whoever takes up Walt Whitman's book as a student of Poetry alone, will not rightly understand it : many and many a line and passage which will appear to him common, insignificant as a drop of water—has like that drop of water latent within it, power enough to furnish forth a flash of lightning and a peal of thunder if only it be taken up where the right conditions for liberating that force are present. I think he will one day win as ardent adhesion from men of science and philosophers, as from lovers of art, and they need him most of all. . . ."

William Michael Rossetti, reverting to the subject of Swinburne (August 7, 1870), writes :—" I disapproved of those poems of Swinburne's against Louis Napoleon (or chiefly of the *publication* of them), not so much (as you do) because L. N. is not worth the powder and shot, as because I dislike cruel gloatings over anybody, and do not think the physical pangs and general personal breakdown of Napoleon ought to be revelled in, any more than the like misfortunes befalling a minor criminal, or a man who does not at all belong to the criminal class. *Now* (though not when Swinburne wrote) L. N. does indeed look as if he were pretty well done for as a potentate ; and his utter extinction in that character will find few more cordial approvals than my own—though one must (I do, at least) admit that Europe owes him one debt of gratitude, in the liberation of Italy.   What will the next thing be?   A Republic?   I deeply hope it may, and think it more probable than not.   But what a military downfall to France !   One can scarcely believe it, though really it seems all but consummated now.   I am most distinctly for Germany in this war as a matter of right ; but, as to general *sympathy*, that has always belonged much more to France than to Germany, and still does.

" I agree with you that Whitman's ' Orotund ' (I doubt indeed whether it is *exclusively* his) is expressive ; but I don't regard it as *language*.   He would *not*, I fancy, have been obliged to me had I set Santa Spirita right :  my impression being that he has turned masculine into feminine with a view to expressing what is called ' the feminine element,' but without that instinct or respect for linguistic forms which tells other men that Latin or Italian words  actually existing can't have their genders topsyturvied, however convenient.

" *Au reste*, I agree with you  that the whole question of diction is, in comparison with  the real grounds and measure of Whitman's greatness, a small affair.

" I very much like and sympathize with (broadly considered) what you say of Whitman and Christ ; it is really the gist of the matter, and ought by rights to have been included in what was printed.   Also I fully concur with you in thinking that to consider Whitman as merely a littérateur among littérateurs, and not in these wider relations, would be a fatal dwarfing of the whole subject, and reduce any sincere expression about Whitman to drivel, if the speaker is an admirer, or to the stupid obtuseness of the ordinary critics, if he is an opponent. Still, I apprehend there is a range of considerations pertinent to the case, in which you and I must differ. I consider that Athenian character and society in the time of Phidias and Plato are at least as noble (I should myself say more noble) than Christian character and society in the time of Aurelius, St. Louis, or Cromwell. And the like, *mutatis mutandis*, as regards Shakspeare, who is perhaps too recent and impersonal to have done a very conspicuous work in society as yet, but whose spirit is at work wherever everything manly and womanly is loved and enjoyed, and its contrary contemned.

"Anybody who has great thoughts, and puts them into great words, seems to be properly a poet : Christ did this, and Whitman does it—and Homer and Shakspeare, to my thinking, did it no less.

"I had a letter lately from a somewhat interesting man, Dixon of Sunderland, the ' Cork cutter ' to whom Ruskin's ' Time and Tide ' is addressed. He says : ' I got quite a treat lately. Whitman sent me his " Democracy, and the Radical," with a lady's opinion on his poems. They are quite the rage here amongst Whitman's readers that know I have them.'"

*September the fifth* the same writer says : " What splendid news — Napoleon gone, and the Republic come ! But the horrid, horrid butchery mars all."

And three months later William Rossetti writes apropos of his friend's illness :—

" My dear Mrs. Gilchrist : I was glad to see your

handwriting the other day. . . . One of these days I shall be getting—what I have not yet had—the sort of illness that makes a frontier line in one's life between youth and good health, and middle-age and invaliding. I shall then sympathize with you more *feelingly*, but scarcely more genuinely.

" You will—or would at a less inopportune time—be pleased to hear that I have lately hunted up some rather curious papers about Shelley at the Record Office—containing an early poem hitherto quite unknown, ' The Devil's Walk,' a manifesto practically not less unknown, the ' Declaration of Rights,' and some correspondence thereanent. I think too the papers furnish a *suggestion* of considerable weight, in explanation of that mysterious attempted assassination at Tanyrallt which has been so much debated by Shelley writers, and often to the casting of a slur upon Shelley himself.

" I shall see about publishing the whole in the *Fortnightly*, with some remarks of my own.

" France is indeed in a horrible condition, but I think one may and must now say not in a disgraced condition, which is a great consolation to myself and others who love a Republic.

" La République has applied herself patriotically and energetically and daringly to retrieving, if possible, the disasters and shame inherited from the Empire —and not altogether unsuccessfully either ; she has made a great fight—an astonishing fight under the circumstances, it seems to me : will apparently be still beaten out and out, but will be entitled to show her horrid wounds and rents with lofty self-respect. And who knows even yet? Great men were living before Agamemnon, and great conquerors have had to turn tail prior to King William of Prussia:—not that I *believe* this augury. I was sorry to see Carlyle's German pæan : doubtless it has its large share of truth; but I think Prussia is quite lucky enough now without being hurraed, and France quite unfortunate enough to be spared taunt and insult. If it turned out that Carlyle made here as miserable a practical mistake as in the American affair, I confess I should exult."

And replying on the fourteenth of September, 1870, from Colne, Anne Gilchrist says : —

" Thanks, dear friend, the letter does give me great pleasure ; so did your last long one in answer to mine.

" I have been laid by with a serious illness since I wrote that ; a month on Saturday since I took to my bed, and no prospect of leaving it at present. The doctor says it is exhaustion of the nervous energy falling on the heart and on the digestion. Have looked death very close in the face—and the action of the heart is still so weak that I lie many days by the hour together unable to move or speak—struggling for life as it were. But the doctor says I shall pull through with patience and caution, but be good for nothing for some months, and I think so too."

Though still very ill, she followed the tragedy of this horrible war :—

" My dear Mr. Rossetti : You say just what I wanted to hear said for the French. I glanced at Carlyle's letter (I could not, and still cannot read any-

thing continuously) and thought it ungenerous and ill-
timed. That 'serves you right' style to either a man
or a nation in misfortune is intolerable because funda-
mentally unjust.

"I feel pretty sure that I have a copy of the 'Devil's
Walk' at Shottermill—a queer-looking, badly-printed,
badly-bound little book it is, with no author's name
on the title-page. If it is *the* 'Devil's Walk' in
question, and you would care to possess a copy, I will
send it to you as soon as I have an opportunity of
getting it."

Anne Gilchrist at length rallied from her prostrating
illness. In the spring of seventy-one she wrote from
London:—

"Dear Mr. Rossetti: You will wonder to see my handwriting so soon, but the truth is, yesterday evening
my conscience smote me for having spoken depreciatingly
of ——; and as I really had unusual opportunities for
obtaining insight into her character let me atone, and do
her and myself (for what is more odious than ungenerous
depreciation?) justice.

"Underneath that soft, languid manner there lurks a
clear-headed, acute, energetic, strong-willed character.
She devotes herself with the most unwearied zeal (spite
of fragile health) to realizing in her husband's home her
ideal of what a —— home should be. And though I
think her ideal a factitious, miserably delusive one
(fanatical believer that I am in a tranquil, sequestered
mode of life, with much solitude and no luxury in it),
it is impossible not to admire and respect the devoted-
ness with which she pursues her aim. She really goes

through an amount of hard work and nervous strain
incredible to any one who has only seen her in society :
and I believe that languid, invalid manner is a wise and
necessary precaution against the nervous exhaustion that
would certainly ensue if she put much briskness and
animation into that perpetual ' playing the agreeable ' to
the streams of guests that flow through their hospitable
home from one year's end to another; in addition to
her other labours.   For she it is who writes almost all
letters for him, manages all business matters, saves him
everywhere from all fatigue and worry, besides what
goes to managing a large establishment and providing
for the luxurious entertainment of that tormenting stream
of admirers and fashionables.

   " But no one can see ——'s profoundly *ennuyé* air
and utter lack of the power of enjoyment without
realizing what a mistake it all is.   Mrs. ——, watching
him with anxious, affectionate solicitude, endeavours to
find a remedy in the very things that cause it—surrounds
him ever closer and closer with the sultry, perfumed
atmosphere of luxury and homage in which his great
soul—and indeed any soul would—droops and sickens.
But there does not breathe a more devoted or a sweeter
tempered wife, I am persuaded. . . ."

   William Michael Rossetti replies :—

   " My dear Mrs. Gilchrist : Your letter to rectify
any impression derogatory to —— is an evidence of
your tender conscience, and I am on all accounts obliged
to you for it.   At the same time I do not think you said
*vivâ voce* anything beyond what still appears to be the
fact—that she attaches to position and appearances a

certain value beyond what you do : and I can most cordially say that in this matter I agree with you, and not with her.    The phrase " High thinking and plain living " has been rather run to death of late years ; but it is a true and high ideal wherein I humbly acquiesce— in opinion, and, I would fain wish, not in opinion only."

# CHAPTER XVIII.

## GEORGE ELIOT.

### 1871—1876.  Age 43—48.

EARLY in the summer of seventy-one, Anne Gilchrist let Brookbank to George Henry Lewes and his wife. Negotiations over the letting led to pleasant correspondence with them both. Lewes wrote from the Priory:—

"Among the supreme pleasures of authorship is that of receiving a spontaneous expression of sympathy from a stranger, and your postscript came with a doubled force, because the contents of the letter itself had excited a conviction that at last we had found the very country refuge we needed."

The Leweses sought out the country refuge:—
"We arrived here yesterday. . . . The weather is delightful, and the place looks *so* tempting. . . .

" Let peace once more settle on your soul, as it has settled on ours in the quiet order now finally established.

"Meanwhile we have been browsing among the varied pasturage of books here. We brought down a huge quantity which might have been lessened by two-thirds had I known what was on the shelves. Already we are

far on with the ' Life of Blake ' (intensely interesting)—
and I have laid hold of Lacroix' Algebra, which I see
was *yours*.

"We have had a drive to the Punchbowl and Liphook,
and found out many delightful walks.

" The weather is perfect, and work goes on smoothly
away from all friendly interruptions.

" Lord Houghton says that it is incomprehensible
how we can live in such Simeon Stylites fashion, as we
often do, all alone—but the fact is we never *are* alone
when alone. And I sometimes marvel how it is I have
contrived to get through so much work living in
London. It's true I am a London child. Mrs. Lewes
never seems at home except under a broad sweep of sky
and the *greenth* of the uplands round her."

George Eliot writes from Brookbank, May the
ninth:—"Everything goes on slowly at Shottermill, and
the mode of narration is that typified in ' This is the
house that Jack built.' But there is an exquisite stillness in the sunshine, and a sense of distance from
London hurry, which encourages the growth of patience.

"Mrs. Garland's pace is proportionate to the other
slownesses, but she impresses me as a worthy person,
and her cooking is of satisfactory quality. But we
find the awkwardness of having only one person in the
house, as well as the advantage (this latter being quietude).
The butcher does not bring the meat, everybody grudges
selling new milk, eggs are scarce, and an expedition we
made yesterday in search of fowls showed us nothing
more hopeful than some chickens six weeks old which
the good woman observed were sometimes 'eaten by the

gentry with asparagus.' Those eccentric people, the gentry !

"But have we not been reading about the Siege of Paris all the winter, and shall we complain while we get excellent bread and butter and many etceteras ?

"You will imagine that we are as fond of eating as Friar Tuck—I am enlarging so on our commissariat.

"If I ever steal anything in my life, I think it will be the two little Sir Joshuas over the drawing-room mantelpiece [Master Lord Burghersh, and little Miss Theophila Gwatkin]. I assure you, I have thought much of the worry we may have caused you while you are in a state of health with which I can sorrowfully sympathize."

George Henry Lewes enjoyed life at Brookbank :—

"As for me, the place agrees with me and I agree with it surprisingly. I shall be loth to leave.

"By all means tell Mr. [George] Smith *who* is the troublesome tenant—perhaps a lurking feeling of gratitude towards George Eliot may make all the difference in his feeling as to postponing his visit until September.

"Mrs. Garland is by no means wooden; on the contrary, she is all pith and no fibre. Kind, attentive, honest, she is, but *on n'est pas aussi bête!* She is as slow as an Oriental (the Orientals regard us Europeans as snobs because we are always in a hurry—perhaps they are right), but she crawls through her work, which owing to our clockwork regularity she is able to get through. But her stupidity and slowness are somewhat trying to the patience of impatient people. . . . I am in

famous case here.   Working harder and more successfully than I have done for years."

George Eliot became fond of Shottermill also, and was
' loth to leave ' Brookbank :—" During the first weeks
of our stay I did not imagine that I should ever be so
fond of the place as I am now [*i.e. July* 3, 1871].
The departure of the bitter winds, some improvement
in my health, and the gradual revelation of fresh and
fresh beauties in the scenery, especially under a hopeful
sky such as we have sometimes had—all these conditions have made me love our little world here and wish
not to quit it until we can settle in our London home.
I have the regret of thinking that it was my original
indifference about it (I hardly ever like things until they
are familiar) that hindered us from securing the cottage
until the end of September, for the chance of coming
to it again after a temporary absence.   But all regrets
ought to be merged in thankfulness for the agreeable
weeks we have had, and probably shall have until the end
of July.   And among the virtues of Brookbank we shall
always reckon this—that our correspondence about it
has been with you rather than with anyone else, so that
along with the country we have had a glimpse of your
ready quick-thoughted kindness."

This was the year (1871, July) and the very month
when George Eliot was writing the *Second Part of
Middlemarch*.   It is pleasant to think of the artist, seated
before her writing-table, in the long irregularly shaped
drawing-room at Brookbank ; honey-suckle and small
red rose peeping in at her through the bow-windows.
The room held antique furniture, and a cloud of Blake-

drawings and engravings graced the walls. She says :
" We have old prints for our dumb companions—charming children of Sir Joshua's, and large hatted ladies of his and Romney's."

The author of " The History of Philosophy " writes a concluding letter in which he says :—" Mrs. Lewes joins with me in the expression of a hope that we may one day make your personal acquaintance. We receive friends every Sunday afternoon, and any Sunday that you may be in the neighbourhood of the Priory it will give us pleasure to see you."

George Eliot, too, sends a farewell note from Cherrimans, the neighbouring house in Shottermill :—

*August* 2, 1871.

" Dear Mrs. Gilchrist : We parted from Brookbank yesterday. . . . After Mr. Lewes had written to you, I was made aware a small dessert or bread and butter dish had been broken. That arch-sinner, the cat, was credited with the guilt. . . .

" This note of course needs no answer, and is intended to make me a clear breast about the crockery. Hoping some day to shake you by the hand in our own home, I remain, yours always sincerely,

M. E. LEWES."

It is to be regretted that the trio never met : to visit a crowded reception was regarded as formidable : as many as sixty people would congregate at the Priory on Sunday afternoon. "Friendly intercourse, in my own home," was the mode of society congenial to Anne Gilchrist.

This was still a time of convalescence with Anne

Gilchrist : in a letter to her son, at Felstead Grammar School, she says :—" How I do enjoy this delicious spring weather and the singing of the birds ; I loiter about for hours in the beautiful [Colne] avenue or some favourite field ; and have such happy thoughts about my dear children, and our future together, now God is making me strong and well again ; and about Walt Whitman and his divine poems. Still, I am feeling rather anxious to be in London again. . . .

" The Tennysons having heard of my illness, wrote a kind letter and sent me a beautifully bound copy of the *Idylls of The King* and *The Holy Grail*."

And from Colne, March 1871, she says :—" Still such delicious weather, is it not? I have been twice into Chalkney wood, into the cleared part where it is dry and sunny, with plenty of felled trees to sit on, and have enjoyed it most thoroughly. It is really beautiful just there, with the Colne winding along through green meadows below you, and the ground rising towards *White* and *Wakes Colne*, and the little spires of the two churches, the cottages dotted about and the vivid green of the young corn on the slopes, also the *Chappel Viaduct* spanning a valley, shows through the trees."

We are quite determined that the garden of Essex shall not be a mere name to the reader ; to William M. Rossetti, writing July 18, 1871, she describes the place more minutely :—" Colne is always a green place, being a damp valley ; but this year, owing to the heavy rainfalls, it is so vividly and deliciously green, that one's eyes have a delightful consciousness of it all day long. My mother's garden too, though not much of a garden, has two pleasant features—the flower borders are a wilderness of roses and ' pretty Betsey ' and tall white July lilies, instead of those eternal rows of calceolaria and scarlet geranium and blue lobelia which are considered the proper thing now in a well-kept garden : and at the end is a green mound thickly shaded by an old yew, whence one looks up a ten-acre green field bordered with an avenue of the stateliest old elms I ever beheld, leading up to a grey church tower, with staircase turret that is as perfect in its kind of beauty as the elms in theirs. . . ."

" . . . I am looking forward to the autumn months at dear little Brookbank—then to finding in London something more of a home than I have had for the last three years. . . ."

When settled in London (Jan. 31, 1872), she mentions in a letter to W. M: Rossetti, having " read somewhere a few extracts from the *Nursery Rhymes*, which were as sweet and spontaneous as a robin's song and made me rejoice : melody of the right kind indeed for the little ones ; who want it as much as they want air and sunshine, or laughter and kisses.  [Rhymes, *i.e. Sing Song*, by Christina Rossetti.]  I have read, too, your brother's grand poem ' Cloud Confines ;' and though I always inwardly rebel against doubt and fear, and respond with joy and eagerness only to an indomitable faith and hope, I know for truth's sake, that mood needs expression too, and has here found one, of the sombre beauty that befits it."

And from *Earl's Colne, August* 28, 1873, Anne Gilchrist writes congratulations to her friend upon his approaching marriage with Miss Lucy Madox Brown.

"My dear Mr. Rossetti: The announcement at the end of your letter rejoices me heartily—earnest believer that I am in the enlarged, deepened, completed life only to be attained through a happy marriage.

"Little as I have seen of Lucy (if I may call her by that pretty name) she is one who draws you to her by a sweetness and charm of look and manner that you feel instinctively to be no acquired graces, but the growth and flower of an inward beauty of heart and soul. I know too that she shares your intellectual tastes and so can give you the close companionship and friendship that yield such a satisfying range and enduring freshness to domestic life. When the happy day for its beginning comes no one will sympathize and rejoice with you both more warmly than I, dear Friend. . . ."

And in the autumn of 1874 she thanks the same friend—"cordially for the copy of your memoir and edition of Blake's Poems, the former of which I have read with admiration and sympathy. . . . Nothing, it seems to me, can be more penetrating and judicious, yet warmed by enthusiasm, than your presentment of Blake's genius. Please tell your dear Wife how I sympathize with her pride in the dedication, which seems to invest the book with subtle fragrance like a flower shut between the leaves."

". . . My dear mother breathed her last very gently and almost without suffering on August 15 [1875]. She had entered her ninetieth year the previous June . . . She realized in her beautiful old age and painless death something of the ideal the Poet we love so much has drawn. . . ."

In the spring of 1876 *The Daily News* reviewed the Centennial Edition of *Leaves of Grass ;* the review was immediately followed by an eloquent letter from Robert Buchanan about Walt Whitman.  In the preceding autumn, William Michael Rossetti and Anne Gilchrist started the project of buying up a portion of the Centennial Edition of *Leaves of Grass.*

"1, *Torriano Avenue ; October* 10, 1875.

"My dear Mr. Rossetti : I have been pondering your letter this day or two.  It had occurred to me that perhaps your excellent scheme might be in part frustrated by some, perhaps a good many, of the Public Libraries declining the proffered gift.  How would it be to invest the money on an edition of Mr. Whitman's forthcoming book *The Two Rivulets ?*

"I know you will say what a pity not to give his very finest poems ! those which may be said to constitute his great message to Humanity, which he himself speaks of having written under the influence of an imperious conviction of the commands of his nature as total and irresistible as those which make ' the sea flow and the globe revolve.'

"But the ' Two Rivulets ' will contain *some* of these very finest things,—as, for instance, the poem Mr. Swinburne singles out for mention ' Out of the Cradle endlessly rocking,' President Lincoln's burial Hymn ' O Captain,' ' To think of Time,' Poems of Joy, ' The Whispers of Heavenly Death ; ' and in general all contained in the ' Passage to India,' besides the noble prose essay, ' Democratic Vistas,' and a good many new pieces. Would it not be better to succeed in making him known through these to a wide circle of readers, who, once having tasted his quality, will, if they be capable of enjoying it, eagerly possess themselves of *Leaves of Grass*, rather than to succeed in circulating a very limited number of the 'Leaves' ?   In truth considering how, as he says, he must himself make the growth by which alone he can be understood, or something to that effect, I think it very needful that such instalments as your Selections (to which I myself owe so incalculable a debt) and this forthcoming book should be widely circulated first as forerunners preparing the way: exhibiting in themselves as they do, and inspiring in the readers such a mingled lofty self-reliance and boundless sympathy and love, as easily and safely enables him to follow this great leader into those regions, hitherto dark and forbidden, which he has laid open to the free air and sunshine in *Leaves of Grass*. . . ."

And whilst staying with her son, Percy, at Blaenavon, June 22, 1876, she writes of the same subject—

" My dear Mr. Rossetti : I am glad to see the list of those who desire to purchase Mr. Whitman's Poems is steadily if not rapidly growing. Many thanks for a copy of the printed particulars. I wonder at not seeing Tennyson's or Browning's name among the others. For Tennyson we know has written friendly letters to the great American . . ."

Alfred Tennyson did buy the Centennial Edition of *Leaves of Grass*, sending five pounds at once to Buchanan, on reading the latter's letter in *The Daily News*, a sum which was duly forwarded to the American

Poet : and the following is an extract from a letter to William Michael Rossetti written by Walt Whitman, June the twenty-sixth, 1876, about this subject :—" I have not written lately to Tennyson, as I supposed him abroad on the Continent ; but I intend to write soon, and send him a set of my books. I am not at all sure that Alfred Tennyson *sees my poems*—but I DO HIS, and strongly, (and there perhaps I have the advantage of him) ; but I think *he sees* ME, and nothing could have evidenced more courtesy, and manliness, and hospitality, than his letters to me have shown, for five years."

A visit to America had been contemplated for some time by Anne Gilchrist, who writes to William Rossetti :—" I hope you will not all have flown on your summer rambles when I return from South Wales in July; for we are veritably going to America this year, we sail in the *Ohio* for Philadelphia, August thirtieth, 1876."

# CHAPTER XIX.

## THE NEW COUNTRY.

### 1876—1879. AGE 48—51.

SEPTEMBER the twelfth, William Michael Rossetti received a card dated from 1929, North 22nd-street, Philadelphia :—" A fairly good voyage. Favourably impressed by Philadelphia, a fine picturesque city."

Anne Gilchrist wrote to the same friend, December the twenty-second :—

" . . . I was never less in the mood for letter-writing than since we have been here; partly because I felt so many friends were expecting to hear, and expecting definite impressions and lively descriptions, and partly because the press of active duties leaves me little leisure.

" As to definite impressions of this vast complex contradictory phenomenon America, I am further from arriving at any such than I was in England. You can see a mountain as a whole—its complete outlines and relative proportions when you are at a distance, but when you are on it these merge into the few square yards around you and the distant prospect beyond.

" As to the bit immediately round us, this city of

Philadelphia, it is more picturesque and more foreign-looking than I expected; long straight streets at right angles to each other, long enough and broad enough to present that always-pleasing effect of vista—converging lines that stretch out indefinitely and look as if they must certainly lead somewhere very pleasant, and being tolerably well planted with trees deserve their names—Girard Avenue, Columbia Avenue, and so forth. Also the clear bright atmosphere, the immunity from soot and smoke (owing to the use of hard coal), and the prevalence of cloudless skies, enable the sunshine to have fair play and bring out in their utmost strength and intensity all colours and forms. One may have too much of a good thing, however, and sometimes this is a little wearying and monotonous; a film of smoke and a cloudy, fitful sky are not unmitigated evils. It is not a distressingly new-looking city however, for the Queen Anne style in vogue when its prosperity began, has been in the main adhered to with Quaker-like precision; good red brick, numerous rather narrow windows with white outside shutters, a block cornice along the top of the façade, and the added American feature of marble steps and entry, have a solid, cheerful and indeed, when the trees were in leaf and the abundant flags hung out, a very gay aspect—both bunting and buncombe are in favour here, says Mr. Burroughs. By-the-by, he came over to see us a few days after we landed, at the hotel; and much we liked him. So also did Mr. Marvin. But of society here we have at present seen very little. There is one delightful family circle to which the Conways gave us an introduction—that of Prof. Lesley (the geologist),

Director of the State Survey, with wife and daughter of the very best type of American women.   But I need not tell you our greatest pleasure is the society of Mr. Whitman, who fully realizes the ideal I had formed from his poems, and brings such an atmosphere of cordiality and geniality with him as is indescribable.   He is really making slow but, I trust, steady progress toward recovery, having been much cheered (and no doubt that has acted favourably on his health) by the sympathy manifested towards him in England and the pleasure of finding so many buyers of his Poems there.   It must be a deep satisfaction to you to have been the channel through which this help and comfort flowed. . . ."

Walt Whitman possesses a richness and breadth of manner, the ideal of democratic freedom and suave dignity of mien.   How pleasant was it to walk with the Poet in Camden or journey over the ferry, and note the jolly greetings exchanged with all sorts and conditions of men.

Of Edward Carpenter Anne Gilchrist writes:—

"*July* 1, 1877.   1929, *N. 22nd-street, Philadelphia.*

"Dear Mr. Rossetti : I have asked the friend who brings this letter to call on you because I think you will like to hear his account of Mr. Whitman, and of us too.   His visit has been quite a delightful episode in our quiet life.   He came to America mainly for the purpose of seeing Mr. Whitman, who brought him up to us ; and what with our sympathy in regard to the Great Poet and what with the wide range of his gifts and accomplishments, we have enjoyed his society heartily. Mr. Carpenter was a Fellow of Trinity College, but threw up his Fellowship because he could not stand the clericalism ; he is now one of the lecturers employed by Cambridge in the University Extension Scheme. He has also written ' Narcissus and other Poems ' which interest me much. I will not add any news of ourselves, because he will tell you all about us. . ."

And to the same friend from 1929, North 22nd-street, December 30, 1877, she writes :—

" When Mr. Whitman gets a letter from England we generally are privileged to share the pleasure of it, and last night he brought us yours. . . . We are having delightful evenings this winter ; how often do I wish you could make one in the circle round our tea table where sits on my right hand every evening but Sunday Walt Whitman. He has made great progress in health and recovered powers of getting about during the year we have been here : nevertheless the lameness —the dragging instead of lifting the left leg continues ; and this together with his white hair and beard give him a look of age curiously contradicted by his face, which has not only the ruddy freshness but the full rounded contours of youth, nowhere drawn or wrinkled or sunk ; it is a face as indicative of serenity and good-ness and of mental and bodily health as the brow is of intellectual power. But I notice he occasionally speaks of himself as having ' a wounded brain,' and of being still quite altered from his former self. . . .

" We saw in *The Athenæum* the description of Madox Brown's fine work recently completed [" *St. Ives* (A.D. 1630)," representing Cromwell on his farm. Painted in 1873-74 in oil, size between 4 and

5 feet]. Cromwell in one of his great moments, greatly realized.

" These things with the thoughts of dear friends they call up, make us long for our return, good as we find it to be here for the present.

" Mr. Whitman took us all to see Joaquin Miller's new play *The Danites*; we think it opens a new vein and gives a lively idea of the Californian miner and his ways. The Danites are emissaries of a secret Mormon Society for avenging the murder of their prophet Joseph Smith. I wish it may find its way on to the English stage and with the same cast too as here, for the acting of the male parts was admirable ; not so of the heroine however. [We remember going with Walt Whitman on this occasion, he sitting in the recess of the box, and now and then nodding approval of the dialogue, but with the reserve of an old play-goer, who has seen the great artists.]

" Joaquin Miller who called on us the other evening spoke with the warmest affection and admiration of you and your brother and sister—of Mr. Madox Brown too : he talks of taking his play to England."

*The Danites* was acted in London, for the first time, on Monday, April 26, 1880, at Sadler's Wells.

When Joaquin Miller came to tea at 1929, Walt Whitman was late in making his appearance from a ' siesta ; ' when, at last, the tall figure of the poet slowly entered the dining-room, Miller rose and exclaimed " he looks like a god, to-night."

Another time, Walt Whitman mentioned that his friend, Miller, delighted to trust strangers in posting

letters and the like small commissions—to cultivate
honesty through good-will: which is the prettiest trait
we can now think of in connection with the author of
*Songs of The Sierras.*

On the twenty-first of January, William Rossetti
answers his friend's last letter of December thirtieth:—
" I read with great pleasure and interest what you say
of Joaquin Miller. . . . I always liked him, and on
certain grounds admire his genius most heartily. His
play ought to be worth reading and seeing. We know
a lady who is (or lately was) particularly desirous of
becoming the owner of a play, for British acting—
purposes herself to act the principal female part: and
your remarks about Miller's play set me speculating a
little on that tack. I refer to Mrs. Petrici, a member of
the Anglo-Greek community (used to be Miss Las-
caridi)—she took to the stage three or four years ago,
her stage-name being Miss Edmeston. . . ."

In the evenings Walt Whitman sometimes read aloud
—rarely his own poems; he was fond of Tennyson;
Ulysses he recited impressively—looked the character.

> ' — all times I have enjoy'd
> Greatly, have suffer'd greatly, both with those
> That loved me, and alone; on shore, and when
> Thro' scudding drifts the rainy Hyades
> Vext the dim sea: I am become a name;
> For always roaming with a hungry heart
> Much have I seen and known;—
>
> .        .        .        .        .        .        .
>
> Yet all experience is an arch wherethro'
> Gleams that untravell'd world, whose margin fades
> For ever and for ever when I move.
>
> .        .        .        .        .        .        .

That ever with a frolic welcome took
The thunder and the sunshine,—'

    .     .     .     .     .     .     .

Walt Whitman frequently examined the collection
of prints grouped upon the walls of 1929, North
22nd-street—the engraved beauties after Sir Joshua
Reynolds and Romney. He was especially fond of Sir
Joshua's full-length portrait of Mrs. Frances Abington,
the comic actress; the Poet spoke of Reynolds's " broad
careless shadows."

In conversation he once admiringly referred to
Sir Edward Thornton apropos of this anecdote :—
"One day when driving through Washington, the
Ambassador noticed a lady intoxicated and surrounded
by a jeering crowd. Sir Edward at once stopped—
stepped from his brougham and escorted the unhappy
person to his carriage, and drove her home. The
incident went the round of Washington and we all
felt willing to do anything for this Englishman." It
should be added, that Sir Edward knew the lady.

The author of *Leaves of Grass* mentioned an incident which occurred at Emerson's house. We re-tell
the story, as it illustrates the Sabbatarianism that existed
in Boston a few years ago. It is not unlikely that some
little qualifying circumstance present in the actual situation has been forgotten in narration. We must keep
present before our mind's eye Emerson's nobility and
natural benignity of manner, nay a graciousness which
imparted a charm to his lightest words — even of
reproof—" Miss Bremer was at Emerson's house, where
conversation turned upon the subject of music, the

qualities which Swedish music lacked. Miss Bremer
went to the piano, and suiting the action to the word,
said—'I will show you that our music does possess these
qualities.' Whereupon some of the party immediately
asked her to desist, even Emerson himself said, 'No,
Miss Bremer, this is Sunday evening, I would rather
not——'

" Miss Bremer blushed and seemed put out ; but like
a good soul she soon recovered and laughed.

" Think of that ! I twice questioned my informer
before I could believe it."

Walt Whitman goes on to say :—

'I remember the Sunday in New York, Jenny Lind
was expected from England; it was afternoon:
people had nothing particular to do, and about five
thousand were seen all making for the wharf—it was
one of the funny sights of America.'

How did Jenny Lind take her reception?

'Very good-naturedly ; two police officers made way
for the unfortunate lion, or *lionne*. Though I do not
think (if the Queen herself were to come here) any
people would go now.'

Why is that?

'Well, America is not so young—and since she has
had wars, internal throes of her own, this curiosity has
lessened. There were a number of youths, boys and
girls who had read a good deal, but had had little
chance of satisfying their curiosity ; so that a star or
great personality attracted them ; but since they have
travelled the impulse has worn off.'

'. . . Count Gurowski was thought rather a bear in

Washington: to me, he did the honour of intrusting his confidences. The Count was aristocratic; his brother having married an Infanta of Spain. He came to America for liberal reasons. Upon one occasion, Count Gurowski was at a soirèe in Boston, where he was introduced to a lady for some special purpose; in the course of conversation it came out that the Count had studied under Hegel. 'Oh! what was the colour of Hegel's eyes?' exclaimed the lady. Count Gurowski could not speak English well, but, animated, vivacious, politely bowing, anxious to understand when the question was repeated—what was the colour of his eyes? His bear nature was too much for him. "Damn his eyes, what do I care for the colour of his eyes!"

Was the Count lionized in Boston?

'He would never consent to be made a lion of.'

'I used to like being with him. He had a head round as an apple, sharply cut features, and one eye had been knocked out in a duel; I was never tired of looking at him. Count Gurowski died in poverty, though actually in the house of Mr. A——, whose daughter he liked—a girl of thirteen. He knew that he must die, and used to speak of approaching death—'it has come—it has come, but a brave man does not fear death.' Miss A——, whom he thought much of, has become fashionable; one who, we thought, might have had glints of the Count's wild savage character—through affinity.'

[Possibly Count Gurowski's character suggested that of Baron Jacobi to the author of *Democracy* (?)].

'. . . Many friends, persons whom I like being

with, have no idea that I am an author; I like it all the better; and give 'Memoranda of the War' to pilot-men and engine-drivers. I have great fun sometimes, for you have no idea what a far-off thing a poet or literary man is to them; a poet is something they have vaguely heard of, and when one comes round talking familiarly, their astonishment is great.'

Apropos of international manners, Walt Whitman said:—

'A friend of mine who has lived in Italy, admires the Italians, believes in them. A butcher, here, the other day brought him a joint.' "He flung it down at my door, as though the fellow meant some injury: an Italian would have handled it gently, as though he felt for it."'

'I often think of that which Thoreau told me:—In one of his long pedestrian trips, Thoreau strayed un-usually far from human habitation; thirsty and tired he lighted upon a farm, where he asked for accommo-dation and food; the farmer (a supercilious man) refused haughtily. Thoreau was vexed at the bad treat-ment; when it suddenly struck him that the farmer was acting a part—and how well he was doing it—as an actor on the stage might! This idea so thoroughly possessed Thoreau, that instead of taking offence at the man's churlishness, he talked to him courteously, till at length the farmer's roughness wore off; Thoreau kept it up, and the two men got on well together, the farmer doing the courtesies of a host irreproachably. I always think of supercilious people as acting a part.'

'That which Edward Carpenter was saying the other

day about the Japanese, interested me, *i.e.*, that an English friend of his in Japan would not mix in Japanese society, because he felt their manners to be above and so far removed from anything he had previously seen.'

'I liked Thoreau, though he was morbid. I do not think it was so much a love of woods, streams, and hills that made him live in the country, as from a morbid dislike of humanity. I remember Thoreau saying once, when walking with him in my favourite Brooklyn —"What is there in the people? Pshaw! what do you (a man who sees as well as anybody) see in all this cheating political corruption?" I did not like my Brooklyn spoken of in this way.'

'. . . Tennyson seems to me to be a superb fellow; only, with a personality such as his, what a pity not to give himself to men. A man cannot invest his capital better than in comradeship. Literary men and artists seem to shrink from companionship; to me, it is exhilarating; affects me in the same way that the light or storm does. . . .'

Another day the Poet gave me these verses, written by him in pencil on the fly-leaf of a book :—

"Gladly would I to be such as he
With his exile and all his persecutions and anguish,
Forego the happiest fortunes of mankind."
         . . . MICHAEL ANGELO (of Dante)."

   .     .     .     .     .     .     .

Did you know Miss Bacon?

'No, I knew people who knew her, and I felt a good deal drawn towards her. She has been described to me as a beautiful woman, magnificent physique—altogether, something interesting about her.'

Hawthorne was good to her.

' Yes, it was one of the good things Hawthorne did.'

Talking about beauty and the figure : —

' Somebody has said, that if we went about nude, no one would look at the face.'

Yes, the figure is neglected now ; and the critics censure Greek artists for subordinating face to figure in their divine statues.

' Depend upon it the Greek sculptors were right.

' Since you were last here, Herbert, I have read Bulwer's *What will He Do with It.*'

Do you like it ?

' Pretty well, it is not a book that I should recommend to any but an American—there is no mincing matters, it is thorough-going Toryism. My friends laugh, and say I am getting Conservative—but I am tired of mock radicalism.'

Do not Bulwer's attitudinising heroes irritate you ?

' No, it is part of the fun.'

Reverting to the Laureate, the author of *Leaves of Grass* added :—" Tennyson, as I always say, is *my Norman*, though I think, that even he, is sometimes shaken in the wind of democracy."

George Eliot was not a favourite with the Poet ; we persuaded him to read *Romola* —" The book is like mosaic, each bit good, but I want a thread, something which carries one on in a novel ; and Romola—I do not see much in her yet ; she is statuesque ; her author always poses her before the reader is allowed to see her, as a photographer does—'your chin a little higher, please!'"

The story is melancholy.

'Ah, when the Greeks treated of tragedy, how differently it was done. They did it in a lofty way, so that there seemed to be fulfilment in defeat; a tragedy as treated by the ancients inspires—fills one with hope.'

Of Henry James's essay upon George Sand :—

"I like his cool, calm judgment, though I think the final summing up tone is too depreciatory."

That is a noticeable passage of James's " concerning the ardent forces of the heart. It is George Sand's merit that she has given us ideas upon them. . . Strange, loveless, seen in this light, are those large, comprehensive fictions 'Middlemarch' and 'Daniel Deronda.' They seem to foreign readers, probably, like vast, cold, commodious, respectable rooms, through whose window-panes one sees a snow-covered landscape, and across whose acres of sober-hued carpet one looks in vain for a fireplace or a fire."

One day, when looking at Bolswert's engraving after Rubens's bold portrait of Cæsar, Walt Whitman said: " What a pity that there is not such a portrait of Lincoln; the portraits of the President are lamentable, horrible, and the worst of it is they are so like!" . . . " I should like to poke about amongst the antiquities of Europe for two years—think I should appreciate the treasures there—that they are for me."

The following gossip we enjoyed with the *Good Gray Poet* in the country, near a perfumed clover-field, within sound of

"The low and sulky murmur of the bee."

' I sometimes think that there never has been a life written of anybody.'

Plutarch's— ?

'I think them of incalculable use ; though probably they give us no idea of that which really happened. During the [Secession] War we would now and then read a special article in the newspapers on an important battle, and we used to shout with laughter—the mistakes and fabrications were so ludicrous. So-called lives are little more than statistics.'

'. . . I remember well once seeing a man fall off a hay-rick ; I ran miles away. But necessity drives off that qualm. There is an operation in camp—the thing *must* be done—hundreds dying for want of attendance.'

'. . . The soldiers' time used to hang heavy on their hands during the winter ; they would devise all sorts of things—make ingenious toys, little knick-knacks.'

" The wild roving life of a soldier, not knowing whether you may die to-morrow or what may happen— the *camaraderie*, being thrown together in that way and under those conditions, is fascinating. I do not think that it has ever been expressed in literature, though the ancients understood it."

" To die,—to sleep ;—
To sleep ! perchance to dream ;—ay, there's the rub; "

The Poet criticised the speech as having morbid tendencies ; in short, that it showed the dividing line between the untroubled health of the ancients and uneasy consciousness of modern thought.

" I have sometimes felt a little vexed that the good

William should have failed to see anything in the common people; for unless it be the faithful servant in As You Like It, there is not a single character, in his plays, of the people who is not a booby (Jack Cade, Bottom), and no doubt they were—only it shows how entirely Shakespeare was absorbed in the feudalism of his time."

When in the open and under the blue sky of America, the author of " Leaves of Grass " quoted freely.

" Well, honour is the subject of my story,"—,was the commencement of a favourite speech with him. Whenever we hear an actor recite it, our mind reverts to the majestic presence and full sweet baritone of Walt Whitman,—

> " The torrent roar'd ; and we did buffet it
> With lusty sinews ; throwing it aside
> And stemming it with hearts of controversy."

A flexible voice, which could sink to the hoarse whisper necessary to the line :—

> " Give me some drink, Titinius."

" . . . . I see that a statue of Burns has been unveiled in Glasgow ; Lord Houghton presided. Convivial Burns—fond of comrades, of talking and joking ; I think that I—nay, that we should all have liked him. What a tragedy his life was, poor fellow !

" Walter Scott is a great favourite of mine ; what happy days and nights I have had from his novels ; the good I have had out of *The Heart of Mid-Lothian !* . . . "

" You remember what I said about painting—? "

Yes, how pleasant it is to be advised to do just that which one is thinking of doing.

" Well, I have never experienced it. When *Leaves of Grass* appeared, the first piece of advice concerning it was from an old fellow —' Yes, there is something in that which you have written, but why don't you study Addison? you ought to read Addison's works !' "

Of travel :—

" There come epochs in our lives, when the breaking up, the tearing oneself away from old scenes, is of incalculable benefit; and one finds upon looking back, that the years which were spent in roving, were the best, the most important of our life."

Two years of quiet life in Philadelphia terminated for the Gilchrists in the spring of 1878. The summer and autumn months were spent at Northampton, Chesterfield, Boston and Concord.

At Northampton Anne Gilchrist wrote *Three Glimpses of a New England Village*, an essay eventually published in *Blackwood*—November, 1884. She also resumed her prose translations from " La Légende Des Siècles."

When staying at Boston she sent a letter to the *Daily Advertiser*, 1878, the year that Jingoism was rampant in England :—

COLONEL HIGGINSON'S ADDRESS AT THE CHESTNUT-
STREET CLUB.

*To the Editors of the Boston Daily Advertiser.*

" I have not the making of a speaker in me, for I left out on Monday the very thing I would best like to have said in answer to Colonel Higginson's remarks on the present and probable future status of England among the nations. He was, I know, only quoting what has been said before, and in England, too, when he observed that England's commercial supremacy was already doomed, and when that was gone she would sink to the rank of a third or fourth-rate power, like Holland. Is then England's commercial supremacy the cause of her greatness? Or is it only one effect, one manifestation and phase of it? What figure did she make among the nations of Europe when her coal was still unworked and her manufactures and export trade non-extant? Certainly not a third or fourth-rate one.

" If we are not degenerating in quality, nor dwindling in numbers; if in moral weight and fibre, in intellectual power, indomitable energy, and last not least, in physical vigour, we are what we were, surely we need not fear the future; need not fear but that we shall find good and ample scope for these qualities and keep the proud position we have now. And if I am told this is a vague, unpractical way of looking at things, I will make bold to answer that not more plastic is clay to the will and imagination of the sculptor than are practical affairs to the national strength, will, and insight underlying them. And that to be great in character and little in destiny does not happen to nations—nor to individuals either, in the long run, spite of transient appearances. History repeats herself, says every one. Nations must decay as soon as they have culminated. History repeats herself; but not in such a way as to make prophesying a safe trade.

" Things are looking pretty dark with us just now;
and Colonel Higginson remarked that it seemed to him
when he was in England, and was admitted by many
with whom he conversed there, that the fact of Lord
Beaconsfield having been able to commit England to the
disastrous course marked out for her in the Berlin Treaty
not merely without the consent, but without the knowledge even of Parliament, proved that we were not a
self-governing people to the extent we had supposed.
But to me it seems that the English people have only
themselves to thank for that disaster. They had had a
good taste of the Premier's quality before the close of
the session. They had had ample proof that he was a
Will-o'-the-Wisp whose nature and delight it was to
dance gaily along over swampy places. And had so
large a proportion of them not suffered themselves to be
deluded by his specious brilliancy and led on by his
fantastic beckoning, he could have been cleared off the
ground in good time : the lawful means are open to us
—and the fit man is there to take his place.

39, Somerset-street, Nov. 20.     ANNE GILCHRIST."

After leaving Boston, the family settled down in New
York for the winter and spring. A letter written from
Brooklyn, December 6, 1878, vividly pictures Concord
and the people living there :—

" My dear Mr. Rossetti : I hardly think I have
written to you since we left Philadelphia in the
Spring; and if so, shall not be repeating myself in
telling you some of our summer and autumn experiences in beautiful New England. Especially has our
autumn been delightful. We went at the beginning

of October to Concord, and boarded there with a sister-in-law of Mrs. Emerson's. Thus we found ourselves at once in the midst of the literary circle : all Concord indeed seems more or less literary, and has ways of its own, and standards of its own ; making money, it seemed to me, of less account than it is in other corners of the civilized world.

"Emerson is of course the central figure, and is personally beloved and honoured by his townsmen in a way that is pleasant to see ; as well he may be. For he unites with his fine genius a fine character, and is full of goodness and amiability. We spent two evenings with him. His conversation reverted continually to Carlyle and their early intercourse. His memory fails somewhat as to recent names and topics, but as is usual in such cases, all the mental impressions that were made when he was in full vigour remain clear and strong. Emerson looks the picture of health and cheerful serenity ; and has just such a home, spacious, comfortable, as one could desire for him. His wife is an animated, graceful, intellectual woman though a sad invalid, and his single daughter, Ellen, devoted to him, and the very soul of goodness and unworldliness. Altogether, few have been the men of genius, I should say, who have had so entirely congenial and favourable a lot in life. His son is practising as a physician in Concord and has two fine children. Indeed on Thanksgiving Day [Emerson] gathers some twenty-two children, grandchildren, and relations of his wife's round his table ; and heartily enjoys the games and merriment of the children, I am told.

" By the by, you probably know there is a portrait of Emerson by David Scott in the Concord Public Library.

" In point of scenery, the charm of Concord lies along its river, whereon, a kind and very agreeable literary friend, Mr. Fred. Holland, rowed us daily. Americans call it a mere stream but we should regard it as a river of respectable dimensions (about as broad as the Kennet). It winds leisurely along, making bold curves through level meadows, past groves of hemlock interspersed (as always throughout Massachusetts) with grey boulders of every shape and size ; past hills, sometimes crowned with vineyards (for Concord is famous for its grapes) sometimes richly wooded, then in all their autumn splendour of scarlet and gold, mirrored in the water as gay as any flower border : now and then the river spreads out and the hills enclose it like a lake. It flows past the famous spot where the first blood was shed in the revolutionary war. A really successful statue— ' The Minute Man '—by a native of Concord, Dan French, marks the spot, an avenue leads up to it, a rustic bridge crosses the river hard by ; and the ' Old Manse,' picturesque, venerable, just as it ought to look is visible through its orchard which slopes to the water —the whole ' just as pretty as it can be ' to use a favourite American phrase.

" But if I run on any longer about Concord, there will be no room for anything else ; so I will only add that ' Sleepy Hollow,' the burial-ground where Hawthorne lies, is the very sweetest last resting-place poet could desire—a green hollow shut in by wooded hills, on the top of one of which is the little stone, planted round with Arbor Vitæ, that marks his grave.

" November we have been spending in Boston, and spending delightfully—for it is a beautiful city ; and it seems to me I have made more new acquaintances in the last two months than in the whole of my life before, and many, nay, most of them people of such intelligence, culture and geniality that I found it tantalizing to have but brief intercourse with them, and hope much to return to Boston before I leave America, that some of these acquaintanceships may ripen into friendship.

" I sent your introduction to Mr. Eliot Norton, who at once called on me ; and a very interesting conversation we had. . . .

" With Mr. Horace Scudder (to whom also you gave me an introduction) I had a delightful time. He and his pretty, graceful wife were as cordial as possible ; and invited a large and interesting circle of friends to meet me—Col. Higginson, Mr. Van Brunt, the architect of Memorial Hall, Mr. Gilman, who is editing, I am told, a very fine edition of Chaucer, and a number of the Harvard professors. . . .

" At Mr. Holland's I met Longfellow, President Eliot, and others. I afterwards called on Mr. Longfellow ; he is the most kindly, good-natured, unaffected man possible, quite unspoiled by his great popularity ; and lives in the jolliest old house with a happy family circle around."

In a letter written from 112, Madison Avenue, a picture of Concord in winter is suggested :—" My dear Mrs. Holland : I feel inclined to write a letter all

questions, for I would dearly like a written picture of
pleasant Concord, of the comings and goings, the
talkings and readings of that friendly delightful circle in
the midst of which I felt more at home after a three
weeks residence than I should after three years here.
And how does the River look? is it a great plain of ice
stretching all over the meadows, with here and there
trees and bushes sticking up through it? And do you
get over to Mrs. Le Brun's for cosy evening chats? and
is the book nearly through the press [*The Reign of
the Stoics*, by Frederick Holland]? and does your
husband walk to the tops of those pleasant hills to take
a look at the wintry world and get as much health out
of it as out of the more luxurious boating? Well, I
do not expect answers to everything, or indeed anything,
till you have leisure and inclination. . . .

"As a place to live in I like it [New York] less than
anywhere else I have been in America; what with its
piled up human habitations, its dirty, noisy streets, its
icy winds, it seems to me behind Boston in everything
but size and noise: I suppose, too, I must add in those
same icy winds and that, that dear old place would be
still more trying to me in that particular. . . ."

The visit to New York, and America, draws to a
close in 1879.

Writing, March the third, to William Rossetti she
says:—"We are having a pleasant winter in New
York. . . . We have had some of our most delightful evenings at Mr. Gilder's. Do you know him
as a young poet? He is one of the editors of
*Scribner's* [now the Editor of *The Century*], and one

of the best friends the young artists have here: he augurs 'a good time' for them soon, and thinks that the appreciation of art is growing rapidly in America.

"Our only drawback here, is that Walt Whitman is so far off: we hear from him pretty often.

". . . My little grandson—I need not tell you, his advent has made me long more than ever to be back in dear old England again. . . .

"We set sail for England June the seventh, 1879."

# CHAPTER XX.

## THE RETURN.

### 1879—1882.  AGE 51—54.

*" Durham, August* 1.

"DEAR MR. ROSSETTI : I do not know whether you have heard from any of our common
friends that we reached old England again a few weeks
ago. . . .

"Our little red tiled village, Lower Shincliffe, lies
among wooded hills, fine corn fields and tall colliery
chimneys, within sight of Durham Cathedral—noblest
sample of Normanesque we have in England.   Eight and
twenty years ago, just after our marriage, my husband
and I spent a week in this most picturesque of English
cities.   And now here I am again after all my wanderings, spending my evenings with my son and his wife
and their beautiful little boy just ten months old. . . .

"You will be glad to hear that Macmillan is at last
willing to undertake a new edition of the Blake. . . .

"Mr. Whitman was still staying in New York when
we left.   He came down to see us the day before, looking well.   He never will entirely recover from his lame-

ness.    I need not tell you we felt the parting from him
very much as he did, I think, from us. . . .

"We saw some grand scenery the last three days of
our voyage; sailing close under the Giants' Causeway . .
up the Firth of Clyde to Greenock—the sun set, the
summer night with its lingering weird kind of daylight
in the sky, and a magnificent sunrise lit up all these wild
grand scenes gloriously. . . ."

Walt Whitman writes from America:—"Thank
you, dear friend, for your letter; how I should indeed
like to see that *Cathedral* [Durham], I don't know which
I should go for first, the Cathedral or *that baby* [Anne
Gilchrist's grandson].    I write in haste, but I am determined  you  shall  have  a  word  at  least  promptly  in
response."

Shottermill was again visited; though not the primitive little Shottermill of 1862.    October the twelfth,
Anne Gilchrist wrote to Emma Holland, a friend gained
in Concord:—"Mr. Tennyson has been to see us and
we have been to lunch with him, and have seen his
beautiful little grandson.    He is now just starting for
Italy.    I send you a leaf of Irish ivy gathered in his
garden in case you have any fancy for such relics."

We remember the visit: Tennyson called at a cottage
on *Lion Green*.    As he sat in the cottage arm-chair in that
small wainscotted room, with flowers near the little case-
ment window, we felt these to be the surroundings which
threw into relief the impressive personality of the bard.
That which is most characteristic of Tennyson, is his
bass voice—deep and resonant—a voice a little like that
of Millais's, only stronger.    Upon this occasion Tenny-

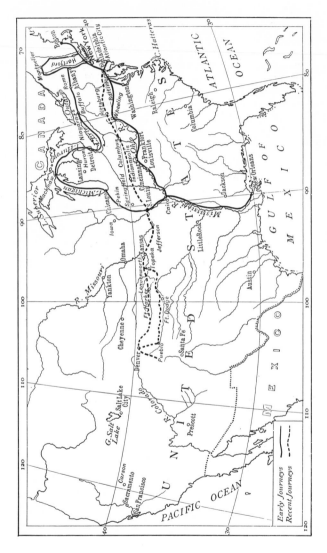

REPRODUCTION OF THE MAP UPON WHICH WALT WHITMAN HAD
TRACED HIS JOURNEY TO THE ROCKY MOUNTAINS.

son talked of Walt Whitman. He mentioned *Niagara Falls* as being to him an inducement to cross the ocean.

Through a friend's suggestion (Mrs. Williams, a lady who has executed some charming pictures), the Gilchrists visited Hampstead, and finally bought a house there.

To William Rossetti, November 25, Anne Gilchrist writes :—" The very morning after I saw you, I had a very interesting letter from Walt Whitman, and what I think (and you will too) very precious, a little map on which he has traced in blue ink all the wanderings of his youth, and in red his recent journey to the Rocky Mountains." The Poet says :—" Wonders, revelations I would not have missed for my life, the great central area 2,000 miles square, the Prairie States *the real America*, I find—and I find that I was not realizing it before." In the postscript of this letter Walt Whitman says : "Lived a couple of weeks on the *Great* Plains —800 miles wide, flat, the greatest curiosity of all. Fifty years from now this region will have a hundred millions of people, the most comfortable, advanced and democratic on the globe ; indeed, it is all *this* and *here* that America is for."

December the tenth Anne Gilchrist writes to Frederick Holland, of Concord :—" How does England seem to me after my long absence and fresh experience ? A land of strange contrasts and paradoxes so great and so small, so old and so young, so sunless and misty, often *murky*. Yet rich in beauty and depth of tone ; so stuffed and crammed with swarms of rude, ignorant, I

fear I must say brutalized people : brutalized by ignorance, poverty and squalor—by the worst possible
physical conditions of life, present and inherited ; people
such as you have a few thousands of in your cities, but
none at all spread over the land, and those in the cities
with better chance of emerging. But teeming too is
old England still with a race of indomitable workers, of
sturdy intellect, sturdy character, not to be beaten in
the race, be it for knowledge, wealth or power ; a people
that will go on fighting the battle of progress a good
while yet, labouring along under a stupendous load of
difficulties and encumbrances inherited from the past ;
also with a very rich heritage, tangible and intangible,
from that same Past. And, to come down from my
high horse, how bitter cold and foggy it is !—the cold
so damp and raw. Don't you Americans grumble
about your climate, for it is splendid ; leave all the
grumbling and some of the boasting to us !

"And how does America look to me from this side
the Atlantic ? A magnificent, sunny land of promise—
splendid with youth, and hope, and inexhaustible pos-
sibilities, which it does one good only to think of, much
more to live amongst. If America does not by and by
attain to a higher ideal than has any where yet been
reached, humanity is a failure and a mistake ; for its
chances there are splendid, physical, social, intellectual.
And as to what America is now to me, when I think of
the genial and congenial friends I found there, of the
intellectual stir and brightness, of the sense of expansion
and encouragement, sunshine without and sunshine
within, I feel as if I must come back among you. . ."

In a letter to Horace Scudder (Jan. 3rd, '80) reference is made to his essay on Blake in *The Century* :—

" Rejoicing to the spirit and the eyes is the article on Blake, which, thanks to you, reached me a few days ago ; with its hearty yet discriminating appreciation, its insight begetting or begotten of sympathy.

" I am specially taken with the description of Blake's ' visionary eye, that far-seeing, vivid and wide-open orb, which looks at one from so many of Blake's figures, and most significantly from his own face.' "

The second edition of the Life of William Blake was now, March 2nd, 1880, taken in hand and pushed energetically through by Anne Gilchrist, upon whom the responsible editing fell. Anent a small discrepancy of date contained in the first edition she says to William Rossetti :—" I am glad to ascertain that Mr. Swinburne's change in the date of Blake's birth rests only on Tatham's authority. He was a mere stripling, I suppose not above seventeen or eighteen, at the time of Blake's death ; and proved in every way such a careless guardian of Blake's precious artistic effects (for all that did not pass into Linnell's hands came into his), destroying the manuscripts on a great scale, as I heard from his own lips, and having the plates stolen from him ; that very little weight indeed is to be attached to his statements except as to Mrs. Blake, after her husband's death. Of her, no doubt, he saw a great deal.

" The date of birth my husband obtained from the baptismal register of St. James's Church (if I am not mistaken) ; how else should he have known the circum-

stance of his having been christened as one in 'a batch
of six'? In fact I remember his search there.

"It is curious there should have been a mistake about
Maria Flaxman, for Mrs. Flaxman's surviving sister,
Miss Denman, was Alec's source of information; but
no doubt he was mistaken, these letters show that Mrs.
Flaxman's name was Anna. . . .

"I have been reading in the *Jerusalem* again, and have
found several more coherent and indeed beautiful passages.
I incline to think Blake's religious enthusiasm (always a
strong feature) took quite a fierce development in the
solitude of Felpham and under the sublime influence of
the sea, and that the *Jerusalem* is in a special sense the
fruit of this. The needful preparation for my tracing
it would be a careful study of Jacob Boehmen and
Swedenborg."

And a month later to Dante Gabriel Rossetti she says:—
"Dear Mr. Rossetti: I gladly send you the new Blake
letters—it is very important you should see them before
we go to press: with one important exception they are
less interesting and beautiful than the Butts letters, but
still a very valuable accession. It is evident from them,
that Blake and Hayley parted very good friends; that
poor old Hayley behaved well from first to last, and
had no other fault than this involuntary one of incapacity
through lack of imagination and of the finer gifts to
understand or really to *see* Blake at all."

Gabriel Rossetti (in reply) writing of the new
letters:—"I fear they will prove rather a disappointment if not somewhat a dissatisfaction to lovers of
Blake. It is painful to find him drawn (doubtless by

an unavoidable predicament) into so much praise and so many expressions of thanks, when we have seen his feelings expressed so differently in private memoranda. The thanks I (like yourself) believe to have been essentially deserved by poor Hayley, but the admiration expressed for Hayley's works must surely be 'turned on.' Alms for dire necessities! Even Blake, I suppose, could not always be above them.

"There is just one letter (that in which the puzzling Truchsessian collection is spoken of) which is in Blake's visionary vein, and an addition to our knowledge of him. . . .

"The allusion to 'Edward of Oxford' is another puzzle, not to be solved as far as I can judge."

Anne Gilchrist answers :—"In regard to the new letters, I felt as you did at first, a good deal disappointed. But I cannot doubt Blake's sincerity, or realize the possibility of his having stooped to conscious flattery: I think the warmth of old Hayley's zeal and friendliness in the Trial and on other occasions really went to Blake's heart, and made him look at his empty verses through a deceptive glow of feeling and endow them with meanings of his own, just as a man of fine gifts often contrives to endow with the like in his imagination a woman who has really nothing within her trivial prettiness. And when the glow faded with time and the deeper sense of Hayley's utter incapacity to understand or perceive greatness alone remained, he may have jotted down those sarcasms in the notebook. I could not help thinking, as I was copying, of the lines

s

' I write the rascal thanks till he and I
  With thanks and compliments are both drawn dry ; '

but there is nothing very black in that, and I think

' Thy friendship oft has made my heart to ache,
  *Do* be my enemy for friendship's sake,'

has a kind of pathetic meaning—such a worthy, kindly
old fellow, yet such a blighting influence on the inner
life !

"The only *Edward of Oxford* we can find a trace of
in the voluminous ' Life of Hayley,' as having been a
guest at Felpham in those years, was Edward Marsh,
of Oriel College; who used to read aloud Hayley's
own poems to him in a very melodious and effective
manner."

Dante Gabriel Rossetti proved a helpful counsellor
in preparing the second edition of the Blake; entering
into it with the same spirit of generous ardour as he had
over the first, being an excellent critic, who looked at
his subject broadly—from the vantage ground which
genius alone commands.

Anne Gilchrist's task of editing the second edition was
not an easy one. It was a tradition in the family to
avoid notes; to recast the text rather than to use them.
Thus, too, as a consequence, her work as editor is not
apparent.

Before bidding adieu to Blake in the present volume
it will not be out of place if we give the reader the chat
that we enjoyed the other day with Mr. George Richmond; the only living man who has conversed with
William Blake—when a student, closed the poet's eyes

and kissed William Blake in death, as he lay upon his bed, in the enchanted work-room at Fountain Court.

The Academician showed us a cast of Blake's head and face, taken by Deville, when Blake was about fifty years old.

" The first mask that the phrenologist took : he wished to have a cast of Blake's head as representative of the imaginative faculty."

Deville's wish was not surprising; (when regarding the mask) we ask if any man ever possessed a fuller temple or a more finely packed brow?—the quivering intensity in the closed eyes and dilated nostrils is wonderful; and when we pass our hand over his stubborn English chin, we understand Hayley's surprise, when calling at the cottage at Felpham, at finding Blake grinding away, graver in hand, during a hot day in August; and the quiet pluck with which he always buckled to etching (for Bookseller Johnson) when Mrs. Blake placed the " empty plate " upon the little round oak table.

Mr. Richmond drew our attention to the position of Blake's ear, which is low down, away from the face near the back of the neck, showing an immense height of head above :—" I have noticed this relation of ear finely characterized in three men—Cardinal Newman, William Blake and Henry Hallam." Mr. Richmond pointed out an engraving after his portrait of Newman, which instanced the noble characteristic happily. " I told Mr. Gladstone that I never understood his character, until the day when I sat in church behind him; then I saw the tremendous bulwark of the statesman's neck."

" That is not like dear Blake's mouth, such a look of severity was foreign to him—an expression of sweetness and sensibility being habitual : but Blake experienced a good deal of pain when the cast was taken, as the plaster pulled out a quantity of his hair.   Mrs. Blake did not like the mask, perhaps the reason being that she was familiar with varying expressions of her husband's fine face, from daily observation : indeed it was difficult to please her with any portrait — she never liked Phillips's portrait ; but Blake's friends liked the mask."

[January number of *The Hobby-Horse*, 1887, gives an admirable photogravure of Mr. Richmond's mask— a Magazine published quarterly.]

We surprised Mr. Richmond by saying that we, too, had stood in Blake's work-room at Fountain Court ; nay, that we had made a drawing of ' that divine window.'

" Why, the room is pulled down ? "

We answered that it was standing in 1880.   Blake's pupil then proceeded to draw a plan to revive his memory :—" The fire-place was in the far right-hand corner opposite the window ; their bed in the left hand, facing the river ; a long engraver's table stood under the window (where I watched Blake engrave the *Book of Job*. He worked facing the light), a pile of portfolios and drawings on Blake's right near the only cupboard ; and on the poet-artist's left—a pile of books placed flatly one on another ; no book-case."

Were there many pictures on the walls?

" No, not many in the work-room but a good num-ber in his show-room, which was rather dark."

" Blake often spoke of the beauty of the Thames, as seen from his window, the river looking ' like a bar of gold.' "

Our host showed a *gesso* water colour, worked in Blake's favourite "fresco" medium — *The Shepherd Abel;* the shepherd is asleep near a wood, moths are hovering about.   The scheme of colour is deep blue and red-brown—a singularly beautiful piece of colour.   It was George Richmond's first picture; one that was submitted to Blake, who made a careful correction-drawing of the shepherd's arm in his pupil's sketch-book.   The picture is dated 1825, and is fresh as the day it was painted !

Fuseli was a close friend of Blake ?

" Yes, Fuseli admired Blake very much.  The former when Blake showed him a design, said,—' Blake, I shall invent that myself.' "

It was Stothard who first gave a nickname to Blake?

"Oh, I do not know that; Blake would say outrageous things to people—answering a fool according to his folly, to those who did not and never would understand either him or his works."

" There ought to be a bust of Blake in the Abbey. Dean Stanley was favourable to placing a bust of the poet-artist there."

Yes, and a painted window (over his bust), of the design—

' When the morning stars sang together, and all the Sons of God shouted for joy.'

Even now, that Rossetti and Palmer have passed

away, there are artists living who could be safely in-
trusted with such a labour of love: only there should
be a stipulation that whoever undertook it, himself
should execute the colour upon glass; not paying others
to have it done at a shop. In 1861 Samuel Palmer
wrote:—" In Westminster Abbey were [Blake's] earliest
and most sacred recollections. I asked him how he would
like to paint on glass, for the great west window, his
*Sons of God shouting for joy*. He said, after a pause,
' I could do it!' kindling at the thought."

A bust of Longfellow has recently been placed in
the Abbey! Has not the time arrived when England
should pay tribute to the " soaring genius " of William
Blake?

Before we left, Mr. Richmond showed us some of his
treasures—pictures by Palmer, Finch, and Calvert, and
a great deal besides. We saw his copy of Romney's
portrait of Mrs. Bentinck, who was a daughter of
Cumberland the poet. "She made that [bewitchingly
becoming] hat herself, and finished it just in time to
wear at a Fête at Vauxhall. . . . "

The ' Life and Works of William Blake ' was at
length finished. In a letter to Horace E. Scudder, the
subject of buying a house is mentioned by Anne Gilchrist: " We are house-hunting, though not house-
building, and have just missed a charming old wainscotted
home with lovely little garden and out-look; so now we
shall probably have to content ourselves with a new one.

" Hampstead is the only suburb of London that is not

suburban; it is really still a picturesque old village, with beautiful views and walks—the steep hill it stands on and the heaths have saved it. I hope one day to explore it with you and Mrs. Scudder. . . .

" If only you could have been with us in Rossetti's studio [the other day]. Assuredly, he is our painter of greatest and most original genius. I wish Boston or New York would possess itself of his 'Vision of the Death of Beatrice;' then they would be convinced that something greater than the greatest French art has been produced in England."

And to William Rossetti she writes :—" Many thanks for all your kind help [over the Blake] : and also for your interest in the question of a house for us. I have been to see the Conways, and think theirs charming ; and that there are many attractions at Turnham Green ; but on the whole not equal to those of Hampstead. The distance from London is twice as great, and you depend entirely on rail at not very frequent intervals; also the country round is a dead flat, on a level with the river, the air therefore somewhat heavy ; so that our breezy heath and sandy soil have great advantages over it in point of healthiness as well as beauty—but I wish we had a Norman Shaw here designing new houses."

Walt Whitman in a letter written from New Jersey in the spring of 1881 mentions that " John Burroughs is reading the proofs of a new book, 'Pepacton'—the Indian name of a beautiful little river. I am out in the woods a great deal to-day, mild but damp and cloudy— a little bird they call the rain-bird is singing softly and coyly on a bush over the road."

While staying at Redcar with her son Percy, Anne Gilchrist writes (May 22) to William Rossetti :—" Miss Blind (whose visit to Hampstead we all enjoyed) brought me also some children of your brain. The sonnet on John Brown is my favourite; it is kindling—great. Next best I like the ' Mary Shelley,' though, indeed, it seems to me you give her doctrinaire father more than his due. . . .

" I am staying with my son Percy and his wife in a little cottage close to the beach here, and much enjoying the ever-varying play of colour—deep greens, deep blues, purples, steely grey, on the sea this sunny breezy weather. I have not been near the sea since I last crossed the Atlantic two years ago. My little grandson also is an endless source of delight, and as sunny and full of ceaseless movement as the summer sea itself. . . "

William Michael Rossetti answers :—" I am delighted at finding that you like these sonnets ; my preference for the John Brown goes with yours. Do you know [John Brown's head] ? I do by a photograph. It is one of the most impressive and peculiar heads of this century, yet not quite what one would pre-suppose ; there is something of Wallenstein in it, and more of Henri Quatre—far finer than either."

Writing to her son from Edinburgh, Anne Gilchrist says :—" I have been running through the ' Life of Kingsley'—find interesting letters to and from Frederic Shields. He seems to have executed his ' Pilgrim's Progress ' designs under Kingsley's auspices, who says to him, ' It seems to me you are about to become one of the finest designers in Europe.' Kingsley improves on close acquaintance; he was truly a finely-gifted genial man."

In the spring of 1882 the artistic world was stunned by the event of Dante Gabriel Rossetti's rather sudden death.

*April* 17, 1882.    *Keats Corner, Hampstead.*

"DEAR MR. ROSSETTI: I do not like to keep silence; though indeed, it is hard to find words fit to be spoken when such a grief befalls.

"To Herby and me, the loss is truly a personal one, nay, of course it is so to all who were capable of receiving the precious gifts he had to bestow—the creations of supreme beauty : but in another sense too; for how generous and helpful a friend he was to us! How did he enhance the preciousness and completeness of my dear Husband's book! Never have I experienced a sweeter, gentler manner than was his to us, when we twice went to see him in the spring of 1880.

"I am glad you elected to lay his remains in that little churchyard within sound of—

'The sea's listless chime :
Time's self it is, made audible,—'

Surely, too, type of a

'Secret continuance sublime—'

"I deeply believe in Nature's great laws of Continuity and Indestructibility for souls as well as for atoms and forces; in her "transfers and promotions;" truth to say, I know not how I could bear the burthen of life since my Beatrice left me, if I did not so believe.

"Yours in full sympathy,

ANNE GILCHRIST."

# CHAPTER XXI.

## MARY LAMB.

### 1882—1885.  AGE 54—57.

A REQUEST from John H. Ingram to write a Life
of Mary Lamb was complied with March 28th:
" I would willingly undertake a Life of Mary Lamb for
the Series you propose.  I must premise, however, that
I had no personal acquaintance with her.  But to my
mind's eye, her sweet, sympathetic, finely attuned
nature, shrouded as it was in the dark shadow of the
tragedy of her youth,—object of her brother's tenderest
solicitude;—at one moment his best companion, at
another his bitterest trial,—has always appeared a singularly interesting, pathetic, beautiful figure. . . ."

It was some months before Anne Gilchrist commenced
writing the Life: the interval allowed leisure for correspondence with John Burroughs.

In the Spring of 1882, John Burroughs visited Eccle-
fechan, thence on to London: after his departure
for America, Anne Gilchrist wrote, July 25 :—" Just
a word to speed you on your homeward voyage, my
friend.  I feel as if you had not had as good a time
in England as you ought—weather partly to blame—

plans partly to blame, too, I think. The human creature is not meant to live on the wing for more than a few weeks at a time, and if you would only have chosen a perch to your mind for the other few weeks, and settled down a bit; say at Hampstead or at Haslemere, where you could have spent the rainy hours in writing, and those delicious refreshing fragrant hours that follow them in our climate, every day in walking; and had thus too given yourself opportunity for a little human intercourse that had time to grow friendly, my national vanity makes me think you would have taken back as cordial a liking for the people as you have for the land.

"... I shall think of you a fortnight hence in the full delight of finding yourselves [Burroughs and his wife] once more at *Home* in the glorious sunny land."

John Burroughs answers from Esopus, New York, October the twenty-second, 1882 :—" I am resting in the hope and expectation that before long you will give yourself up and write the article on Walt Whitman, that we are all looking for. I feel sure that you will cut your way to the heart of this matter as no one has yet done. . . .

" I find I am not quite able to shake off the attractions of London even at this distance, and feel that I shall be back there again in a year or two. What is the secret of the attraction that London has, to such a city hater as I am ? I often ask myself this question; it seems to attract most people who have been there in the same way : it seems to me it is because of its thoroughly domestic and home look and air. It is a vast aggregation of actual homes, and seems to exist not for commerce or trade, like New York, but for life; there is something in the air and in the expression of things, that is different from—more tender and majestic—than anything I have experienced in cities at home.

"When you find time to write me—which I hope you will before long—tell me what you think about it— what this subtle charm of London, apart from its obvious advantages and benefits, is.

"Tell Herbert I recall our tramp with fondness, and only regret that we did not have more of them. . . ." The naturalist alludes to a walk from Rochester to Canterbury.

December the third, John Burroughs's last letter is answered :—"I am rejoiced old London has such a good pull upon you, and will draw you over here again before so very long. As to explaining the secret of its power, I cannot. It is too much a part of me, born and bred as I was there, for it to be possible for me to look at it from without, or to question it as a whole : it is a curious miscellaneous bundle of experiences and associations to me; happy, unhappy, indifferent; and sometimes it looks grand to me, and sometimes almost demoniac—with its miles of misery seething in the yellow murky air—and its hard and cruel prosperity—miles of that too : but I suppose neither the one nor the other is half so bad as it looks, and that there is a solid good heart and the best of brains within the monster.

"I have at last finished my little book ; a Life of Mary Lamb, the writing of which has been a great solace to me. It was a task that came to me unsought; but I

have not found it task-work : and now I am going to
put my heart into an article on Walt [Whitman] ; I
do not the least know whether or where I shall get it
published ; but anyhow I must try once more and give a
reason for the faith that is in me.    There is an article in
this month's *Nineteenth Century :* which I have not yet
seen, but Herby says it is good ; and that in spite of
some carping there is clear recognition of a new great
force in Walt.    [The article referred to is called *Walt
Whitman*, written by G. C. Macaulay.]

   " I like heartily your letter to the *Critic* on English
nature—but ' so as with a difference.'    I like the subtle
delicate discrimination, the fresh hearty enjoyment of our
beauties.    But why identify sublimity with size ?    And
nature knows how to take care of herself, and keeps a
bit of her own wildness even here—nay, with a sort of
rebound and ecstasy at her escape from the cares we
lavish on her.    A great painter can put sublimity in a
small canvas, if he has it in him, and so can nature.

   "I do much want you to see more of English humanity
when you come again, not ' society '—but a few men
and women in easy, friendly intercourse, such as
perhaps we can gather here from time to time ;
and I can answer for their taking cordially to you and
you to them."

   In July (1883) she was correcting the proofs of Mary
Lamb in conjunction with William Haines :—" Sometimes, in these last sheets I have feared my diligently
gathered scraps were not sufficiently *welded* and might
read *scrappy*—but perhaps getting it in sheets enhances
that defect.    I was so bent on making the *dramatis*

*personæ* speak themselves whenever possible, that I sacrificed to that, the idea of a *flowing* narrative—which would no doubt have been a tame flow, after all, compared to their pungencies and delightful idiosyncrasies.

"One thing I feel sure of, that this research into the domestic side of Lamb's life, has brought a very beautiful part of his nature into stronger relief than before; and also a very interesting period of his life—from twenty to thirty-five, before he had any literary fame." And to Mrs. Watson :—"Lamb's editors and biographers since Talfourd and Procter, have, it always seemed to me, dwelt unduly on his jokes (things which ill bear printing and reiterating) and left out of sight the serious and beautiful side of his character, and especially his friendship with Coleridge, which happily for me comes into strong relief in treating of Mary." And to William Rossetti she says :—"I think I must have owed it to a suggestion from you, that Mr. Ingram came to me to write the Life of Mary Lamb." Rossetti did propose his friend's name for the *Eminent Women Series*, though not specially in connection with Mary Lamb.

Many years ago, Cary (in a talk with Alexander Gilchrist) mentioned the "curious swiftness of Lamb's reading—'looked at a page as one does at a printed notice on a wall, not following line by line or word by word; one at first thought he was only looking over it.' 'Oh yes, Charles is reading it,' said Miss Lamb."

In 1883, the Life of Mary Lamb was published : Mary Cowden-Clarke wrote to the author (from Genoa), acknowledging a copy of the volume :—"Since its perusal, I am more than ever impatient to thank you;

for the exquisitely tender spirit in which you have achieved your task, the affectionate appreciation and loving reverence you have shown for that noble brother and sister,—the true insight you have yourself, and have given your readers, into the beautiful simplicity with large wisdom of *her* character,—move me to cordial gratitude and admiration; the way in which you have let passages from their own poems form a series of autobiographical revelations, the keen eloquent estimates you have given of their intellectual powers and heart-strength in few but pregnant lines at modestly rare intervals,—the delicacy, brevity, and justice of your reference at page 80,—the quiet but comprehensive sentence with which you close your book,—all win my warmest, my sincerest approbation, and combine to make me regard it as one of the most perfect pieces of biographical composition I ever read."

To H. Buxton Forman (a helpful friend in lending Lamb authorities) Anne Gilchrist writes, apropos of a volume in the *Series :*—" . . . I am so sorry you are not pleased with the *George Sand*. In regard to the charge of want of candour, it seems to me that, had Miss Thomas been dealing with the manuscript material inaccessible to the public, she would certainly have been open to the charge of uncandid suppression of damaging facts. But, having dealt only with printed material, and all those who care to know being familiar with the shady as well as the sunny side of George Sand's large nature, and these little books being on the face of them selections, condensations, small epitomes, and what the world wants above everything being to have its sym-

pathies drawn to what is great, noble, beautiful,—ideal;
I think it was more than justifiable, it was wise to dis-
miss very briefly, merely to hint at unprofitable details.
What say you to that long sentence of mine—and will
not you and Mrs. Forman be able to give us an evening before you go?"

To John Burroughs, on reading his essay on Carlyle,
she writes from Keats Corner, Hampstead, *September
the second* 1883 :—" Dear FRIEND : Just finished your
article on ' Carlyle ' in *The Century* ;" it grasps the subject masterfully and gives abundant food for reflection ;
so that I do not like to write hastily of it : but my
belief is that you have penetrated into the reality of
the man, and furnished some excellent clues to the
student of his life and writings.

"Curiously enough, I think you make a very bad
start in that quotation from Emerson, ' He has manly
superiority rather than intellectuality,' which is surely
as wide of the mark as it was possible to go. For
Carlyle's boundless complainings and wailings were *in
part* certainly a deficient manliness. And as for his
' intellectuality,' it is stupendous. But Emerson valued
abstract ideas above everything else, and if I may be
permitted to say so, did not realize that, after all, they
are only something *abstracted* from the actual—not
greater than it but a part of it, and that to see them
incarnated in man, in life, in the universe, is the gigantic
brain work, not to discourse ever so eloquently about
them *as* abstractions.

"I am venturing on great topics very hurriedly and
crudely—take it as only tea-table talk.

"One more point: Carlyle has not only not said the last word about Lamb, he has never even said one true word about him. And I think, could he return, the only words he has written he would passionately desire to blot out, are those about Lamb; for in them he has fixed himself to the gaze of posterity, as throwing mud at a hero. If courage, tenderness, long, long sustained endurance, generosity in thought, word and deed, un-repining acceptance of a hard destiny, and heart full to the brim of human love—be marks of the hero, Car-lyle was not worthy to untie the latchet of his shoes in regard to beauty of character. But I am glad to think, admiring and loving Carlyle as I do, that he wrote in ignorance—the true story of Lamb's life and character was not published, I think, till long after Carlyle wrote those words.

"As to Coleridge, I do not think he has said the last word either, far from it, but there was more excuse for his severe judgment. Nevertheless, Coleridge has left half-a-dozen perfect poems, and the memory of some beautiful friendships; and I do not think the world is so rich in those things it can afford to forget him.

"Good wishes and good-byes. ANNE GILCHRIST."

The acquaintance of Robert Perceval Graves (author of "The Life of Sir William R. Hamilton"), Sub-Dean of the Chapel Royal, Dublin, and formerly Curate-in-charge of Windermere, was made through Edward Dowden, in 1884 :—

*August the Third.*

"Dear Mr. Graves: Your letter and the book which came with it have carried on the intercourse

begun on those two days which will always stand out in
our memory lit up with unexpected sunshine—strangers
that we were one moment, and almost the next linked
with such bonds of sympathy, admiring and enjoying
together as old friends !

"The 'Reminiscences' of Wordsworth reinforce just
as one would desire the conception of him we form after
a careful and meditative study of his works ; of all his
works, his prose no less than his Poems. Indeed, I
think ' the strong intellect, strong feeling, sturdy, massive individuality ' you felt so conscious of in his presence
reveal themselves wonderfully in that noble essay on
*The Convention of Cintra.* I would cheerfully barter for
it the poems of his later life if need be. There is a
generous ardour, clear-sightedness, grasp, a lofty eloquence in it not easy to match. It really took me by
storm this winter.

"Many besides myself have and will, I doubt not, feel
very grateful to you for your just and sympathetic
explanation of what was unthinkingly or ungenerously
called his personal vanity and egotism. It is a charge
that has been laid at the door of other great poets. If
they did not believe in themselves and were not strongly
absorbed in the workings of their own genius, and did
not know that they have given the best expression they
were capable of to the subjects they have treated, they
would not be great poets. Add to this that they are
generally characterized by a candour amounting to
naïveté, and one sees what a handle they may give to
the thoughtless or the cynical ! "

Many years ago, Thomas Carlyle, when in conversation with Alexander Gilchrist, compared 'a man of genius to a burning ship which has been set on fire for the glorification of the spectators on land,' a saying which seems to illuminate the subject—with Carlyle's wonted flash of wit.

The study of Lamb brings the student into contact with Coleridge : the author of the Life of Mary Lamb felt the fascination of the poet's genius, indeed at this time thought of writing his life, only, as the following letter to Mrs. Watson shows, she was not in full sympathy with Coleridge's orthodoxy.

*November* 22 1884 :—" As to his Poetry, that the best he did is as perfect as anything in the language, brother poets and critics all agree. He is already a classic. In regard to his place as a philosopher, time and time only will decide the amount of permanent value in his work.

" In Poetry each perfect work remains a separate and enduring monument; what comes after adds to the world's riches, but does not supersede what went before. But in philosophy, which is at bottom, I suppose, the search for and the orderly setting forth of knowledge concerning the profoundest verities of man's nature and environment and their relations to each other, it sometimes happens that the new destroys, or at any rate renders of small value the old—the new light makes the old statements palpably inadequate or false. I have a deep conviction in my own mind that the new insight into nature and into the physical half of man, conquered on the one hand by Darwin in research, and on the other by the physicists, with their wondrous revelations of the active energetic nature of what we have regarded as dead inert matter (all its atoms in ceaseless, varied, complex movement) are bringing to light such an entirely new *point of departure* for the philosopher that he will leave behind all the old systems as abortive.

"Were Coleridge's master-mind (with the right physical temperament added to it) in its prime working here to-day, no doubt he would be the pioneer in a magnificent philosophical movement forward. But, as I said, time and great masters in these fields of thought must settle this.

"No candid, thoughtful mind can deny, I think, that Coleridge had in him the making, the gifts of a great philosopher, and also that the main calamity and weakness of his life so handicapped him, so undermined his powers of continuous concentration, that he has not left behind him any philosophical work which does the same justice to his splendid endowments of that kind, that his work as a Poet does; do not you think so? . . ."

[This letter was written before Traill's Life of the poet was published.]

Coleridge's biographer " should set before the reader the living breathing figure of the man, who was more ardently loved by the greatest men of his time and land than it has ever fallen to the lot of any poet to be—the man to whom Wordsworth wrote—

> " There is no grief, no sorrow, no despair
> No languor, no dejection, no dismay,
> No absence scarcely can there be for those
> Who love as we do ! "

And for whom Lamb cherished a life-long ardour of

affection and admiration that was the greatest joy of his sad, storm-clouded life. . . "

In this, her last letter to John Burroughs (*January* 19 1885) Carlyle is again discussed :—" Dear Friend : I feel not a little refreshed by your ' Carlyle,' which I have just read. It arrived at the busy Christmas time, since when the quiet moment for enjoying it was not easy to find. May it silence the host of little whipper-snappers who are crowing so loud here over what they take to be the humiliation of a great and proud spirit in the Froude Confessional.

" I agree in almost everything you say (and say so vigorously), with here and there an inward protest, that would make lively talk if we were together. By the by, I see with regret you adhere to your old dictum about Lamb. Lamb was to be judged by his life first, and his writings afterwards read in the light of that tragic story. And you must remember that when Carlyle wrote the mean judgment you quote, the story of his life was still unknown. Its silent uncomplaining heroism would have brought a blush of shame to Carlyle's cheek had he ever been at the pains to read it. . . .

" Did you notice in the last volume a passage from Carlyle's Journal about America that might have been written by Walt? I have it not at hand to quote, but the substance was this :—' American Anarchy. Yes ; it is huge, loud, ugly to soul and sense, raging wildly in that manner from shore to shore. But I ask myself sometimes, Could your Frederic Wilhelm, your wisest Frederic, by the strictest government, by any conceivable skill in the art of charioteering, guide America forward in what is its real task at present—task of turning a savage immensity into arability, utility, and readiness for becoming *human*, as fast and well as America itself, with its very anarchies, gasconadings, vulgarities, stupidities, is now doing? No; not by any means. That withal is perfectly clear to me this good while past.'"

Returning to the subject of *Elia*, she says :—" I wish before finally making up your mind about Lamb, you would read my little book and see if it does not make you like him better."

Walter White is an old friend whose acquaintance the reader made in Chapter five. Upon his retirement from assistant Secretaryship of the Royal Society, Anne Gilchrist says :—" It is, no doubt, wise to lay down the burthen of such large responsibilities as those you have carried so long and so successfully before they become overwhelming. And I think and hope the calmness and sense of freedom will bring good compensation for the loss of active interest and participation in the important work carried on by the Royal Society. If ever a man might feel his leisure well earned W. W. may.

" Perhaps you will take up the pen and write a brief autobiography by and by—always a valuable bequest to society from a sincere man."

Upon receiving a copy of *The Life of Sir William Rowan Hamilton*, from the author, she writes : " My dear Mr. Graves: It is a noble gift you have sent me. Accept my grateful thanks. Proud and full of pleasure in it do I feel—the pleasure only beginning, as I turn the leaves hastily, arrested here and there by something of especial interest. Although there is, I need not say, much that I am too ignorant to understand, yet I have such a strong interest and curiosity respecting those high and abstruse scientific topics he treats of, that I persevere and do not miss a line for the sake of the glimpses and hints I am now and then able to seize. Especially do I wrestle with the fragments on what he calls the metaphysics of physics, singularly attracted always by them.

" I rejoice to find there is quite a considerable number of Herschel's letters too. Have you seen a really magnificent portrait of him from a photograph, by Mrs. Cameron, in the June *Century* ? Also an interesting one of Sir William Herschel, the wonderful intensity of whose face reminds one curiously of Blake's.

" I trust you are feeling rested and refreshed by the trip to London. It is a delightful thing to be engaged in such a task,—in the study of and close companionship as it were of such a mind as Sir William Hamilton, and I cannot but think that some regrets will mingle with rejoicing when the work is completed. I see you have in this volume handled the delicate subject of Hamilton's one failing, and if I may be permitted to say so, have done it with that tenderness and consideration of the circumstances which is as essential to justice as to kindness."

On the premature death of the beloved and gifted nephew, Sidney Gilchrist Thomas, she writes to William Rossetti, *March* 15 1885 :—" I believe I may say that Sidney Thomas's death is a loss that extends far beyond the circle of his relations and friends.

Painted by Herbert Harlakenden Gilchrist. 1885.

ANNE GILCHRIST

" He naɑ conquered one tough problem in the realm of metallurgv, and would have conquered others ; for he haɑ very remarkable abilities, and his energy, industry and resource were inexhaustible, but he wore himself out prematurely."

And to the same friend, two months later, from Keats Corner, Hampstead : —" Mr. Aldrich's letter (which you have kindly sent me to read) does indeed confirm what I was surmising, that Walt Whitman's pecuniary resources are more than ever straitened; and it seems a kind of disgrace to his admirers (let alone his country) that the little needed to make his remaining years comfortable should not be in sòme way or other supplied to him. . . ."

The Aldrich here spoken of is ' The Hon. Chas. Aldrich, of Webster City, Iowa ' —a Farmer, and donor to his State Library of an important autograph-collection. He called in 1885 upon Mr. Rossetti, who had previously presented him with a considerable number of autographs.

*June the sixteenth* Anne Gilchrist writes :—" I am sorry to say my difficult breathing makes it a great effort to me to get about, but I am fairly well and busy at home."

A line taken from a letter to William Michael Rossetti, August the fourteenth, ends a correspondence which is the record of a memorable friendship :—" I am rejoiced to see your name on the Committee for the Hyde Park Demonstration "—held in connection or through the agency of Thomas Stead.

Mr. and Mrs. Frederick Wedmore, Mr. and Mrs.

James Sully, Miss Blind, Dr. Richard Garnett, Mr. Francis Edgeworth and others in the walks of science and letters, often called on Sunday afternoon at Keats Corner.

One Sunday in November, seated in the drawing-room opposite two masks, one of Keats, the other of Dante, she said: 'I cannot admire Keats's face, it is ignoble by that of Dante's." And of an engraved portrait by Houbraken of Lord Bacon (a print Walt Whitman had often admired for its "freedom and delicacy"),—"I am fond of my portrait of Bacon, yet, there is a curious twist—a moral squint—in his eyes, which is very painful to me.'

Amongst sympathizing friends—those who realize the serious nature of their friend's illness at this time, is Helen Zimmern. She writes to Grace Gilchrist, *November the fourteenth:*—". . . No one can know your mother, however slightly, without valuing her highly. I have honoured her from the first, and though I have not seen her often, have come to feel her presence a source of strength, and have looked to her judgment and calm wisdom as a support. . . ."

Early in 1882 Anne Gilchrist looked upon approaching death calmly; cheerfully finishing her "Life of Mary Lamb," then to write "A Confession of Faith," a "Life of Blake," for Leslie Stephen's Biographical Dictionary; and lastly to study Carlyle, his life and works, with a view to removing some of the mud heaped upon the hero's grave: but, for this last task her strength failed.

Towards the end of September difficult breathing

became more and more laboured—until, THE END—
Sunday evening, November the twenty-ninth; twenty-
four years, save a day, after her husband's death. . . .

It is impossible not to feel that a powerful brain has
gone to rest prematurely; that had the decided bent
of her mind towards science received early and special
training, fostered by favourable circumstances of life—
she would have contributed her quota of research. But
who shall regret that the actual conditions of life caused
her to move amongst poets and artists; that well
equipped, she bravely, successfully addressed herself to
the work or duty nearest at hand?

A little above the average height, she walked with an
even, light step. Brown hair concealed a full and
finely-chiselled brow, and her hazel eyes bent upon you
a bright and penetrating gaze. Whilst conversing her
face became radiant as with an experience of golden
years: humour was present in her conversation—flecks
of sunshine, such as sometimes play about the minds of
deeply religious natures. Her animated manner seldom
flagged, and charmed the taciturn to talking in his or
her best humour. Once, when speaking to Walt
Whitman of the beauty of the human speaking voice,
he replied 'The voice indicates the soul.' Hers,
with its varied modulations and blended tones, was the
tenderest, most musical voice ever to bless our ears.

  .  .  .  .  .  .

  " So angels walk'd unknown on earth,
   But when they flew were recognized."

*December* 1885, we received the following lines from
John Burroughs :—" Few men have had such a mother

as you : she was the only woman I have ever seen to whose strength of mind and character I humbly bowed. As I think of her death, a shadow comes over the whole of that beautiful land ; now she is gone I see how much she stood to me for all England. I have had many misgivings about her health ever since I saw her in '82. I feared that shortness of breath proceeded from some deep-seated danger. . . ."

Edward Dowden, in the same month, says :—" I shall always have the memory of her brightness, kindness, wisdom ; and of the varied learning and culture which appeared, as it were, under and through a genial humanity that put a spell on one beyond culture or learning.

" I had not known what the ' Academy ' told, that even then, though so bright, she knew that the shadow of death was advancing towards her. . . ?"

The Poet is last to linger over a grave covered with flowers :—

> " 15th December 1885.
>> Camden, United States, America.
>
> DEAR HERBERT,
>> I have received your letter.
>
> Nothing now remains but a sweet and rich memory —none more beautiful all time, all life all the earth—
>
> I cannot write anything of a letter to-day, I must sit alone and think.
>
>> WALT WHITMAN."

HOPE.

# ESSAYS.


## AN ENGLISHWOMAN'S ESTIMATE OF WALT WHITMAN.


## THREE GLIMPSES OF A NEW ENGLAND VILLAGE.


## A CONFESSION OF FAITH.

# AN ENGLISHWOMAN'S ESTIMATE OF WALT WHITMAN.

[FROM LATE LETTERS BY AN ENGLISH LADY TO WILLIAM MICHAEL ROSSETTI.]

*London; November* 20 1869.

THE great satisfaction which I felt in arranging, about two years ago, the first edition (or rather selection) of Walt Whitman's poems published in England has been, in due course of time, followed by another satisfaction—and one which, rightly laid to heart, is both less mixed and more intense. A lady, whose friendship honours me, read the selection last summer, and immediately afterwards accepted from me the loan of the complete edition, and read that also. Both volumes raised in her a boundless and splendid enthusiasm, ennobling to witness. This found expression in some letters which she addressed to me at the time, and which contain (I affirm it without misgiving, and I hope not without some title to form an opinion) about the fullest, farthest-reaching, and most eloquent appreciation of Whitman yet put into writing, and certainly the most valuable, whether or not I or other readers find cause for critical dissent at an item here and there. The most valuable, I say, because this is the expression of what *a woman* sees in Whitman's poems,—a woman who has read and thought much, and whom to know is to respect and esteem in every relation, whether of character, intellect, or culture.

I longed that what this lady had written should be published for the benefit of English, and more especially of American readers. She has generously acceded to my request. The ensuing reflections upon Whitman's poems contain several passages reproduced verbatim from the letters in question, supplemented by others which the same lady has added so as more fully to define and convey the impression which those unparalleled and deathless writings have made upon her.

W. M. ROSSETTI.

*June* 22 1869.—I was calling on [Mr. Madox Brown] a fortnight ago, and he put into my hands your edition of Walt Whitman's poems. I shall not cease to thank him for that. Since I have had it, I can read no other book : it holds me entirely spell-bound, and I go through it again and again with deepening delight and wonder.

*June* 23.—I am very sure you are right in your estimate of Walt Whitman. There is nothing in him that I shall ever let go my hold of. For me the reading of his poems is truly a new birth of the soul.

I shall quite fearlessly accept your kind offer of a loan of a complete edition, certain that great and divinely beautiful nature has not, could not infuse any poison into the wine he has poured out for us. And as for what you specially allude to, who so well able to bear it—I will say, to judge wisely of it—as one who, having been a happy wife and mother, has learned to accept all things with tenderness, to feel a sacredness in all? Perhaps Walt Whitman has forgotten—or, through some theory in his head, has overridden—the truth that our instincts are beautiful facts of nature, as well as our bodies; and that we have a strong instinct of silence about some things.

*July* 11.—I think it was very manly and kind of you to put the whole of Walt Whitman's poems into my hands; and that I have no other friend who would have judged them and me so wisely and generously.

I had not dreamed that words could cease to be words, and become electric streams like these. I do assure you that, strong as I am, I feel sometimes as if I had not bodily strength to read many of these poems. In the series headed " Calamus," for instance, in some of the " Songs of Parting," the " Voice out of the Sea," the poem beginning " Tears, tears," &c., there is such a weight of emotion, such a tension of the heart, that mine refuses to beat under it—stands quite still—and I am obliged to lay the book down for a while. Or again, in the piece called " Walt Whitman," and one or two others of that type, I am as one hurried through stormy seas, over high mountains, dazed with sunlight, stunned with a crowd and tumult of faces and voices, till I am breathless, bewildered, half-dead. Then come parts and whole poems in which there is such calm wisdom and strength of thought, such a cheerful breadth of sunshine, that the soul bathes in them renewed and strengthened. Living impulses flow out of these that make me exult in life, yet look longingly towards " the superb vistas of

Death." Those who admire this poem, and do not care for that, and talk of formlessness, absence of metre, and so forth, are quite as far from any genuine recognition of Walt Whitman as his bitter detractors. Not, of course, that all the pieces are equal in power and beauty, but that all are vital; they grew—they were not made. We criticise a palace or a cathedral; but what is the good of criticising a forest? Are not the hitherto-accepted masterpieces of literature akin rather to noble architecture; built up of material rendered precious by elaboration; planned with subtle art that makes beauty go hand in hand with rule and measure, and knows where the last stone will come, before the first is laid; the result stately, fixed, yet such as might, in every particular, have been different from what it is (therefore inviting criticism), contrasting proudly with the careless freedom of nature, opposing its own rigid adherence to symmetry to her wilful dallying with it? But not such is this book. Seeds brought by the winds from north, south, east, and west, lying long in the earth, not resting on it like the stately building, but hid in and assimilating it, shooting upwards to be nourished by the air and the sunshine and the rain which beat idly against that,—each bough and twig and leaf growing in strength and beauty its own way, a law to itself, yet, with all this freedom of spontaneous growth, the result inevitable, unalterable (therefore setting criticism at naught), above all things vital,—that is, a source of ever-generating vitality: such are these poems:—

" Roots and leaves themselves alone are these,
    Scents brought to men and women from the wild woods
        and from the pond-side,
    Breast sorrel and pinks of love, fingers that wind around
        tighter than vines,
    Gushes from the throats of birds hid in the foliage of
        trees as the sun is risen,
    Breezes of land and love, breezes set from living shores
        out to you on the living sea,—to you, O sailors !
    Frost-mellowed berries and Third-month twigs,
        offered fresh to young persons wandering out in
        the fields when the winter breaks up,
    Love-buds put before you and within you, whoever you
        are,
    Buds to be unfolded on the old terms.
    If you bring the warmth of the sun to them, they will
        open, and bring form, color, perfume, to you :
    If you become the aliment and the wet, they will become
        flowers, fruits, tall branches and trees."

And the music takes good care of itself too.   As if
it *could* be otherwise !   As if those " large, melodious
thoughts," those emotions, now so stormy and wild, now
of unfathomed tenderness and gentleness, could fail to
vibrate through the words in strong, sweeping, long-
sustained chords, with lovely melodies winding in and
out fitfully amongst them !   Listen, for instance, to the
penetrating sweetness, set in the midst of rugged
grandeur, of the passage beginning—

    " I am he that walks with the tender and growing
        night ;
    I call to the earth and sea half held by the night.

I see that no counting of syllables will reveal the

mechanism of the music; and that this rushing spontaneity could not stay to bind itself with the fetters of metre. But I know that the music is there, and that I would not for something change ears with those who cannot hear it. And I know that poetry must be one of two things,—either own this man as equal with her highest, completest manifestors, or stand aside, and admit that there is something come into the world nobler, diviner than herself, one that is free of the universe, and can tell its secrets as none before.

I do not think or believe this; but see it with the same unmistakable definiteness of perception and full consciousness that I see the sun at this moment in the noonday sky, and feel his rays glowing down upon me as I write in the open air. What more can you ask of the words of a man's mouth than that they should " absorb into you as food and air, to appear again in your strength, gait, face,"—that they should be " fibre and filter to your blood," joy and gladness to your whole nature?

I am persuaded that one great source of this kindling, vitalizing power—I suppose *the* great source—is the grasp laid upon the present, the fearless and comprehensive dealing with reality. Hitherto the leaders of thought have (except in science) been men with their faces resolutely turned backwards; men who have made of the past a tyrant that beggars and scorns the present, hardly seeing any greatness but what is shrouded away in the twilight, underground past; naming the present only for disparaging comparisons, humiliating distrust that tends to create the very barrenness it complains of;

bidding me warm myself at fires that went out to mortal eyes centuries ago ; insisting, in religion above all, that I must either " look through dead men's eyes," or shut my own in helpless darkness. Poets fancying themselves so happy over the chill and faded beauty of the past, but not making me happy at all,—rebellious always at being dragged down out of the free air and sunshine of to-day.

But this poet, this " athlete, full of rich words, full of joy," takes you by the hand, and turns you with your face straight forwards. The present is great enough for him, because he is great enough for it. It flows through him as a " vast oceanic tide," lifting up a mighty voice. Earth, " the eloquent, dumb, great mother," is not old, has lost none of her fresh charms, none of her divine meanings ; still bears great sons and daughters, if only they would possess themselves and accept their birthright,—a richer, not a poorer, heritage than was ever provided before,—richer by all the toil and suffering of the generations that have preceded, and by the further unfolding of the eternal purposes. Here is one come at last who can show them how ; whose songs are the breath of a glad, strong, beautiful life, nourished sufficingly, kindled to unsurpassed intensity and greatness by the gifts of the present.

" Each moment and whatever happens thrills me with joy.

" O the joy of my soul leaning poised on itself,— receiving identity through materials, and loving them,—observing characters, and absorbing them ! O my soul vibrated back to me from them !

" O the gleesome saunter over fields and hillsides!
 The leaves and flowers of the commonest weeds, the
   moist, fresh stillness of the woods,
 The exquisite smell of the earth at daybreak, and all
   through the forenoon.

" O to realize space!
 The plenteousness of all—that there are no bounds;
 To emerge, and be of the sky—of the sun and moon
   and the flying clouds, as one with them.

" O the joy of suffering,—
 To struggle against great odds, to meet enemies
   undaunted,
 To be entirely alone with them—to find how much
   one can stand!"

I used to think it was great to disregard happiness, to
press on to a high goal, careless, disdainful of it. But
now I see that there is nothing so great as to be capable
of happiness; to pluck it out of " each moment and
whatever happens;" to find that one can ride as gay
and buoyant on the angry, menacing, tumultuous waves
of life as on those that glide and glitter under a clear
sky; that it is not defeat and wretchedness which
come out of the storm of adversity, but strength and
calmness.

See, again, in the pieces gathered together under the
title " Calamus," and elsewhere, what it means for a
man to love his fellow-man. Did you dream it before?
These " evangel-poems of comrades and of love" speak,
with the abiding, penetrating power of prophecy, of a
" new and superb friendship;" speak not as beautiful
dreams, unrealizable aspirations to be laid aside in sober

moods, because they breathe out what now glows within
the poet's own breast, and flows out in action toward the
men around him.    Had ever any land before her poet,
not only to concentrate within himself her life, and, when
she kindled with anger against her children who were
treacherous to the cause her life is bound up with, to
announce and justify her terrible purpose in words of
unsurpassable grandeur (as in the poem beginning,
"Rise, O days, from your fathomless deeps"), but
also to go and with his own hands dress the wounds,
with his powerful presence soothe and sustain and
nourish her suffering soldiers, — hundreds of them,
thousands, tens of thousands,—by day and by night, for
weeks, months, years?

"I sit by the restless all the dark night; some are so
        young,
    Some suffer so much: I recall the experience sweet
        and sad.
    Many a soldier's loving arms about this neck have
        crossed and rested,
    Many a soldier's kiss dwells on these bearded lips :—"

Kisses, that touched with the fire of a strange, new,
undying eloquence the lips that received them!    The
most transcendent genius could not, untaught by that
"experience sweet and sad," have breathed out hymns
for her dead soldiers of such ineffably tender, sorrowful,
yet triumphant beauty.

    But the present spreads before us other things besides
those of which it is easy to see the greatness and beauty ;
and the poet would leave us to learn the hardest part of
our lesson unhelped if he took no heed of these ; and

would be unfaithful to his calling, as interpreter of man
to himself and of the scheme of things in relation to
him, if he did not accept all—if he did not teach "the
great lesson of reception, neither preference nor denial."
If he feared to stretch out the hand, not of condescend-
ing pity, but of fellowship, to the degraded, criminal,
foolish, despised, knowing that they are only laggards
in "the great procession winding along the roads of the
universe," "the far-behind to come on in their turn,"
knowing the "amplitude of Time," how could he
roll the stone of contempt off the heart as he does, and
cut the strangling knot of the problem of inherited
viciousness and degradation?   And, if he were not bold
and true to the utmost, and did not own in himself the
threads of darkness mixed in with the threads of light,
and own it with the same strength and directness that he
tells of the light, and not in those vague generalities
that everybody uses, and nobody means, in speaking on
this head,—in the worst, germs of all that is in the
best; in the best, germs of all that is in the worst,—
the *brotherhood* of the human race would be a mere
flourish of rhetoric.   And brotherhood is naught if it
does not bring brother's love along with it.   If the
poet's heart were not "a measureless ocean of love"
that seeks the lips and would quench the thirst of all, he
were not the one we have waited for so long.   Who
but he could put at last the right meaning into that
word "democracy," which has been made to bear such
a burthen of incongruous notions?

"By God! I will have nothing that all cannot have
    their counterpart of on the same terms!"

flashing it forth like a banner, making it draw the
instant allegiance of every man and woman who loves
justice.   All occupations, however homely, all developments of the activities of man, need the poet's recognition, because every man needs the assurance that for
him also the materials out of which to build up a great
and satisfying life lie to hand, the sole magic in the use
of them, all of the right stuff in the right hands.
Hence those patient enumerations of every conceivable
kind of industry :—

" In them far more than you estimated—in them far
    less also."

Far more as a means, next to nothing as an end ;
whereas we are wont to take it the other way, and think
the result something, but the means a weariness.   Out
of all come strength, and the cheerfulness of strength.
I murmured not a little, to say the truth, under these
enumerations, at first.   But now I think that not only
is their purpose a justification, but that the musical ear
and vividness of perception of the poet have enabled
him to perform this task also with strength and grace,
and that they are harmonious as well as necessary parts
of the great whole.

   Nor do I sympathize with those who grumble at the
unexpected words that turn up now and then.   A
quarrel with words is always, more or less, a quarrel
with meanings ; and here we are to be as genial and as
wide as nature, and quarrel with nothing.   If the thing
a word stands for exists by divine appointment (and
what does not so exist ?), the word need never be

ashamed of itself; the shorter and more direct, the
better.   It is a gain to make friends with it, and see it
in good company.  Here, at all events, "poetic diction"
would not serve,—not pretty, soft, colourless words,
laid by in lavender for the special uses of poetry, that
have had none of the wear and tear of daily life; but
such as have stood most, as tell of human heart-beats,
as fit closest to the sense, and have taken deep hues of
association from the varied experiences of life—those are
the words wanted here.   We only ask to seize and be
seized swiftly, overmasteringly, by the great meanings.
We see with the eyes of the soul, listen with the ears of
the soul ;  the poor old words that have served so many
generations for purposes, good, bad, and indifferent,
and become warped and blurred in the process, grow
young again, regenerate, translucent.   It is not mere
delight they give us,—*that* the "sweet singers," with
their subtly wrought gifts, their mellifluous speech, can
give too in their degree; it is such life and health as
enable us to pluck delights for ourselves out of every
hour of the day, and taste the sunshine that ripened the
corn in the crust we eat—I often seem to myself to do
that

Out of the scorn of the present came scepticism ;
and out of the large, loving acceptance of it comes
faith.   If *now* is so great and beautiful, I need no
arguments to make me believe that the *nows* of the past
and of the future were, and will be, great and beautiful
too.

" I know I am deathless.

I know this orbit of mine cannot be swept by the carpenter's compass.

I know I shall not pass, like a child's carlacue cut with a burnt stick at night.

I know I am august.

I do not trouble my spirit to vindicate itself or be understood.

" My foothold is tenoned and mortised in granite :

I laugh at what you call dissolution,

And I know the amplitude of Time."

" No array of terms can say how much I am at peace about God and Death."

You argued rightly that my confidence would not be betrayed by any of the poems in this book. None of them troubled me even for a moment; because I saw at a glance that it was not, as men had supposed, the heights brought down to the depths, but the depths lifted up level with the sunlit heights, that they might become clear and sunlit too. Always, for a woman, a veil woven out of her own soul—never touched upon even, with a rough hand, by this poet. But, for a man, a daring, fearless pride in himself, not a mock-modesty woven out of delusions—a very poor imitation of a woman's. Do they not see that this fearless pride, this complete acceptance of themselves, is needful for her pride, her justification? What! is it all so ignoble, so base, that it will not bear the honest light of speech from lips so gifted with " the divine power to use words? " Then what hateful, bitter humiliation for her, to have to give herself up to the reality! Do you think there is ever a bride who does not taste more or less this bitterness in her cup? But who put it there? It must surely be man's fault, not God's, that she has to say to herself, "Soul, look another way—you have no part in this. Motherhood is beautiful, fatherhood is beautiful; but the dawn of fatherhood and motherhood is not beautiful." Do they really think that God is ashamed of what He has made and appointed? And, if not, surely it is somewhat superfluous that they should undertake to be so for Him.

"The full-spread pride of man is calming and excellent
    to the soul,"

Of a woman above all. It is true that instinct of silence I spoke of is a beautiful, imperishable part of nature too. But it is not beautiful when it means an ignominious shame brooding darkly. Shame is like a very flexible veil, that follows faithfully the shape of what it covers,—beautiful when it hides a beautiful thing, ugly when it hides an ugly one. It has not covered what was beautiful here; it has covered a mean distrust of a man's self and of his Creator. It was needed that this silence, this evil spell, should for once be broken, and the daylight let in, that the dark cloud lying under might be scattered to the winds. It was needed that one who could here indicate for us "the path between reality and the soul" should speak. That is what these beautiful, despised poems, the "Children of Adam," do, read by the light that glows out of the rest of the volume: light of a clear, strong faith in God, of an unfathomably deep and tender love for humanity,—light shed out of a soul that is "possessed of itself."

" Natural life of me faithfully praising things,
  Corroborating for ever the triumph of things."

Now silence may brood again ; but lovingly, happily,
as protecting what is beautiful, not as hiding what is un-
beautiful ; consciously enfolding a sweet and sacred
mystery—august even as the mystery of Death, the
dawn as the setting : kindred grandeurs, which to eyes
that are opened shed a hallowing beauty on all that
surrounds and preludes them.

" O vast and well-veiled Death !
" O the beautiful touch of Death, soothing and benumbing a few moments, for reasons ! "

He who can thus look with fearlessness at the beauty
of Death may well dare to teach us to look with fearless,
untroubled eyes at the perfect beauty of Love in all its
appointed realizations.    Now none need turn away their
thoughts with pain or shame ; though only lovers and
poets may say what they will,—the lover to his own,
the poet to all, because all are in a sense his own.    None
need fear that this will be harmful to the woman.  How
should there be such a flaw in the scheme of creation
that, for the two with whom there is no complete life,
save in closest sympathy, perfect union, what is natural
and happy for the one should be baneful to the other ?
The utmost faithful freedom of speech, such as there is
in these poems, creates in her no thought or feeling that
shuns the light of heaven, none that are not as innocent
and serenely fair as the flowers that grow ; would lead,
not to harm, but to such deep and tender affection as
makes harm or the thought of harm simply impossible.

Far more beautiful care than man is aware of has been
taken in the making of her, to fit her to be his mate.
God has taken such care that *he* need take none ; none,
that is, which consists in disguisement, insincerity, painful hushing-up of his true, grand, initiating nature.
And, as regards the poet's utterances, which, it might be
thought, however harmless in themselves, would prove
harmful by falling into the hands of those for whom
they are manifestly unsuitable, I believe that even here
fear is needless.   For her innocence is folded round
with such thick folds of ignorance, till the right way and
time for it to accept knowledge, that what is unsuitable
is also unintelligible to her ; and, if no dark shadow
from without be cast on the white page by misconstruc-
tion or by foolish mystery and hiding away of it, no
hurt will ensue from its passing freely through her
hands.

This is so, though it is little understood or realized
by men.   Wives and mothers will learn through the
poet that there is  rejoicing grandeur and beauty there
wherein their hearts have so longed to find it ; where
foolish men, traitors to themselves, poorly comprehend-
ing the grandeur of their own or the beauty of a
woman's nature, have taken such pains to make her
believe there was none,—nothing but miserable discrepancy.

One of the hardest things to make a child understand
is, that down underneath your feet, if you go far
enough, you come to blue sky and stars again ; that
there really is no " down " for the world, but only in
every direction an " up."   And that this is an all-

embracing truth, including within its scope every created thing, and, with deepest significance, every part, faculty, attribute, healthful impulse, mind, and body of a man (each and all facing towards and related to the Infinite on every side), is what we grown children find it hardest to realize too. Novalis said, " We touch heaven when we lay our hand on the human body ; " which, if it mean anything, must mean an ample justification of the poet who has dared to be the poet of the body as well as of the soul,—to treat it with the freedom and grandeur of an ancient sculptor.

" Not physiognomy alone nor brain alone is worthy of
    the muse :—I say the form complete is worthier far.

" These are not parts and poems of the body only, but
    of the soul.

" O, I say now these are soul."

But while Novalis—who gazed at the truth a long wav off, up in the air, in a safe, comfortable, German fashion—has been admiringly quoted by high authorities, the great American who has dared to rise up and wrestle with it, and bring it alive and full of power in the midst of us, has been greeted with a very different kind of reception, as has happened a few times before in the world in similar cases. Yet I feel deeply persuaded that a perfectly fearless, candid, ennobling treatment of the life of the body (so inextricably intertwined with, so potent in its influence on the life of the soul) will prove of inestimable value to all earnest and aspiring natures, impatient of the folly of the long prevalent belief that it is because of the greatness of the

spirit that it has learned to despise the body, and to
ignore its influences; knowing well that it is, on the
contrary, just because the spirit is not great enough, not
healthy and vigorous enough, to transfuse itself into the
life of the body, elevating that and making it holy by
its own triumphant intensity; knowing, too, how the
body avenges this by dragging the soul down to the
level assigned itself. Whereas the spirit must lovingly
embrace the body, as the roots of a tree embrace the
ground, drawing thence rich nourishment, warmth, impulse. Or, rather, the body is itself the root of the
soul,—that whereby it grows and feeds. The great
tide of healthful life that carries all before it must surge
through the whole man, not beat to and fro in one
corner of his brain.

"O the life of my senses and flesh, transcending my
senses and flesh!"

For the sake of all that is highest, a truthful recognition of this life, and especially of that of it which
underlies the fundamental ties of humanity,—the love
of husband and wife, fatherhood, motherhood,—is
needed. Religion needs it, now at last alive to the fact
that the basis of all true worship is comprised in " the
great lesson of reception, neither preference nor denial,"
interpreting, loving, rejoicing in all that is created,
fearing and despising nothing.

" I accept reality, and dare not question it."

The dignity of a man, the pride and affection of a
woman, need it too. And so does the intellect. For
science has opened up such elevating views of the

mystery of material existence that, if poetry had
not bestirred herself to handle this theme in her
own way, she would have been left behind by her
plodding sister. Science knows that matter is
not, as we fancied, certain stolid atoms which the
forces of nature vibrate through and push and pull
about; but that the forces and the atoms are one
mysterious, imperishable identity, neither conceivable
without the other. She knows, as well as the poet,
that destructibility is not one of nature's words; that it
is only the relationship of things—tangibility, visibility
—that are transitory. She knows that body and soul
are one, and proclaims it undauntedly, regardless, and
rightly regardless, of inferences. Timid onlookers,
aghast, think it means that soul is body,—means death
for the soul. But the poet knows it means body is
soul,—the great whole imperishable; in life and in death
continually changing substance, always retaining identity. For, if the man of science is happy about the
atoms, if he is not baulked or baffled by apparent decay
or destruction, but can see far enough into the dimness
to know that not only is each atom imperishable, but
that its endowments, characteristics, affinities, electric
and other attractions and repulsions—however suspended, hid, dormant, masked, when it enters into new
combinations—remain unchanged, be it for thousands
of years, and, when it is again set free, manifest themselves in the old way, shall not the poet be happy about
the vital whole? shall the highest force, the vital, that
controls and compels into complete subservience for its
own purposes the rest, be the only one that is destruc-

x

tible? and the love and thought that endow the whole
be less enduring than the gravitating, chemical, electric
powers that endow its atoms? But identity is the
essence of love and thought,—I still I, you still you.
Certainly no man need ever again be scared by the
" dark hush " and the little handful of refuse.

" You are not scattered to the winds—you gather
　　certainly and safely around yourself."

" Sure as Life holds all parts together, Death holds all
　　parts together."

" All goes onward and outward: nothing collapses."

" What I am, I am of my body; and what I shall be,
　　I shall be of my body."

" The body parts away at last for the journeys of the
　　soul."

　　Science knows that whenever a thing passes from a
solid to a subtle air, power is set free to a wider scope
of action. The poet knows it too, and is dazzled as he
turns his eyes toward " the superb vistas of death."
He knows that " the perpetual transfers and promotions " and " the amplitude of time " are for a man as
well as for the earth. The man of science, with unwearied, self-denying toil, finds the letters and joins
them into words. But the poet alone can make complete sentences. The man of science furnishes the
premises; but it is the poet who draws the final conclusion. Both together are " swiftly and surely preparing a future greater than all the past." But, while
the man of science bequeaths to it the fruits of his toil,

the poet, this mighty poet, bequeaths himself—" Death making him really undying." He will " stand as nigh as the nighest" to these men and women. For he taught them, in words which breathe out his very heart and soul into theirs, that " love of comrades" which, like the " soft-born measureless light," makes wholesome and fertile every spot it penetrates to, lighting up dark social and political problems, and kindling into a genial glow that great heart of justice which is the life-source of Democracy. He, the beloved friend of all, initiated for them a " new and superb friendship;" whispered that secret of a god-like pride in a man's self, and a perfect trust in woman, whereby their love for each other, no longer poisoned and stifled, but basking in the light of God's smile, and sending up to Him a perfume of gratitude, attains at last a divine and tender completeness. He gave a faith-compelling utterance to that " wisdom which is the certainty of the reality and immortality of things, and of the excellence of things." Happy America, that he should be her son! One sees, indeed, that only a young giant of a nation could produce this kind of greatness, so full of the ardour, the elasticity, the inexhaustible vigour and freshness, the joyousness, the audacity of youth. But I, for one, cannot grudge anything to America. For, after all, the young giant is the old English giant,—the great English race renewing its youth in that magnificent land, " Mexican-breathed, Arctic-braced," and girding up its loins to start on a new career that shall match with the greatness of the new home.

# THREE GLIMPSES OF A NEW ENGLAND VILLAGE.

DOES the reader chance to know that bit of England round about Haslemere, but an hour and a half's journey from the heart of London, where three counties meet, and the traveller may see at a glance, from many a hill-top, the most rich and beautiful parts of Sussex, the wildest and most picturesque of Surrey and Hampshire? At his feet lies spread the weald of Sussex, whilst the dark-wooded promontories and long purple ridges of Blackdown, Marley, and Ironhill curve round or jut out into this broad sea of fertility, and the distant South Downs close the view with wavy outline and fluted sides, bare of everything save fine turf, nibbling sheep, and the shadows of the clouds. Turning round, Surrey culminates, as it were, in Hind Head, with triple summit—no mere hill, but a miniature mountain in bold individuality of form. And when he climbs this vantage-ground, Hampshire lies unfolded before him as well as Surrey; Wolmer Forest—forest no longer, but brown moorland; ranges of chalk hills, conspicuous among them one with a white scar on its dark flank, which hides Selborne amid its trees; solemn distances seen against the sunset sky, clothed with a deep purple bloom, which haunt the memory like a strain of noble music.

No less beautiful and strikingly similar in general character is that part of Western Massachusetts wherein stands our New England village—Northampton,—village in size and rural aspect, though the capital of Hampshire county. But the New England valley has one advantage over the weald of Sussex in its broad and beautiful river, with Indian name, Connecticut—Quonnektacut, the long river—which winds through it. Mount Holyoke and Mount Tom, the Sugar Loaf and the Pelham range, are its Blackdown, Marley, Hind Head, and South Downs. These hills are a couple of hundred feet or so higher than their English prototypes, ranging from 1000 to 1300 feet above the sea, and their old ribs are of harder and more ancient stuff than the chalk and greensand of the South Downs and Surrey hills; witness the granite or rather gneiss boulders scattered broadcast over the land, sometimes in rugged upright masses, looking like some grey ruin, sometimes in small rounded fragments, bestrewing the uplands like a flock of sheep, and more rarely the black and still harder blocks of trap. In the museum at Amherst, just over the river, are preserved slabs with the famous bird-tracks—colossal footprints two feet long, found in the trias of this part of the Connecticut valley—all tending to prove that the sun shone down upon dry land here for some ages whilst the mother-country was still mostly a waste of waters; and that, geologically speaking, and so far as these parts at any rate are concerned, New England is old, and old England new, by

comparison. Broad, fertile, level meadows border the
river, and the hills are richly clothed with chestnut, birch,
hemlock (somewhat like the yew in aspect), hickory (a
kind of walnut), beech, oak, and so forth. It is hard to
say whether the likeness or the unlikeness to an English
landscape strikes the traveller more. There is the all-
pervading difference of a dry and brilliant atmosphere,
which modifies both form and colour, substituting the
sharp-edged and definite for the vague and rounded in
distant objects, and brilliancy and distinctness of hue
for depth and softness. Apart, too, from the brilliant
and searching light, the leaves are absolutely of a lighter
green, and grow in a less dense and solid mass ; the
foliage looks more feathery, the tree more spiral. Especially is this so with the American oak, which has
neither the dome-like head, the sturdiness of bough, nor
the dark bluish-green foliage of the English oak. If it
be spring-time, no gorse is to be seen with golden
blossom set among matted thorns, perfuming the sunshine ; but everywhere abounding masses of the delicate
pink-clustered, odourless, waxlike kalmia, called there
laurel and growing to the full size of our laurels ; and
more shyly hidden, the lovely azalea or swamp-pink, as
the country people call it. Instead of the daisy, the
delicate little Housatonia, like Venus's looking-glass but
growing singly, stars the ground ; and for fragrance we
must stoop down and seek the pale pink clusters of the
trailing arbutus or May-flower, which richly reward the
seeker. In July we miss the splendid purpling of the
hills with heather blossom ; but the pink spikes of the
hardhack abound ; gay lilies, lady's ear-rings, blue-

fringed gentians, glowing cardinal flowers (*Lobelia car-dinalis*), with slender petals of a deeper crimson than the salvia, and a host more new friends, or old friends with new ways grown democratic as befits them, scatter their beauty freely by the wayside and the margins of the brooks, instead of setting up as exclusives of the garden.

Nor are the differences less marked in the aspect of the cultivated land. The fertile valley has perhaps a look of greater breadth from not being intersected with hedges and having few fences of any kind, one crop growing beside another, and one owner's beside another's, like different beds in a nursery-garden. But the effect of these large undivided fields is to dwarf the appearance of the crops themselves. The patches of tall tasselled Indian corn, the white-blossomed buckwheat, and large-leaved tobacco, look diminutive. No haystacks, no wheat-ricks are to be seen; only here and there a lonely, prison-like tobacco barn or drying-house, full of narrow loopholes to let in air without light. Everything else is housed in the big barn that adjoins the farmhouse, which stands, not amid its own fields, but on the outskirts of the nearest town or village. Of wheat little is grown; of root-crops still less, for sheep-farming is not in favour. Tobacco, with its large, glossy dark leaves, like those of the mangel-wurzel, thrives well on the rich alluvial soil of the Connecticut valley; but, fluctuating as it is in value, exhaustive of the soil, and easily damaged by weather, the great gains of one year are often more than counterbalanced by the losses of the next. The Indian corn remains long upon

the ground in autumn after it is cut, to ripen in stooks,
much as beans do with us ; and then come to light the
pumpkins which were sown amongst it, and now lie
basking and glowing in the sun like giant oranges.
Glowing, too, in the splendid sunshine, are the apple-
orchards, laden with fruit half as large and quite as red
as full-blown peonies. Never, even in the vale of
Evesham or in Herefordshire, have I seen any so
beautiful.

As to the living creatures—feathered, four-legged, or
no-legged—there are some conspicuous differences which
it does not take a naturalist to discover. Ten to one,
indeed, if we come upon a rattlesnake ; but a few are
still left in snug corners of Mount Holyoke and Mount
Tom, as anxious to avoid us as we them. The lively
little chipmuck, diminutive first cousin to the squirrel,
with black stripe along the back, is sure to make our
acquaintance, for his kind seems as multitudinous as the
rabbit with us, and is a worse foe to the farmer, because
he has more audacity and a taste for the kernels of things,
instead of merely the leaves. Strange new sounds greet
the ear from katydid " working her chromatic reed " ;
from bull-frog with deep low, almost a roar ; from
grasshoppers and locusts, whose loud brassy whirr
resounds all through the sunny hours with such persistency it seems at last a very part of the hot sunshine.
The chirp of our grasshoppers is the mere ghost of a
sound in comparison. At night fireflies glance in and
out of the darkness ; and, if we remain under the trees,
mosquitoes soon make us unpleasantly aware of their
existence. As to the birds, the flame-coloured oriole,

the delicately shaped blue-bird, flit by now and then as
flashes of surprise and delight from the south; the rose-
breasted grossbeak has a sweet note; the robin, not
round as a ball and fierce and saucy, but grown tall, and
slim, and mild—his breast not so red, his song not so
sweet, his eye not so bright—is there.   He is indeed a
robin only in name,—really a species of thrush.   A
cheerful twittering, chirping, whistling, the tuning of the
orchestra, a short sweet snatch or two of song I heard;
but the steady, long-sustained outpour of rich melody
from throats never weary, the chorus trilling joyously,
with which our woods and hedgerows resound in spring
and early summer, I listened for in vain.   Perhaps the
pathlessness of the woods and hills prevented my penetrating to the secluded haunts of the sweetest singers,
such as the hermit-thrush, and I speak only of New
England.   Remembering what John Burroughs has
said on the subject, I will not venture to generalise the
comparison.

GLIMPSE THE FIRST.

About two hundred and forty years ago, towards the
close of Cromwell's life, and thirty-four years after the
landing of the Pilgrim Fathers, the Boston and Plymouth
Settlement found itself vigorous enough to send out off-
shoots; and having heard from the Dutch settlers of
New York of this rich and well-watered valley discov-
ered by them in 1614, the General Court appointed
John Pynchon, Elizur Holyoke, and Samuel Chapin,
of Springfield, settled seventeen years before, to nego-
tiate with the Indians for that tract of land called

Nonotuck, where now stand six small towns and villages, chief and first built of which was Northampton.
The price paid was a hundred fathoms of wampum
(equal to about £20), ten coats, some small gifts, and
the ploughing up of sixteen acres on the east side of the
river. Wampum (Indian for white) consisted of strings
of beads made of white shells and *suckauhock* black or
blue money, of black or purple shells. Both were
used for more purposes than trading with the Indians,
coin being scarce. Eight white and four black beads
were worth a penny ; and a man as often took out a
string of beads as a purse to pay an innkeeper or a
ferryman, or to balance a trading account.

But Nonotuck was paid for with a good deal besides
the wampum and the ploughing. For a hundred and
twenty-four years there was almost incessant warfare
with the Indians. Treacherous ambuscades lay in wait
for the trader on his journey, stealthy dark-skinned
assassins for the solitary husbandman, and not a few of
these fertile fields were watered by the blood of its first
tillers. He carried his weapons with him to his work
and to the meeting-house, and expressed his gratitude
for hairbreadth escapes, Puritan fashion, by the pious
names he gave his children. Preserved Clapp, Submit
Grout, Comfort Domo, Thankful Medad, are names
that figure in the records of this and the neighbouring
villages ; where we read also that one- Praise-Ever
Turner, and his servant Uzackaby Shakspeare, were
killed by the Indians. Within sight of Northampton
it was, just over the river, in the sister settlement of
Hadley,—that beautiful old village, with street eighteen

rods wide, set with a double avenue of superb elms, greensward in the middle and a road on either side, looking more like the entrance to a fine park than a village street,—here it was that a "deliverance" occurred, long believed by the people to have been miraculous. One Sunday, when nearly the whole scant population was gathered for worship in the meeting-house, a large body of Indians fell upon them, and, what with the panic and the want of a leader, all seemed lost, when a majestic, venerable figure, dressed in a strange rich garb, fully armed, appeared suddenly in their midst, assumed the command, rallied their scattered numbers, and led them on to victory ; then vanished as suddenly as he had appeared, no man knew where or whence.* No man but one—Mr. Russell, the minister. This venerable apparition was Goffe, once a general in Cromwell's army, and, like Whalley, his companion in exile, one of the judges who condemned Charles to death, now forced, even in that far land, to hide for his life, since an active quest was maintained, in obedience to the Home Government, for both Goffe and Whalley. For twelve years did good Mr. Russell shelter them, unknown to all but his own family. Whalley died in his house ; but Goffe subsequently disappeared, and the rest of his career is unknown.

Altogether the hardy band found ample scope for carrying into practice the noble maxim of the Pilgrim Fathers rehearsed at Leyden. "All great and honour-

---

* Sir Walter Scott, Fenimore Cooper, Miss Sedgwick, and Hawthorne in his story of "The Gray Champion," have all made use of this striking incident.

ESSAYS.

able actions are accompanied with great difficulties, and must be enterprised and overcome with answerable courages." In order to secure protection from Indians and wolves, the little community built its dwellings, not each isolated on its own farm-lands, but side by side, so as to form at once the main street; each house having its "home lot" or strip of "interval," as the rich meadow-land stretching down to the river was called, and its "wood lot" on the hillside. Having chosen her "select men to direct all the fundamental affairs of the town; to prevent anything which they judge shall be of damage, and to order anything which shall be for the good of the town; to hear complaints, arbitrate controversies, lay out highways, see to the scouring of ditches, the killing of wolves, and the training of children," Northampton proceeded at once to build herself a meeting-house " of sawen timber 26 feet long and 18 feet wide," for the sum of £14 sterling, to be paid in work or corn. There was no clock in the settlement: so the worshippers were called together, sometimes by a large cow-bell, sometimes by drum, and finally by trumpet, for the blowing of which Jedediah Strong had a salary of eighteen shillings a year. There was no minister for some years; and more finding in themselves a vocation for preaching than for listening, or at any rate for criticising than for meekly imbibing, disputes arose, the General Court was appealed to, and its decision enforced that the service should consist, besides praying and singing, of "the reading aloud of known godly and orthodox books;" and for those who failed to obey with seemly decorum the summons of Mr. Jedediah Strong's

trumpet, severe was the chastisement. Joe Leonard
and Sam Harmon, for instance, " who were seen to whip
and whisk one another with a stick before the meeting-
house door," were fined five shillings; and Daniel, " for
idle watching about and not coming to the ordinances
of the Lord," was adjudged worthy of stripes to the
number " of five, *well laid on*." In 1672 the town voted
that there be some sticks set up in the " meeting-house,
with fit persons placed near, to use them as occasion
shall require, to keep the youth from disorder." Which
staves were fitted with a hare's foot at one end and his
tail at the other; the former to give a hard rap to mis-
behaving boys, the latter a gentle reminder to sleeping
women.

Something besides repression was done, however, for
the benefit of the youth of Northampton. The first
school was started in 1663,—the master to receive £6
a-year and his charges for tuition. Bridges were built
and roads made by calling out every man to labour
according to his estate; and those who did not labour
paid in grain at the rate of half-a-crown a day for ex-
emption. For more than sixty years Northampton had
no doctor, only a bone-setter: on the whole, a lucky
circumstance perhaps, considering what were the remedies
then chiefly in vogue. Sylvester Judd, from whose
' History of Hadley,' and also from Dr. Holland's
' History of Western Massachusetts,' the foregoing
details have been gathered, gives a curious list, taken
from medical prescriptions of the time :—the fat of a
wild cat, blood of a goat, of an ass, of a white pigeon
taken from under the wing, the tongue and lungs of a

fox, liver of an eel and of a wolf, horns of a bug (beetle), teeth of a sea-horse, bone from the heart of a stag, the left foot of a tortoise, and so forth.

After the Indian and the French and Indian wars were over, there was but a short interval of rest before the War of Independence began. The long rugged battle with the savage and the wilderness had done its work well in training men for the struggle which was to sunder all bonds, and convert the colony into a new nation, master of its own destiny. Northampton was not the scene of any battles; but bore its part in furnishing some brave and leading men, and money, or money's worth, to the army. After the war was over, came a time of depression and disorganisation in public affairs and in trade, which culminated hereabouts in what is known as Shay's Rebellion, so named from its leader; but it was soon quelled, and peace and prosperity settled down upon Northampton and upon the whole land.

## GLIMPSE THE SECOND.

If we lift a corner of the veil of time at the opening of the present century, we find our handful of settlers become a population of 4000,—there was no immigration in those days to swell the numbers by thousands and tens of thousands at a blow,—and possessed of resources for their social and intellectual welfare pretty much on a par with those of an English country town at that date of the same size: a little behind still in material comforts and luxuries, a little ahead in the amount of mental activity and the spirit of progress generated partly by more complete self-dependence, by the great and stirring times men had just passed through, and by hereditary influences from the parent stock, which was the pick of Old England in these qualities.

The spirit of fellowship thrives where all are fellow-workers. There comes, it would seem, a happy transition time between the struggles, privations, isolation of the pioneers, and the wealth, luxury, and poverty (grim skeleton in the cupboard of advancing prosperity), when there yet remains a good measure of that sense of neighbourship necessarily developed, when no man is independent of the free help and good will of others, no man is born with a silver spoon in his mouth,—a time, in short, when sociability is and "society" is not, and those to whom the lines have fallen in pleasant places can stretch out a friendly hand to the less fortunate without suspicion of condescension or patronage.

For sample, we will take a single group, the door of whose hospitable house has been set open for us by the privately printed memoirs of Mrs. Anne Jean Lyman. The inmates are a judge, his wife, and a large family of children of all ages, for he has been twice married. The judge is a genuine product of the soil, his family having for at least three generations back been settled in North-ampton. His wife, who is from the neighbourhood of Boston, of Scotch ancestry on one side, and on the other descended from Anne Hutchinson (the eloquent woman-preacher, who, banished for heterodoxy from their settlement by the Pilgrim Fathers, was killed by the Indians in 1643), may be taken as a good but a typical instance of the New England woman of that day—capable, practical, aspiring, intellectual, friendly above all.

There are no stirring adventures, no record of any achievements of genius in these memoirs, but the unpretending pages reflect a clear image of two fine characters, well adjusted to the social conditions amid which they lived. Both had beauty and dignity of person, warm sympathies, good brains, abundant energy, and a spirit of hospitality which made their home the focus where the worth and intellect of the village were wont to gather and to shine brightest and warmest. Northampton has now its row of thriving stores, to which the people from neighbouring villages flock on market-days, making a cheerful bustle. The elms, planted by the pioneers on either side the street, from the boughs of one of which Jonathan Edwards had preached to the Indians, now spread a goodly shade. A four-horse stage from Boston, ninety miles distant, comes in every evening with bugle-horn sounding gaily. The driver is the personal friend of the whole town, for his tenacious memory never lets slip a single message or commission —save on one memorable occasion, when he forgot to bring back his wife who had been visiting in Boston, and so furnished the village with a long-enduring joke. The social judge, when he hears the horn, takes his hat and with alert step and cheerful face glowing in the evening light, hastens to Warner's Tavern where the coach draws up, to welcome the arrivals and bring any friend who may be among them to his own home—and any stranger too, who seems in ill-health or sorrow, and not likely to be made comfortable at an inn. When

Y

the judge and his wife go yearly to Boston, a throng of neighbours flock into the library overnight, where the packing goes on, not only to take an affectionate leave, but to bring parcels of every size and commissions of every variety,—a pattern with request to bring back dresses for a family of five; and "could they go to the orphan asylum and see if a good child of ten could be bound out till she was eighteen? and if so, bring her back." One requests them to call and seek a sick mother at Sudbury, another a sick sister at Ware. Finally, a little boy, with bundle as large as himself, asks "if this would be too big to carry to grandmother?" "I'll carry anything short of a cooking-stove," says the kind lady; and wherever the stage stops to change horses, she runs round to hunt up the sick friend or deliver the parcel.

Here is a picture, in brief, of a day of home-life at a later period when the children are mostly grown up and the judge has retired from the Bench. It is the grey dawn of a summer's day, and the mother is already up and doing, while the rest of her large family, all but the husband, are still asleep. Dressed in short skirt and white *sacque*, she goes with broom and duster to her parlour and dining-room, opens wide the windows to the sweet morning air and the song of the birds, and puts all in order. At six o'clock she calls up her two maids, puts on her morning-dress and white cap, takes the large work-basket that always stands handy in the corner— for she mends not only for the family but for the maids and the hired man—and works till breakfast, when often fifteen or twenty cheerful souls assemble round the table.

After which, with help of children and grandchildren, the dishes are swiftly washed, the table cleared, and husband and wife are then wont to take their seat at the front door, that they may greet the passers-by or send messages to neighbours: she with the work-basket and the book that always lay handy under the work— some essay, poem, history, novel (for she is an omnivorous reader, and her letters intelligently discuss current literary topics)—or with the peas and beans to shell and string for dinner; he with the newspaper. Among the passers-by with whom they chat come, at certain seasons of the year, the judges of the Supreme Court and other notable men,—Baron Renné, Henry Clay, Daniel Webster, Emerson, too, while he was yet a young unknown Unitarian minister. Seldom does the large family sit down to dinner without guests, for anyone who drops in is asked to stay, or some wearied-looking passer-by is pressed to step in. In the afternoon the mother's chosen seat is at the window of the west parlour looking towards the hills, and then the young people flock around while she reads aloud through the long summer afternoons. All must share in her enjoyment, and often is the wayfarer, some "good neighbour" or "intellectual starveling," beckoned in "just to hear this rich passage we are reading,—it won't take long." If she finds any with a strong desire for knowledge, she never rests till the means to supply the want are found, and more than one youth of promise afterwards fulfilled owed his first good chance in life to this wise, generous-hearted woman.

GLIMPSE THE THIRD.

Northampton to-day carries her two hundred and thirty odd years lightly, and, save for the lofty and venerable elms, looks as young as the youngest of towns.   How, indeed, can anything but the trees ever look old in America, since the atmosphere does not furnish old Time with moisture enough to write the record of his flight in grey tones and weather stains, and lichens, and worn and crumbling edges?   Hawthorne's "old mause" at Concord was the only ancient-looking house I saw.   Either it had never been painted, or the paint was all worn off, and so the wooden walls had taken a silver-grey colour, and, with its picturesque situation close to the Concord river and by the side of the field in which was fought the first battle in the War of Independence, it well deserves the honour and renown that have settled on it, both as associated with Emerson's ancestors, his own early days, and with Hawthorne's romance.   But in general the yearly fresh coat of paint is a sort of new birth to the old houses, which makes them indistinguishable from modern ones, wood being still the material used in country-places for detached houses.   But step inside some one or two of these pretty modest-looking cottages, under the shade of the Northampton elms, and you will find the low ceiling, the massive beams, small doors and windows, corner cupboards, and queer ups and downs along the passages, which tell that they were put up by hands long since mouldered in the grave, and make you feel as if you were at home again in some old Essex village.

Socially, the little town may be regarded as a kind of Cranford—but Cranford with a difference. There is the same preponderance of maiden ladies and widows—for what should the men do there? New England farming is a very slow and unprofitable affair compared with farming in the West, and there are no manufactures of any importance. There are the same tea-parties, with a solitary beau in the centre, " like the one white flower in the middle of a nosegay ;" the same modest goodness, kindliness, refinement, making the best of limited means and of restricted interests. But even under these conditions the spirit of enterprise and of public spirit lurks in an American Cranford, and strikes out boldly in some direction or other. What would Miss Jenkyns have said to the notion of a college which should embody the most advanced ideas for giving young women precisely the same educational opportunities as young men? · She would justly have felt that it was enough to make Dr. Johnson turn in his grave. Yet such a scheme has been realised by one of the maiden ladies of Northampton or its immediate neighbourhood, in Smith College—a really noble institution ; where, also, the experiment is being tried of housing the students, not in one large building, but in a cluster of pretty-looking, moderate-sized homes, standing amid lawn and garden, where they are allowed, under certain restrictions, to enter into and receive the society of the village, so that their lives may not be a too monotonous routine and " grind."

Another maiden lady has achieved a still more remarkable success, for she had no wealth of her own to

enable her to carry out her idea—which was, to perfect
and to introduce on a large scale the method, devised in
Spain some hundred years ago, developed by Heinicke,
a German, by Bell of Edinburgh, and by his son, in a
system of "visible speech,"—for enabling the deaf and
dumb to speak, not with the fingers but the voice,
dumb no longer, and to hear with the eyes, so
to speak, by reading the movements of the lips.
Miss Harriet Rogers, who had never witnessed this
method in operation, began by teaching a few pupils
privately till her success induced a generous inhabitant
of Northampton, Mr. Clarke, to come forward with
£10,000 to found a Deaf and Dumb Institution, of
which her little school formed the nucleus, and her unwearied devotion and special gifts the animating soul.
Step into a class-room in one of these cheerful-looking
houses, surrounded by gay flower borders and well-kept
lawns, standing on a hill just outside the town,—for
here, too, the plan of a group of buildings has been
adopted. About twenty children, boys and girls, are
ranged, their faces eagerly looking towards a lady who
stands on a raised platform. Her presence conveys a
sense of that gentle yet resistless power which springs
from a firm will, combined with a rich measure of sympathy and affection. She raises her hand a little way,
and then moves it slowly along in a horizontal direction.
The children open their mouths and utter a deep sustained tone, a plaintive, minor, wild, yet not unmusical
sound. She raises it a little higher, and again moves it
slowly along. The children immediately raise the pitch
of their voices and sustain a higher tone. Again the

voices, following the hand, sustain a yet higher, almost a shrill note. Then the hand waves up and down rapidly, and the tones faithfully follow its lead in swift transition, till they seem lost in a maze of varying inflexions; but always the voices are obedient to the waving hand. The teacher then makes a round O with thumb and forefinger, gradually parting them like the opening of the mouth. This is the sign for crescendo and diminuendo. The voices begin softly, swell into a great volume of sound, then die away again, still with those peculiar plaintive tones; yet much do the children seem to enjoy the exercise, though, to most of them, remember, the room is all the while soundless as the grave. They learn to vary the pitch of their voices partly by feeling with the hand the vibrations of the throat and chest,—quick and in the throat for high tones, slow and in the chest for low ones,—partly by help of Bell's written signs, which represent the position peculiar to each sound of the various organs of speech —throat, tongue, lips, and back of the mouth. This was a class of beginners chiefly learning to develop and control their hitherto unused voices. Inexhaustible is the patience, wonderful the tact employed by Miss Rogers and her able assistants in the far more difficult task of teaching actual speech. A small percentage of the children will prove too slow and blunt of perception ever to master it, and will have to be sent where the old finger alphabet is still the method in use. Some, on the other hand, will succeed so brilliantly that it will be impossible for a stranger to detect that they were once deaf mutes,—that they seize your words with their eyes, not with their ears, and have never heard the sound of human speech, though they can speak. And the great bulk will return to their homes capable of understanding in the main what is going on around them, and of making themselves intelligible to their friends without recourse to signs.

Our actual Cranford over the sea, then, has a considerable advantage over the Cranford of romance, in that her heroines do not wait for the (in fiction) inevitable, faithful, long-absent, mysteriously-returning-at-the-right-moment lover to redeem their lives from triviality, and renew their faded bloom. And, in the present state of the world's affairs, what is more needed than the single woman who succeeds in making her life worth living, honourably independent, and of value to others ? Through such will certainly be given new scope and impetus to the development of woman generally, and in the long-run, therefore, good results for all.

Among the solid achievements of Northampton must also be mentioned an excellent free library, with spacious airy reading-room, such as any city might be proud of. There is also a State lunatic asylum, with large farm attached, which not only supplies the most restorative occupation for those of the inmates who are capable of work, but defrays all the expenses of the institution, with an occasional surplus for improvements.

If I were asked what, after some years spent in America, impressed me most unexpectedly, I should say of the people, as of the New England landscape, So like ! yet so different ! I speak, of course, not of superficial differences, but of mental physiognomy and temperament. Given new conditions of climate, soil, space, with their subtle, slow, yet deep and sure modifying influences,—new qualities to the pleasures of life, new qualities to its pains and struggles, new social and political conditions, new mixing of old races, different antecedents, the primitive wrestle with nature by a people not primitive but inheriting the habits and characteristics of advanced civilisation,—and how can there but result the shaping of a new race out of old world stock, a fresh instrument in the great orchestra of humanity ? Indicate these differences, these traits ! says the impatient reader. They are too subtle for words, like the perfume of flowers, the flavour of fruit,—too much intermingled with individual qualities also, at any rate for mere descriptive words, though no doubt in time the imaginative literature of America will creatively embody them.

One lesson whoever has lived in, not merely travelled through America, must learn perforce. It is that the swift steamers bringing a succession of more or less keen observers, the telegrams and newspapers, which we fondly imagine annihilate space and make us fully cognisant of the character and affairs of our far-off kindred, are by no means such wonder-workers. In spite of newspapers, and telegrams, and travellers, and a common language and ancestry, we are full of misconceptions about each other. Nay, I found the actual condition of my own country drift slowly out of intelligible sight after a year or two's absence. Even if every word uttered and printed were true, that which gives them their significance cannot be so transmitted ; whilst the great forces that are shaping and building up a people's life and character work silently beneath the surface, so that truly may it be said of a nation, as of an individual, " The heart knoweth its own bitterness, and a stranger intermeddleth not with its joy." Save by the help of vital literature—in that, at last, the souls of the nations speak to one another.

# A CONFESSION OF FAITH.

" OF genius in the Fine Arts," wrote Wordsworth, " the only infallible sign is the widening the sphere of human sensibility for the delight, honour, and benefit of human nature. Genius is the introduction of a new element into the intellectual universe, or, if that be not allowed, it is the application of powers to objects on which they had not before been exercised, or the employment of them in such a manner as to produce effects hitherto unknown. What is all this but an advance or conquest made by the soul of the poet? Is it to be supposed that the reader can make progress of this kind like an Indian prince or general stretched on his palanquin and borne by slaves? No; he is invigorated and inspirited by his leader in order that he may exert himself, for he cannot proceed in quiescence, he cannot be carried like a dead weight. Therefore to create taste is to call forth and bestow power."

A great poet, then, is " a challenge and summons; " and the question first of all is not whether we like or dislike him, but whether we are capable of meeting that challenge, of stepping out of our habitual selves to answer that summons. He works on Nature's plan: Nature, who teaches nothing but supplies infinite material to learn from; who never preaches but drives

home her meanings by the resistless eloquence of effects.
Therefore the poet makes greater demands upon his
reader than any other man. For it is not a question of
swallowing his ideas or admiring his handiwork merely,
but of seeing, feeling, enjoying, as he sees, feels, enjoys.
" The messages of great poems to each man and woman
are," says Walt Whitman, " come to us on equal terms,
only then can you understand us. We are no better than
you ; what we enclose you enclose, what we enjoy you
may enjoy "—no better than you potentially, that is ; but
if you would understand us the potential must become
the actual, the dormant sympathies must awaken and
broaden, the dulled perceptions clear themselves and let
in undreamed of delights, the wonder-working imagination must respond, the ear attune itself, the languid soul
inhale large draughts of love and hope and courage,
those " empyreal airs " that vitalize the poet's world.
No wonder the poet is long in finding his audience ; no
wonder he has to abide the " inexorable tests of Time,"
which, if indeed he be great, slowly turns the handful
into hundreds, the hundreds into thousands and at last
having done its worst, grudgingly passes him on into the
ranks of the Immortals.

Meanwhile let not the handful who believe that such
a destiny awaits a man of our time cease to give a reason
for the faith that is in them.

So far as the suffrages of his own generation go Walt
Whitman may, like Wordsworth, tell of the " love, the
admiration, the indifference, the slight, the aversion and
even the contempt " with which his poems have been
received ; but the love and admiration are from even a

smaller number, the aversion, the contempt more vehement, more universal and persistent than Wordsworth
ever encountered. For the American is a more daring
innovator; he cuts loose from precedent, is a very
Columbus who has sailed forth alone on perilous seas to
seek new shores, to seek a new world for the soul, a
world that shall give scope and elevation and beauty to
the changed and changing events, aspirations, conditions
of modern life. To new aims, new methods; therefore
let not the reader approach these poems as a judge,
comparing, testing, measuring by what has gone before,
but as a willing learner, an unprejudiced seeker for
whatever may delight and nourish and exalt the soul.
Neither let him be abashed nor daunted by the weight of
adverse opinion, the contempt and denial which have been
heaped upon the great American even though it be the
contempt and denial of the capable, the cultivated, the
recognized authorities; for such is the usual lot of the
pioneer in whatever field. In religion it is above all to
the earnest and conscientious believer that the Reformer
has appeared a blasphemer, and in the world of literature
it is equally natural that the most careful student, that
the warmest lover of the accepted masterpieces, should
be the most hostile to one who forsakes the methods by
which, or at any rate, in company with which, those
triumphs have been achieved. " But," said the wise
Goethe, " I will listen to any man's convictions; you
may keep your doubts, your negations to yourself, I have
plenty of my own." For heartfelt convictions are rare
things. Therefore I make bold to indicate the scope
and source of power in Walt Whitman's writings,

starting from no wider ground than their effect upon an individual mind. It is not criticism I have to offer; least of all any discussion of the question of form or formlessness in these poems, deeply convinced as I am that when great meanings and great emotions are expressed with corresponding power, literature has done its best, call it what you please. But my aim is rather to suggest such trains of thought, such experience of life as having served to put me *en rapport* with this poet may haply find here and there a reader who is thereby helped to the same end. Hence I quote just as freely from the prose (especially from "Democratic Vistas" and the preface to the first issue of "Leaves of Grass," 1855) as from his poems, and more freely, perhaps, from those parts that have proved a stumbling-block than from those whose conspicuous beauty assures them acceptance.

Fifteen years ago, with feelings partly of indifference, partly of antagonism,—for I had heard none but ill words of them—I first opened Walt Whitman's poems. But as I read I became conscious of receiving the most powerful influence that had ever come to me from any source. What was the spell? It was that in them humanity has, in a new sense, found itself; for the first time has dared to accept itself without disparagement, without reservation. For the first time an unrestricted faith in all that is and in the issues of all that happens has burst forth triumphantly into song.

"... The rapture of the hallelujah sent
From all that breathes and is ..."

rings through these poems. They carry up into the region of Imagination and Passion those vaster and more profound conceptions of the universe and of man reached by centuries of that indomitably patient organized search for knowledge, that " skilful cross-questioning of things " called science.

> " O truth of the earth I am determined to press my way toward you.
> Sound your voice! I scale the mountains, I dive in the sea after you,"

cried science; and the earth and the sky have answered, and continue inexhaustibly to answer her appeal. And now at last the day dawns which Wordsworth prophesied of: " The man of science," he wrote, " seeks truth as a remote and unknown benefactor; he cherishes and loves it in his solitude. The Poet, singing a song in which all human beings join with him, rejoices in the presence of truth as our visible friend and hourly companion. Poetry is the breath and finer spirit of all knowledge; it is the impassioned expression which is in the countenance of all science, it is the first and last of all knowledge; it is immortal as the heart of man. If the labours of men of science should ever create any material revolution, direct or indirect, in our condition, and in the impressions which we habitually receive, the Poet will then sleep no more than at present; he will be ready to follow the steps of the man of science not only in those general indirect effects, but he will be at his side carrying sensation into the midst of the objects of science itself. If the time should ever come when what is now called science, thus familiarized to man, shall be ready to put on, as it were, a form of flesh and blood, the Poet will lend his divine spirit to aid the transfiguration, and will welcome the being thus produced as a dear and genuine inmate of the household of man." That time approaches: a new heaven and a new earth await us when the knowledge grasped by science is realized, conceived as a whole, related to the world within us by the shaping spirit of imagination. Not in vain, already, for this Poet have they pierced the darkness of the past, and read here and there a word of the earth's history before human eyes beheld it; each word of infinite significance, because involving in it secrets of the whole. A new anthem of the slow, vast, mystic dawn of life he sings in the name of humanity:—

" I am an acme of things accomplish'd, and I am an
    encloser of things to be.

My feet strike an apex of the apices of the stairs;
On every step bunches of ages, and larger bunches be-
    tween the steps;
All below duly travell'd and still I mount and mount.

Rise after rise bow the phantoms behind me:
Afar down I see the huge first Nothing—I know
I was even there;
I waited unseen and always, and slept through the
    lethargic mist,
And took my time, and took no hurt from the fetid
    carbon.

Long I was hugg'd close—long and long.

Immense have been the preparations for me,
Faithful and friendly the arms that have help'd me.

Cycles ferried my cradle, rowing and rowing like cheer-
ful boatmen ;
For room to me stars kept aside in their own rings,
They sent influences to look after what was to hold me.

Before I was born out of my mother, generations guided
me ;
My embryo has never been torpid—nothing could
overlay it.

For it the nebula cohered to an orb,
The long slow strata piled to rest it on,
Vast vegetables gave it sustenance,
Monstrous sauroids transported it in their mouths and
deposited it with care.

All forces have been steadily employ'd to complete and
delight me ;
Now on this spot I stand with my robust Soul."

Not in vain have they pierced space as well as time
and found " a vast similitude interlocking all."

" I open my scuttle at night and see the far-sprinkled
systems,
And all I see, multiplied as high as I can cypher, edge
but the rim of the farther systems.

Wider and wider they spread, expanding, always expanding,
Outward, and outward, and for ever outward.

My sun has his sun, and round him obediently wheels,
He joins with his partners a group of superior circuit,
And greater sets follow, making specks of the greatest
inside them.

z

There is no stoppage, and never can be stoppage;
If I, you, and the worlds, and all beneath or upon their
　　　surfaces, were this moment reduced back to a pallid
　　　float, it would not avail in the long run ;
We should surely bring up again where we now stand,
And as surely go as much farther—and then farther and
　　　farther."

Not in vain for him have they penetrated into the
substances of things to find that what we thought poor,
dead, inert matter is (in Clerk Maxwell's words), " a
very sanctuary of minuteness and power where mole-
cules obey the laws of their existence, and clash together
in fierce collision, or grapple in yet more fierce embrace,
building up in secret the forms of visible things ;" each
stock and stone a busy group of Ariels plying obediently their hidden tasks.

" Why ! who makes much of a miracle?
As to me, I know of nothing else but miracles,
　　　　　.　　　　　.　　　　　.
To me, every hour of the light and dark is a miracle,
Every cubic inch of space is a miracle,
Every square yard of the surface of the earth is spread
　　　with the same,　　　.　　　.　　　.　　　.
Every spear of grass—the frames, limbs, organs, of men
　　　and women, and all that concerns them,
All these to me are unspeakably perfect miracles."

The natural *is* the supernatural, says Carlyle. It is
the message that comes to our time from all quarters
alike ; from poetry, from science, from the deep brooding of the student of human history. Science material-
istic ?　Rather it is the current theology that is material-

istic in comparison. Science may truly be said to have annihilated our gross and brutish conceptions of matter, and to have revealed it to us as subtle, spiritual, energetic beyond our powers of realization. It is for the Poet to increase these powers of realization. He it is who must awaken us to the perception of a new heaven and a new earth here where we stand on this old earth. He it is who must, in Walt Whitman's words, indicate the path between reality and the soul.

Above all is every thought and feeling in these poems touched by the light of the great revolutionary truth that man, unfolded through vast stretches of time out of lowly antecedents, is a rising, not a fallen creature; emerging slowly from purely animal life; as slowly as the strata are piled and the ocean beds hollowed; whole races still barely emerged, countless individuals in the foremost races barely emerged: "the wolf, the snake, the hog" yet lingering in the best; but new ideals achieved, and others come in sight, so that what once seemed fit is fit no longer, is adhered to uneasily and with shame; the conflicts and antagonisms between what we call good and evil, at once the sign and the means of emergence, and needing to account for them no supposed primeval disaster, no outside power thwarting and marring the Divine handiwork, the perfect fitness to its time and place of all that has proceeded from the Great Source. In a word that Evil is relative; is that which the slowly developing reason and conscience bid us leave behind. The prowess of the lion, the subtlety of the fox, are cruelty and duplicity in man.

" Silent and amazed, when a little boy,
I remember I heard the preacher every Sunday put God
     in his statements,
As contending against some being or influence."

says the poet.    And elsewhere, " Faith, very old now,
scared away by science "—by the daylight science lets
in upon our miserable inadequate, idolatrous conceptions
of God and of His works, and on the sophistications,
subterfuges, moral impossibilities, by which we have
endeavoured to reconcile the irreconcilable—the co-
existence of omnipotent Goodness and an absolute
Power of Evil,—" Faith must be brought back by the
same power that caused her departure : restored with
new sway, deeper, wider, higher than ever."    And what
else, indeed, at bottom, is science so busy at ?    For
what is Faith ?    " Faith," to borrow venerable and unsurpassed words, " is the substance of things hoped for,
the evidence of things not seen."    And how obtain
evidence of things not seen but by a knowledge of
things seen ?    And how know what we may hope for,
but by knowing the truth of what is, here and now ?
For seen and unseen are parts of the Great Whole :
all the parts interdependent, closely related ; all alike have
proceeded from and are manifestations of the Divine
Source.    Nature is not the barrier between us and the
unseen but the link, the communication ; she too has
something behind appearances, has an unseen soul ; she
too is made of " innumerable energies."    Knowledge is
not faith, but it is faith's indispensable preliminary and
starting ground.    Faith runs ahead to fetch glad tidings
for us ; but if she start from a basis of ignorance and

illusion, how can she but run in the wrong direction? "Suppose" said that impetuous lover and seeker of truth, Clifford, "Suppose all moving things to be suddenly stopped at some instant, and that we could be brought fresh, without any previous knowledge, to look at the petrified scene. The spectacle would be immensely absurd. Crowds of people would be senselessly standing on one leg in the street looking at one another's backs; others would be wasting their time by sitting in a train in a place difficult to get at, nearly all with their mouths open, and their bodies in some contorted, unrestful posture. Clocks would stand with their pendulums on one side. Everything would be disorderly, conflicting, in its wrong place. But once remember that the world is in motion, is going somewhere, and everything will be accounted for and found just as it should be. Just so great a change of view, just so complete an explanation is given to us when we recognize that the nature of man and beast and of all the world is *going somewhere*. The maladaptions in organic nature are seen to be steps toward the improvement or discarding of imperfect organs. The *baneful strife which lurketh inborn in us, and goeth on the way with us to hurt us*, is found to be the relic of a time of savage or even lower condition." "Going somewhere!" That is the meaning then of all our perplexities! That changes a mystery which stultified and contradicted the best we knew into a mystery which teaches, allures, elevates; which harmonises what we know with what we hope. By it we begin to

"  .  .  .    see by the glad light,
And breathe the sweet air of futurity."

The scornful laughter of Carlyle as he points with one
hand to the baseness, ignorance, folly, cruelty around us,
and with the other to the still unsurpassed poets, sages,
heroes, saints of antiquity, whilst he utters the words
" progress of the species ! " touches us no longer when
we have begun to realize " the amplitude of time ; "
when we know something of the scale by which Nature
measures out the years to accomplish her smallest
essential modification or development ; know that to
call a few thousands or tens of thousands of years
antiquity, is to speak as a child, and that in her chron-
ology the great days of Egypt and Syria, of Greece
and Rome are affairs of yesterday.

" Each of us inevitable ;
Each of us limitless—each of us with his or her right
    upon the earth ;
Each of us allow'd the eternal purports of the earth ;
Each of us here as divinely as any are here.

You Hottentot with clicking palate !   You woolly
    hair'd hordes !
You own'd persons, dropping sweat-drops or blood-
    drops !
You human forms with the fathomless ever-impressive
    countenances of brutes !
I dare not refuse you—the scope of the world, and of
    time and space are upon me.

        .       .       .       .       .       .

I do not prefer others so very much before you either ;
I do not say one word against you, away back there,
    where you stand ;

(You will come forward in due time to my side.)

My spirit has pass'd in compassion and determination
around the whole earth ;

I have look'd for equals and lovers, and found them
ready for me in all lands ;

I think some divine rapport has equalized me with
them.

O vapors ! I think I have risen with you, and moved
away to distant continents and fallen down there, for
reasons ;

I think I have blown with you, O winds ;

O waters, I have finger'd every shore with you.

I have run through what any river or strait of the globe
has run through ;

I have taken my stand on the bases of peninsulas, and
on the high embedded rocks, to cry thence.

     *Salut au monde !*

What cities the light or warmth penetrates, I penetrate
those cities myself ;

All islands to which birds wing their way I wing my way
myself.

     Toward all,

I raise high the perpendicular hand—I make the signal,

To remain after me in sight forever,

For all the haunts and homes of men."

But "Hold!" says the reader, especially if he be one
who loves science, who loves to feel the firm ground
under his feet, "That the species has a great future
before it we may well believe ; already we see the indi-
cations. But that the individual has is quite another
matter. We can but balance probabilities here, and the
probabilities are very heavy on the wrong side ; the

poets must throw in weighty matter indeed to turn the
scale the other way !" Be it so : but ponder a moment
what science herself has to say bearing on this theme ;
what are the widest, deepest facts she has reached down
to. INDESTRUCTIBILITY : Amidst ceaseless change and
seeming decay all the elements, all the forces (if indeed
they be not one and the same) which operate and sub-
stantiate those changes, imperishable ; neither matter
nor force capable of annihilation. Endless transforma-
tions, disappearances, new combinations, but diminution
of the total amount never ; missing in one place or shape
to be found in another, disguised ever so long, ready
always to re-emerge. " A particle of oxygen," wrote
Faraday, " is ever a particle of oxygen ; nothing can in
the least wear it. If it enters into combination and dis-
appears as oxygen, if it pass through a thousand combinations, animal, vegetable, mineral,— if it lie hid for a
thousand years and then be evolved, it is oxygen with
its first qualities neither more nor less." So then out
of the universe is no door. CONTINUITY again is one
of Nature's irrevocable words ; everything the result and
outcome of what went before; no gaps, no jumps ;
always a connecting principle which carries forward the
great scheme of things as a related whole, which subtly
links past and present, like and unlike. Nothing breaks
with its past. " It is not," says Helmholtz, " the
definite mass of substance which now constitutes the
body to which the continuance of the individual is
attached. Just as the flame remains the same in appearance and continues to exist with the same form and
structure although it draws every moment fresh combus-

tible vapour and fresh oxygen from the air into the vortex of its ascending current; and just as the wave goes on in unaltered form and is yet being reconstructed every moment from fresh particles of water, so is it also in the living being. For the material of the body like that of flame is subject to continuous and comparatively rapid change,—a change the more rapid the livelier the activity of the organs in question. Some constituents are renewed from day to day, some from month to month, and others only after years. That which continues to exist as a particular individual is, like the wave and the flame, only the *form of motion* which continually attracts fresh matter into its vortex and expels the old. The observer with a deaf ear recognizes the vibration of sound as long as it is visible and can be felt, bound up with other heavy matter. Are our senses in reference to life like the deaf ear in this respect?"

"You are not thrown to the winds—you gather certainly
　　and safely around yourself;

　　·　　　　·　　　　·　　　　·　　　　·　　　　·

It is not to diffuse you that you were born of your
　　mother and father—it is to identify you;
It is not that you should be undecided, but that you
　　should be decided;
Something long preparing and formless is arrived and
　　form'd in you,
You are henceforth secure, whatever comes or goes.

　　·　　　　·　　　　·　　　　·　　　　·　　　　·

O Death! the voyage of Death!
The beautiful touch of Death, soothing and benumbing
　　a few moments for reasons;

Myself discharging my excrementitious body to be
    burn'd or reduced to powder or buried.
My real body doubtless left me for other spheres,
My voided body, nothing more to me, returning to the
    purifications, farther offices, eternal uses of the earth."

Yes, they go their way, those dismissed atoms with
all their energies and affinities unimpaired. But they
are not all ; the will, the affections, the intellect are just
as real as those affinities and energies, and there is strict
account of all; nothing slips through ; there is no door
out of the universe. But they are qualities of a personality, of a self, not of an atom but of what uses and dis-
misses those atoms. If the qualities are indestructible
so must the self be. The little heap of ashes, the puff
of gas, do you pretend that is all that was Shakespeare?
The rest of him lives in his works, you say? But he
lived and was just the same man after those works were
produced. The world gained, but he lost nothing of
himself, rather grew and strengthened in the production
of them.

Still farther, those faculties with which we seek for
knowledge are only a part of us, there is something behind which wields them, something that those faculties
cannot turn themselves in upon and comprehend ; for
the part cannot compass the whole. Yet there it is with
the irrefragable proof of consciousness. Who should
be the mouthpiece of this whole? Who but the poet,
the man most fully " possessed of his own soul," the
man of the largest consciousness ; fullest of love and
sympathy which gather into his own life the experiences

of others, fullest of imagination; that quality whereof
Wordsworth says that it

> ".  .  . in truth
> Is but another name for absolute power,
> And clearest insight, amplitude of mind
> And reason in her most exalted mood."

Let Walt Whitman speak for us :—

" And I know I am solid and sound;
To me the converging objects of the universe perpetually
    flow:
All are written to me, and I must get what the writing
    means.

I know I am deathless;
I know this orbit of mine cannot be swept by the car-
    penter's compass;
I know I shall not pass like a child's carlacue cut with
    a burnt stick at night.

I know I am august;
I do not trouble my spirit to vindicate itself or be
    understood;
I see that the elementary laws never apologize;
(I reckon I behave no prouder than the level I plant my
    house by, after all.)

I exist as I am—that is enough;
If no other in the world be aware I sit content;
And if each one and all be aware, I sit content.

One world is aware, and by far the largest to me, and
    that is myself;
And whether I come to my own to-day, or in ten
    thousand or ten million years,
I can cheerfully take it now, or with equal cheerfulness
    I can wait.

My foothold is tenon'd and mortis'd in granite ;
I laugh at what you call dissolution ;
And I know the amplitude of time."

What lies through the portal of death is hidden from
us ; but the laws that govern that unknown land are not
all hidden from us, for they govern here and now ; they
are immutable, eternal.

"Of and in all these things
I have dream'd that we are not to be changed so
    much, nor the law of us changed,
I have dream'd that heroes and good doers shall be
    under the present and past law,
And that murderers, drunkards, liars, shall be under
    the present and past law,
For I have dream'd that the law they are under now
    is enough."

And the law not to be eluded is the law of consequences,
the law of silent teaching. That is the meaning of
disease, pain, remorse. Slow to learn are we ; but
success is assured with limitless Beneficence as our
teacher, with limitless time as our opportunity. Already
we begin—

" To know the Universe itself as a road—as many roads
As roads for travelling souls.
For ever alive ; for ever forward.
Stately, solemn, sad, withdrawn, baffled, mad, turbulent,
    feeble, dissatisfied ;
Desperate, proud, fond, sick ;
Accepted by men, rejected by men.
They go ! they go ! I know that they go, but I know
    not where they go.

But I know they go toward the best, toward something
   great ;
The whole Universe indicates that it is good."

Going somewhere !   And if it is impossible for us to
see whither, as in the nature of things it must be, how
can we be adequate judges of the way ?  how can we but
often grope and be full of perplexity ?   But we know
that a smooth path, a paradise of a world, could only
nurture fools, cowards, sluggards.   " Joy is the great
unfolder," but pain is the great enlightener, the great
stimulus in certain directions, alike of man and beast.
How else could the self-preserving instincts, and all that
grows out of them, have been evoked ?   How else those
wonders of the moral world, fortitude, patience, sympathy ?   And if the lesson be too hard comes Death,
come " the sure-enwinding arms of Death " to end it,
and speed us to the unknown land.

       " . . . . Man is only weak
   Through his mistrust and want of hope,"

wrote Wordsworth.   But man's mistrust of himself is,
at bottom, mistrust of the central Fount of power and
goodness whence he has issued.   Here comes one who
plucks out of religion its heart of fear, and puts into it
a heart of boundless faith and joy; a faith that beggars
previous faiths because it sees that All is good, not part
bad and part good; that there is no flaw in the scheme
of things, no primeval disaster, no counteracting power;
but orderly and sure growth and development, and that
infinite Goodness and Wisdom embrace and ever lead
forward all that exists.   Are you troubled that He is an

unknown God; that we cannot by searching find Him
out? Why, it would be a poor prospect for the Universe if otherwise; if, embryos that we are, we could
compass Him in our thoughts:

"I hear and behold God in every object, yet understand
      God not in the least."

It is the double misfortune of the churches that they
do not study God in his works—man and Nature and
their relations to each other; and that they do profess
to set Him forth; that they worship therefore a God of
man's devising, an idol made by men's minds it is true,
not by their hands, but none the less an idol. "Leaves
are not more shed out of trees than Bibles are shed out
of you," says the poet. They were the best of their
time, but not of all time; they need renewing as surely
as there is such a thing as growth, as surely as knowledge nourishes and sustains to further development; as
surely as time unrolls new pages of the mighty scheme of
existence. Nobly has George Sand, too, written "Everything is divine, even matter; everything is superhuman,
even man. God is everywhere. He is in me in a measure
proportioned to the little that I am. My present life
separates me from Him just in the degree determined by
the actual state of childhood of our race. Let me
content myself in all my seeking to feel after Him, and
to possess of Him as much as this imperfect soul can
take in with the intellectual sense I have. The day will
come when we shall no longer talk about God
idly; nay, when we shall talk about Him as little as
possible. We shall cease to set Him forth dogmatically,

to dispute about His nature. We shall put compulsion on no one to pray to Him, we shall leave the whole business of worship within the sanctuary of each man's conscience. And this will happen when we are really religious."

In what sense may Walt Whitman be called the Poet of Democracy? It is as giving utterance to this profoundly religious faith in man. He is rather the prophet of what is to be than the celebrator of what is. "Democracy," he writes, "is a word the real gist of which still sleeps quite unwakened, notwithstanding the resonance and the many angry tempests out of which its syllables have come from pen or tongue. It is a great word, whose history, I suppose, remains unwritten because that history has yet to be enacted. It is in some sort younger brother of another great and often used word, Nature, whose history also waits unwritten." Political democracy, now taking shape, is the house to live in, and whilst what we demand of it is room for all, fair chances for all, none disregarded or left out as of no account, the main question, the kind of life that is to be led in that house is altogether beyond the ken of the statesmen as such, and is involved in those deepest facts of the nature and destiny of man which are the themes of Walt Whitman's writings. The practical outcome of that exalted and all accepting faith in the scheme of things, and in man, toward whom all has led up and in whom all concentrates as the manifestation, the revelation of Divine Power is a changed estimate of himself; a higher reverence for, a loftier belief in the heritage of himself; a perception that pride, not humility, is the true homage to his Maker; that "noblesse oblige" is for the Race, not for a handful; that it is mankind and womankind and their high destiny which constrain to greatness, which can no longer stoop to meanness and lies and base aims, but must needs clothe themselves in "the majesty of honest dealing" (majestic because demanding courage as good as the soldier's, self-denial as good as the saint's for every-day affairs), and walk erect and fearless, a law to themselves, sternest of all lawgivers. Looking back to the palmy days of feudalism, especially as immortalized in Shakespeare's plays, what is it we find most admirable? what is it that fascinates? It is the noble pride, the lofty self-respect; the dignity, the courage and audacity of its great personages. But this pride, this dignity rested half upon a true, half upon a hollow foundation; half upon intrinsic qualities, half upon the ignorance and brutishness of the great masses of the people, whose helpless submission and easily dazzled imaginations made stepping-stones to the elevation of the few, and "hedged round kings," with a specious kind of "divinity." But we have our faces turned towards a new day, and toward heights on which there is room for all.

"By God, I will accept nothing which all cannot have their counterpart of on the same terms"

is the motto of the great personages, the great souls of to-day. *On the same terms*, for that is Nature's law and cannot be abrogated, the reaping as you sow. But all shall have the chance to sow well. This is pride indeed! Not a pride that isolates, but that can take no rest till our common humanity is lifted out of the mire everywhere, " a pride that cannot stretch too far because sympathy stretches with it : "—

" Whoever you are ! claim your own at any hazard !
These shows of the east and west are tame, compared to you ;
These immense meadows—these interminable rivers—
You are immense and interminable as they ;
These furies, elements, storms, motions of Nature, throes of apparent dissolution—you are he or she who is master or mistress over them,
Master or mistress in your own right over Nature, elements, pain, passion, dissolution.

The hopples fall from your ankles—you find an unfailing sufficiency ;
Old or young, male or female, rude, low, rejected by the rest, whatever you are promulges itself ;
Through birth, life, death, burial, the means are provided, nothing is scanted ;
Through angers, losses, ambition, ignorance and ennui, what you are picks its way."

This is indeed a pride that is " calming and excellent to the soul " ; that " dissolves poverty from its need and riches from its conceit."

And humility ? Is there, then, no place for that virtue so much praised by the haughty ? Humility is the sweet spontaneous grace of an aspiring, finely developed nature which sees always heights a-head still unclimbed, which outstrips itself in eager longing for excellence still unattained. Genuine humility takes good care of itself as men rise in the scale of being ; for every height climbed discloses still new heights beyond. Or it is a wise caution in fortune's favourites lest they themselves should mistake, as the unthinking crowd around do, the glitter reflected back upon them by their surroundings for some superiority inherent in themselves. It befits them well if there be also due pride, pride of humanity behind.   But to say to a man ' Be humble ' is like saying to one who has a battle to fight, a race to run, ' You are a poor, feeble creature ;  you are not likely to win and you do not deserve to.'   Say rather to him, ' Hold up your head !   You were not made for failure, you were made for victory :  go forward with a joyful confidence in that result sooner or later, and the sooner or the later depends mainly on yourself.'

" What Christ appeared for in the moral-spiritual field for humankind, namely, that in respect to the absolute soul there is in the possession of such by each single individual something so transcendent, so incapable of gradations (like life) that to that extent it places all beings on a common level, utterly regardless of the distinctions of intellect, virtue, station, or any height or lowliness whatever " is the secret source of that deathless sentiment of Equality which how many able heads imagine themselves to have slain with ridicule and contempt, as Johnson, kicking a stone, imagined he had demolished Idealism when he had simply attributed to the word an impossible meaning.   True, *In*equality is one of Nature's words :  she moves forward always by means of the exceptional.   But the moment the move is accomplished, then all her efforts are towards equality, towards bringing up the rear to that standpoint.   But social inequalities, class distinctions, do not stand for, or

represent Nature's inequalities.   Precisely the contrary
in the long run.   They are devices for holding up many
that would else gravitate down and keeping down many
who would else rise up; for providing that some should
reap who have not sown, and many sow without reaping.
But literature tallies the ways of Nature; for though
itself the product of the exceptional, its aim is to draw
all men up to its own level.   The great writer is
" hungry for equals day and night," for so only can he
be fully understood.   " The meal is equally set "; all
are invited.   Therefore is literature, whether consciously
or not, the greatest of all forces on the side of Democracy.

Carlyle has said there is no grand poem in the world
but is at bottom a biography—the life of a man.  Walt
Whitman's poems are not the biography of a man, but
they are his actual presence.   It is no vain boast when
he exclaims,

> " Camerado ! this is no book ;
> Who touches this touches a man."

He has infused himself into words in a way that had not
before seemed possible; and he causes each reader to
feel that he himself or herself has an actual relationship
to him, is a reality full of inexhaustible significance and
interest to the poet.   The power of his book, beyond
even its great intellectual force, is the power with which
he makes this felt ; his words lay more hold than the
grasp of a hand, strike deeper than the gaze or the flash
of an eye ; to those who comprehend him he stands
" nigher than the nighest."

America has had the shaping of Walt Whitman, and he repays the filial debt, with a love that knows no stint. Her vast lands with their varied, brilliant climes and rich products, her political scheme, her achievements and her failures, all have contributed to make these poems what they are both directly and indirectly. Above all has that great conflict, the Secession War, found voice in him. And if the reader would understand the true causes and nature of that war, ostensibly waged between North and South, but underneath a tussle for supremacy between the good and the evil genius of America (for there were just as many secret sympathisers with the secession-slave-power in the North as in the South) he will find the clue in the pages of Walt Whitman. Rarely has he risen to a loftier height than in the poem which heralds that volcanic upheaval :—

" Rise, O days, from your fathomless deeps, till you
      loftier and fiercer sweep !
Long for my soul, hungering gymnastic, I devour'd
      what the earth gave me ;
Long I roam'd the woods of the north—long I watch'd
      Niagara pouring ;
I travel'd the prairies over, and slept on their breast—
I cross'd the Nevadas, I cross'd the plateaus ;
I ascended the towering rocks along the Pacific, I sail'd
      out to sea ;
I sail'd through the storm, I was refresh'd by the storm ;
I watch'd with joy the threatening maws of the waves ;
I mark'd the white combs where they career'd so high,
      curling over ;
I heard the wind piping, I saw the black clouds ;
Saw from below what arose and mounted, (O superb !
      O wild as my heart, and powerful !)

Heard the continuous thunder, as it bellow'd after the
    lightning;
Noted the slender and jagged threads of lightning, as
    sudden and fast amid the din they chased each other
    across the sky;
—These, and such as these, I, elate, saw—saw with
    wonder, yet pensive and masterful;
All the menacing might of the globe uprisen around me;
Yet there with my soul I fed—I fed content, supercilious.

'Twas well, O soul! 'twas a good preparation you gave
    me!
Now we advance our latent and ampler hunger to fill;
Now we go forth to receive what the earth and the sea
    never gave us;
Not through the mighty woods we go, but through the
    mightier cities;
Something for us is pouring now, more than Niagara
    pouring;
Torrents of men (sources and rills of the Northwest, are
    you indeed inexhaustible?)
What, to pavements and homesteads here—what were
    those storms of the mountains and sea?
What, to passions I witness around me to-day? Was
    the sea risen?
Was the wind piping the pipe of death under the black
    clouds?
Lo! from deeps more unfathomable, something more
    deadly and savage;
Manhattan, rising, advancing with menacing front—
    Cincinnati, Chicago, unchain'd;
—What was that swell I saw on the ocean? behold
    what comes here!
How it climbs with daring feet and hands! how it
    dashes!

How the true thunder bellows after the lightning ! how
  bright the flashes of lightning !
How DEMOCRACY, with desperate, vengeful port strides
  on, shown through the dark by those flashes of
  lightning !
(Yet a mournful wail and low sob I fancied I heard
  through the dark,
In a lull of the deafening confusion.)

Thunder on ! stride on, Democracy ! stride with vengeful
  stroke !
And do you rise higher than ever yet, O days, O cities !
Crash heavier, heavier yet, O storms ! you have done
  me good ;
My soul, prepared in the mountains, absorbs your
  immortal strong nutriment,
—Long had I walk'd my cities, my country roads,
  through farms, only half satisfied ;
One doubt, nauseous, undulating like a snake, crawl'd
  on the ground before me,
Continually preceding my steps, turning upon me oft,
  ironically hissing low ;
—The cities I loved so well, I abandon'd and left—I
  sped to the certainties suitable to me ;
Hungering, hungering, hungering for primal energies,
  and nature's dauntlessness ;
I refresh'd myself with it only, I could relish it only ;
I waited the bursting forth of the pent fire—on the
  water and air I waited long ;
—But now I no longer wait—I am fully satisfied—I
  am glutted ;
I have witness'd the true lightning—I have witness'd
  my cities electric ;
I have lived to behold man burst forth, and warlike
  America rise ;

Hence I will seek no more the food of the northern
    solitary wilds,
No more on the mountains roam, or sail the stormy sea."

But not for the poet a soldier's career. "To sit by
the wounded and sooth them, or silently watch the
dead" was the part he chose. During the whole war he
remained with the army, but only to spend the days and
nights, saddest, happiest of his life, in the hospital tents.
It was a beautiful destiny for this lover of men, and a
proud triumph for this believer in the People ; for it
was the People that he beheld, tried by severest tests.
He saw them " of their own choice, fighting, dying for
their own idea, insolently attacked by the secession-slàve-
power." From the workshop, the farm, the store, the
desk, they poured forth, officered by men who had to
blunder into knowledge at the cost of the wholesale
slaughter of their troops. He saw them " tried long
and long by hopelessness, mismanagement, defeat ;
advancing unhesitatingly through incredible slaughter ;
sinewy with unconquerable resolution. He saw them by
tens of thousands in the hospitals tried by yet drearier,
more fearful tests—the wound, the amputation, the
shattered face, the slow hot fever, the long impatient
anchorage in bed ; he marked their fortitude, decorum,
their religious nature and sweet affection." Finally,
newest, most significant sight of all, victory achieved,
the Cause, the Union safe, he saw them return back to
the workshop, the farm, the desk," the store, instantly
reabsorbed into the peaceful industries of the land : —

" A pause—the armies wait.
A million flush'd embattled conquerors wait.

The world, too, waits, then soft as breaking night and
    sure as dawn
They melt, they disappear."

  " Plentifully supplied, last-needed proof of Democracy
in its personalities ! " ratifying on the broadest scale
Wordsworth's haughty claim for average man—" Such
is the inherent dignity of human nature that there belong
to it sublimities of virtue which all men may attain, and
which no man can transcend."

  But, aware that peace and prosperity may be even
still severer tests of national as of individual virtue and
greatness of mind, Walt Whitman scans with anxious,
questioning eye the America of to-day. He is no
smooth-tongued prophet of easy greatness.

" I am he who walks the States with a barb'd tongue
    questioning every one I meet ;
Who are you, that wanted only to be told what you
    knew before ?
Who are you, that wanted only a book to join you in
    your nonsense ? "

He sees clearly as any the incredible flippancy, the blind
fury of parties, the lack of great leaders, the plentiful
meanness and vulgarity ; the labour question beginning
to open like a yawning gulf. . . . " We sail a dangerous
sea of seething currents, all so dark and untried. . . .
It seems as if the Almighty had spread before this
nation charts of imperial destinies, dazzling as the sun,
yet with many a deep intestine difficulty, and human
aggregate of cankerous imperfection, saying lo ! the
roads ! The only plans of development, long and varied,
with all terrible balks and ebullitions ! You said in your

soul, I will be empire of empires, putting the history of
old-world dynasties, conquests, behind me as of no
account—making a new history, a history of democracy
. . . I alone inaugurating largeness, culminating time.
If these, O lands of America, are indeed the prizes, the
determinations of your soul, be it so.   But behold the
cost, and already specimens of the cost.   Thought you
greatness was to ripen for you like a pear ?   If you
would have greatness, know that you must conquer it
through ages . . . must pay for it with proportionate
price.   For you, too, as for all lands, the struggle, the
traitor, the wily person in office, scrofulous wealth, the
surfeit of prosperity, the demonism of greed, the hell
of passion, the decay of faith, the long postponement,
the fossil-like lethargy, the ceaseless need of revolutions,
prophets, thunderstorms, deaths, new projections and
nvigorations of ideas and men."

"Yet I have dreamed, merged in that hidden-tangled
problem of our fate, whose long unravelling stretches
mysteriously through time—dreamed, portrayed, hinted
already—a little or a larger band, a band of brave and
true, unprecedented yet, arm'd and equipt at every
point, the members separated, it may be by different
dates and states, or south or north, or east or west, a
year, a century here, and other centuries there, but
always one, compact in soul, conscience-conserving,
God-inculcating, inspired achievers not only in literature, the greatest art, but achievers in all art—a new
undying order, dynasty from age to age transmitted, a
band, a class at least as fit to cope with current years,
our dangers, needs, as those who, for their time, so long,

so well, in armour or in cowl, upheld and made illustrious that far-back-feudal, priestly world."

Of that band, is not Walt Whitman the pioneer ? Of
that New World literature, say, are not his poems the
beginning ? A rude beginning if you will. He claims no
more and no less. But whatever else they may lack
they do not lack vitality, initiative, sublimity. They
do not lack that which makes life great and death, with
its " transfers and promotions, its superb vistas," exhilarating,—a resplendent faith in God and man which
will kindle anew the faith of the world :—

" Poets to come ! Orators, singers, musicians to come !
Not to-day is to justify me, and answer what I am for;
But you, a new brood, native, athletic, continental,
     reater than before known,

Arouse ! Arouse—for you must justify me—you must
     answer.

I myself but write one or two indicative words for the
     future,
I but advance a moment, only to wheel and hurry back
     in the darkness.

I am a man who, sauntering along, without fully
     stopping, turns a casual look upon you, and then
     averts his face,
Leaving it to you to prove and define it,
Expecting the main things from you."

ANNE GILCHRIST.

# INDEX TO BIOGRAPHY.

PAGE

Abel; and Peto .. .. .. 159
Abington, Frances .. .. .. 233
Aders's collection of Blakes .. 132
Airlie, Lady; and Thackeray .. 81
Aldrich, J. C.; and W. Rossetti .. 281
Angelo, Michael: quoted .. 59, 237
Arkwright; Carlyle upon .. .. 65
Ashburton, Lady; Jane W. Carlyle
describes .. .. .. .. 82
Ashburton, Lord; Carlyle mentions 53

Babington, Dr.; and Mrs. Gabriel
Rossetti .. .. .. .. 88
Bacon, Lord .. .. 38, 282
Bacon, Miss .. .. .. 237
Baillee, Captain Matthew .. .. 82
Barford: and Pimm .. .. 119
Barlow .. .. .. .. 81
Basic Process: Thomas-Gilchrist .. 153
Bayle; and D'Aulnoy .. .. 52
Belper, Lord: mentioned by Carlyle 66
Bentinck, Mrs.; and G. Richmond. 262
Bielefeld .. .. .. .. 48
Blake, Catherine; versus Linnell 130, 259
Blake, Miss; and Tatham .. .. 129
Blake, William: his new letters .. 257
—— account of by Richmond 258, 261
Blind, Mathilde .. .. .. 264
Boileau: Satires .. .. .. 29
Bowdler .. .. .. .. 178

Boyd, Miss; C. Rossetti .. .. 161
Bremer, Miss; and Emerson .. 233
Brown, F. Madox; letter from 110,
152, 154
Brown, John: Sonnet on by W.
Rossetti .. .. .. .. 264
Brown, Miss; and Carlyle .. .. 60
Brown, Miss Lucy Madox [Mrs.
Rossetti] .. .. .. .. 222
Brown, Marshal: Irish Jacobite .. 61
Browning, Robert .. .. .. 143
Brunt, Mr. Van .. .. .. 247
Buchanan, Robert: letter in Daily
News .. .. .. .. 223
Buller: Carlyle mentions .. .. 62
Bulwer [Lord L.]; and Walt Whit-
man .. .. .. .. 238
Bunn, Poet; and "Poet Close" .. 202
Buranelli; and Carlyle .. .. 85
Burghersh, Lord .. .. .. 217
Burns: Carlyle's opinion of.. .. 75
Burroughs, John .. .. 274, 284
—— letter which speaks of Whitman 268
Burrows, Mrs. .. .. .. 2, 154
Butler, Mrs.: miniature painter .. 8
Butts, Captain; and Blake.. .. 136

Cahusac, Miss .. .. 19, 21
Caley; and Rossetti .. .. 174

PAGE

Cameron, Mrs. .. .. .. 280

Carpenter, Edward ; in Philadelphia 229

Carl VI. .. .. .. .. 53

Carlyle, J. W. ; letter .. .. 67

—— her conversation .. 72, 83

—— letters from 79, 85, 98, 103,

105, 106, 107

—— letter from, about Brookbank 139

Carlyle, Thomas ; described by A.G. 36

—— first letter from .. .. 40

—— eight letters from .. .. 44

—— his opinion of Blake .. .. 59

—— his conversation .. .. 60

—— talk with Lady Stanley .. 61

—— speaks of *Monthly Magazine* .. 63

—— his liking for Ruskin.. .. 82

—— letter about *Blake* .. .. 141

—— his opinion of *The Ring and the*

*Book* .. .. .. 174

—— as a *leader of thought* .. 188

—— quoted .. .. .. 279

Carr .. .. .. .. 53

Carwardine, Henry.. .. .. 3, 27

Carwardine, John, J.P.: *Secession*

*War* .. .. .. .. 149

Carwardine, Thomas ; and Cunning-

ham .. .. .. .. 7

Cawarden, Sir Thomas .. .. 6, 7

Chapman ; and *Life of Blake* .. 59

*Cheyne Walk :* Rossetti moved there

1862 .. .. .. .. 127

*Cheshire Cheese, The* .. .. 88

Chodowiecky : Carlyle upon .. 46

Christ .. .. .. .. 203

Cloud Confines .. .. .. 221

Colne Priory founded A.D. 1100 3, 220

Comte : Carlyle mentions.. .. 73

PAGE

Conway, M.D., Whitman speaks of

179, 263

Cowden-Clarke, Mrs.; letter .. 271

*Cromwell ;* Carlyle pleased with 43, 7, 208

Cunningham .. .. .. 7, 54

Czarina, Elizabeth ; Carlyle mentions 44

*Danites, The* .. .. .. 231

D'Aulnoy, Countess .. .. 51

*Declaration of Rights* .. .. 209

*Democracy ;* Baron Jacobi .. .. 235

Deville : Blake's mask .. .. 259

Dickens, Charles ; and Jane Carlyle. 81

—— quoted .. .. .. 119

Disraeli [Lord B.] ; his Blakes .. 132

Dixon, of Sunderland .. .. 208

Dowbiggin ; and Lord Panmure .. 51

Dowden, Edward .. .. .. 284

Edgeworth, Francis.. .. .. 282

Edgeworth, Miss ; A. G.'s opinion of 29

*Elijah* .. .. .. .. 134

Eliot, George .. .. 86, 216, 238

Emerson, R. W. ; at Concord .. 245

Emerson, W.; the Mathematician 64

Etty, William, R.A. .. .. 35

—— Life, published 1855.. .. 40

Eugenius, Prince ; and Carlyle .. 53

Evans, General Sir de Lacy .. 51

Everett ; and Barnum : Carlyle on.. 75

Fechter : mentioned by J. W. Carlyle 86

Ferdinand and Miranda .. .. 135

Forman, H. Buxton ; is written to .. 271

Forster ; the biographer, Mrs. Carlyle 80

Francke ; and psalm-singing .. 48

PAGE

Frederick : orders—bad spelling .. 49

French, Dan : *The Minute Man* .. 246

Gilchrist, Anne, born 1828, d. 1885 1, 2
—— babyhood .. .. .. 11
—— *Magnet Stories*.. .. .. 12
—— description of drowning .. 17
—— loses her father .. .. 19
—— goes to school at Highgate .. 19
—— her first letter.. .. .. 22
—— loses her only brother .. 24
—— thinks deeply on religion .. 25
—— marriage .. .. .. 32
—— describes house at Guildford .. 40
—— removal to London .. .. 55
—— first Essay noticed by Dickens 64
—— *Glance at Vegetable Kingdom* .. 66
—— *Whales and Whalemen* .. 71
—— *Memoir* quoted .. 39, 55, 57, 97, 102
—— first letter to W. M. Rossetti.. 123
—— speaks of Carlyle .. .. 142
—— meets Christina Rossetti .. 149
—— her opinion of Hallam .. 150
—— *The Indestructibility of Force* .. 153
—— meets with carriage accident.. 157
—— letters, autobiographical 125, 153
—— reads *Selections from Whitman* 177
—— serious illness of .. .. 210
—— visits America .. .. 228
—— visit to New England.. .. 242
—— translates Hugo .. .. 242
—— writes to *Daily Advertiser* .. 242
—— begins second edition of Blake 255
—— describes Hampstead .. .. 262
—— writes *Life of Mary Lamb* .. 268
—— interesting letter on London .. 269
—— letter about Coleridge .. 276

PAGE

Gilchrist, Anne : last words .. 282
—— buried at Kensal Green (grave
No. 16,877, Square 83, Row 5,
3 ft. north of Frampton, 11,839).
Gilchrist, Alex. : marriage.. .. 31
—— letter to Miss Newton .. 37
—— letter describing Carlyle ..41, 42
—— born April 25, 1828; died
Nov. 30, 1861 .. .. 101
Gilchrist, Dr.; and the Carlyles .. 74
Gilchrist, P. C. .. .. 37, 153
Gladstone, W. .. .. .. 259
Godiva ; alluded to by Anne Gilchrist 191
Goethe .. .. .. .. 193
Graves, Robert Perceval .. 274, 279
Gurowski, Count ; and Walt Whit-
man .. .. .. .. 235
Gwatkin, Miss ; and George Eliot .. 217

Haines, William .. .. 123, 125
Hallam, Henry .. .. .. 259
Hamilton, Sir William .. .. 279
Harlakenden, Dorothy .. .. 5
Harlakenden, William .. .. 5
Hawthorne, Nathaniel .. .. 238
Hayley, W. : letter to Carwardine .. 8
—— extract of letter .. .. 20
—— his composition—at Eartham.. 154
—— versus Blake .. .. .. 258
Hegel : and Count Gurowski .. 235
*Henri, Vie du Prince* .. .. 48
Henry VIII. ; and Sir Thomas Carden 6
Hextalls, manor of .. .. .. 5
Higginson, Colonel.. 242, 244, 247
*Hobby-Horse, The* .. .. .. 260
Hogarth : Carlyle mentions .. 46
Holgate, Ann [Mrs. Carwardine] .. 5, 7

PAGE

Holinshed and Giant Albion .. 133
Holland, Emma .. .. .. 252
Holland, Frederick ; letter to .. 246, 253
Hotten : publisher, Walt Whitman 181
Hüffer, Dr... .. .. .. 176
Hugo, Victor .. .. 173, 194
Humphrey, Ozias .. .. .. 8
Hutchinson, Jonathan ; Surgeon .. 174

Ingelow, Jean .. .. .. 148
Ingram, J. H. .. .. .. 267
*Instructions Militaires* .. .. 44
Ireland, Mrs. Edwin [No relation to
     Alexander Ireland] ..101, 107, 115

Jacobi, Baron ; *Democracy* .. .. 235
James, Henry, Jun. ; quoted .. 239
Jersey, Lady : J. W. Carlyle mentions 73
Jewsbury, Geraldine .. 85, 114
Johnston, Mr.; mentioned by Carlyle 47
Johnson, Dr. .. .. 94, 129
Jones, Mrs. E. Burne .. 87, 148

Kemp, Alfred John .. .. 7
Kent, Charles; and W. M. Rossetti 183
Kingsley : his opinion of F. J. Shields 264
*Kolin :* battle of .. .. .. 50

Lacroix : Algebra, and G. H. Lewes 216
*L'Allegro* .. .. .. .. 144
Lamb, Charles : Cary speaks of, 271, 274
                                         277
Lamb, Mary .. 267, 269, 271
*Letter on Patriotism* .. .. .. 45
Lewes, G. H.; and Carlyle .. 72
—— letters from .. .. .. 215
Ligne, Prince de .. .. .. 46

PAGE

Lind, Jenny .. .. .. 234
Lindsay, Sir Coutts.. .. .. 54
Linnell, William : his notes .. 132
*Llandaff ;* D. G. Rossetti .. .. 93
Locker, Frederick ; *Lyrics* quoted.. 9
*London ;* John Burroughs .. .. 268
Longfellow ; described .. .. 247
Lowe, Robert [Lord S.] : and Lindsay 54
Luke : and Paul .. .. .. 205
*Lyme Regis* .. .. .. .. 39

Macaulay, G. C. ; his article .. 270
Macaulay, Lord ; Carlyle upon .. 42
Macmillan, A. .. .. .. 128
*Magnet Story ;* extract from .. 8
*Main du Maitre* .. .. .. 50
Malakhoff, Duke : and Lady C. .. 73
Manchester, Duke of .. .. 65
Maria Anna .. .. .. 53
Marochetti ; Tennyson .. .. 169
Marsh, Edward ; and Hayley .. 258
*Mém. de Bareith* .. .. .. 49
*Memoranda of the War* .. .. 236
Meredith, George .. .. 95, 137
Meyrick, Sir Samuel .. .. 54
*Middlemarch* .. .. 218, 239
Miller, Joaquin : and Walt Whitman 231
Milnes, M. [Lord H.] 80, 84, 123
                                    216, 241
Milton .. .. .. .. 58
*Mitchell Papers* .. .. .. 49
*Modern Painters* .. .. .. 31
Montalembert ; Carlyle upon .. 60
More, William .. .. .. 7
Morèri; and D'Aulnoy .. .. 52
Morris, William .. .. .. 91
Müller : Silesian Wars .. .. 48

PAGE

Muloch, Miss; *reader* for Macmillan    59

Mynheer; Carlyle speaks of     ..    48

Newcastle, Duke of; and Carlyle ..    45

Newman, Cardinal; and George Richmond    ..    ..    ..    259

Newton, Julia    ..    .. 20—37, 108

Norton, Eliot    ..    ..    .. 247

O'Connor, W. D.: letter to Rossetti    187

—— the Radical ..    ..    ..    201

Palmer, Samuel    ..    108, 109, 143

—— letter from    ..    ..    ..    58

—— quoted from ..    ..    ..    262

Panmure, Lord; and Dowbiggin    ..    51

Patmore; and D. G. Rossetti    ..    88

*Pennycuick* ..    ..    ..    ..    82

Peto; and House of Commons    ..    159

Petrici, Mrs.    ..    ..    ..    232

Planchè    ..    ..    ..    ..    64

Plato    ..    ..    ..    ..    208

Plint; Leeds, Stockbroker    ..    93

*Plutarch*    ..    ..    ..    ..    240

Pugh, Mrs., née Carwardine    ..    20

Quarles: Emblems    ..    ..    5

*Record Office*    ..    ..    ..    209

Richmond, George, R.A. .. 58, 258, 261

*Riesbuk*: Advocate ..    ..    ..    50

*Rochester*; John Burroughs    ..    269

*Roderick Random*; read by Carlyle ..    63

Rogers, poet; Carlyle mentions    ..    51

Romney, George ..    ..    ..    7

Rossetti, Christina; spoken of    ..    145

—— letters from    .. 147, 160, 173, 175

PAGE

Rossetti, D. G. ; first letters,  87, 99, 110, 111, 121, 134

—— speaks of *My Spectre* ..    ..    136

—— last letter from    ..    ..    256

—— death of    ..    ..    ..    265

Rossetti, Mrs. D. G.    ..    ..    145

Rossetti, W. M.; *Catalogue Raisonné*    134

—— explanation of *Mental Traveller*    138

—— writes about Whitman, 179, 186, 281

Rousseau; *Confessions*    ..    ..    22

Rubens; Walt Whitman admires ..    239

Ruskin, John    ..    31, 82, 89, 208

Sand, George; and H. James    239, 272

Scott, Sir Walter ..    ..    ..    241

Scudder, H. E.    ..    241, 247, 262

*Secession War*; John Carwardine 149, 208, 240

*Selections from Whitman*    ..    ..    177

*Serena and Toland* ..    ..    ..    47

Shakespeare; quoted    30, 167, 208, 240

Shelley; rare book..    ..    191, 209

Shields, Frederic J.    ..    ..    264

Simmons, James, J.P. .. 149, 164, 171

*Sing-Song* ..    ..    ..    ..    221

" Skittles," the Courtezan ..    ..    73

Smetham, James ..    ..    ..    57

Smith and Elder ..    ..    ..    89

Smith: Carlyle mentions ..    ..    46

Smith, George; and George Eliot..    217

Spencer, Herbert ..    .. 36, 166, 170

Stanley, Lady, of Alderley..    ..    60

Stillman; meets Whitman..    ..    191

Stowe, Mrs.; mentioned by Rossetti    186

Strutt; mentioned by Carlyle    ..    66

Swinburne, Algernon    ..137, 193, 195

Symonds, J. A.; ancestry, 5 (Rossetti) 183

**PAGE**

*Tanyrallt* ; Shelley ..  ..  .. 209

Tatham, Frederick..  ..  .. 128

Tenniel, John  ..  ..  .. 21

Tennyson, [Lord] Alfred ..  .. 74

—— calls at Brookbank ..  .. 162

—— speaks of Tom Campbell  .. 163

—— Walt Whitman speaks of him 225

—— speaks of Whitman ..  .. 252

Thackeray : and *The Cornhill*  .. 81

*Thinghill Court*, in Herefordshire; pulled

   down a hundred years ago  .. 6

Thomas, Bertha  ..  ..  .. 272

Thomas, Sidney Gilchrist  .. 153, 280

Thoreau : mentioned by Whitman 236

Thornton, Sir Edward  ..  .. 233

Thurlow, Lord  ..  ..  .. 7

Toland ; mentioned by Carlyle  .. 47

*Tolleshunt-Knights* ..  ..  ..13, 18

*Treaty of Ryswick* ..  ..  .. 47

Turner ; *Hind-Head Hill*  ..  .. 118

*Ulysses*; Walt Whitman recites  .. 232

*Union Debating Club, Oxford*  .. 90

Vere, Alberic de  ..  ..  .. 5

Vestris, Madame ; Carlyle mentions 64

**PAGE**

Voltaire ; Old Palace  ..  48, 251

Wale, Mary : and Ann Holgate  .. 5, 7

Wale, Thomas ; *My Grandfather's*

   *Pocket-Book* ; quoted  ..  .. 5

Watson, Mrs.; quoted from  .. 66

Weigall ; and Rossetti  ..  .. 89

Wells, Mrs.; obituary  ..  .. 94

Wells, R. A.; Rossetti mentions .. 110

Whitman, Walt; first mention of .. 177

—— letter to W. Rossetti..  .. 179

—— speaks of Tennyson ..  .. 225

—— is described  ..  ..  .. 229

—— conversation ..  233, 238, 242

—— fragment of letter 252, 253,

          263, 281, 282, 284

White, Walter  ..  40, 120, 152, 279

Wilhelmina : Frederick's sister  .. 49

William the Conqueror  ..  .. 4

Williams, Mrs. Robert  ..  .. 253

Windermere ; described  ..  .. 34

Woodward ; Architect  ..  .. 89

Woolner  ..  ..  ..  .. 169

*Wye* ; A. Gilchrist mentions  .. 35

Zimmern, Helen ; letter quoted  .. 282

Ziska ; and Carlyle..  ..  .. 72